Ife

NEW ASPECTS OF ARCHAEOLOGY

Edited by Sir Mortimer Wheeler

Ife in the History of West African Sculpture

Frank Willett

13 Color Plates
110 Monochrome Plates
41 Line Drawings

McGRAW-HILL BOOK COMPANY NEW YORK

Library of Congress Catalog Card Number: 67–14151
Color and Monochrome Illustrations Printed in Switzerland
Text Printed in Great Britain
Bound in Holland
70303

Contents

General Editor's Preface

THE CENTRAL POINT of this book is inevitably the ancient town of Ife, set amongst the forests of south-western Nigeria in the territories of the Yoruba. Here the author lived for some years as an officer of the Nigerian Department of Antiquities, and was able to study closely the astonishing sculptures which have made Ife famous, with the environment from which they have been derived. But round this central point he has explored widely; to the north, where his colleague Bernard Fagg collected the earlier terracottas of Nok, and to the east where in 1897 a famous punitive expedition advertized to the world the later bronzes and ivories of the Benin court. He is aware, too, of further horizons; and his book is in one way and another a new synthesis of his own discoveries and those of others in the broad field of West African art. To many, the result must come as something of a revelation.

The Benin sculptures have indeed been broadcast amongst the museums of Europe and are generally familiar. But, with rare exceptions, those of Nok and Ife have still to be sought in their homeland: at Lagos, at Ife itself, at Jos. The pilgrimage is an arduous and costly one for the European or American student. Nevertheless, the study of art in its broad context is sadly incomplete without a proper cognizance of these West African schools. The 'Ife phase' at least, though still problematic in its details, is now recognized as a classic episode of art-history.

That this should be so continues, in spite of a slowly developing awareness of the inner minds of Africa, to perplex the unprepared European critic. Professor Willett records from experience that 'European visitors to Ife frequently ask how it could have been possible for people living in mud houses with grass roofs to have made such beautiful objects as the bronze and terracotta sculptures which are exhibited in the museum'. The notion that subtle thinking and artistic sensibility must in some obscure way subsume skills in domestic planning and plumbing dies hard. It may or may not be true that the prehistoric builders of Stonehenge around 1500 BC or earlier were in fact constructing a proto-computer on evolved mathematical premises; it is certainly a fact that our Celtic forerunners on the wind-swept hilltops of north-western Europe had a vivid appreciation of Greek art, and could themselves combine Classical and Scythian elements in a splendid *art nouveau* of their own. If a dog-kennel could house a philosopher at Athens or Corinth, there is certainly no reason why in an African glade a grass hut should not serve as a perfectly adequate studio for the geniuses who cast their wonderful *cire perdue* bronzes (or brasses) at Ife. That in fact it did so is beyond argument.

There is, however, much else about this diverse art that may profitably be argued. And 'diverse' is a just word. If the restrained and sensitive modelling and advanced technique of the Ife heads bring them most completely within the compass of the classical European tradition, there are others, whether later or earlier, which suggest the deliberate rejection of such sophistication. The varied and often dramatic emphasis which marks certain of the Nok terracottas or Benin bronzes accords more nearly with certain modern trends in the West, and the accordance is not entirely accidental. But it is above all the wide range of African aesthetic in its own right that impresses the serious student. The old misconception that all 'African' art was vaguely an expression of 'folk fetish' still demands constant and public refutation, as does, alas, the slowly dying nigger-minstrel notion of negro mentality, whatever that may be. This book may, it is to be hoped, mark another step towards a fuller understanding.

West Africa can fairly claim a clear primacy in the non-European art of the continent, regarded momentarily as a whole. The reasons for this are scarcely yet susceptible to objective analysis, but some of them can perhaps be guessed. The broad belt of tropical forest which comprises the southern zone of the region provides a refuge for traditions and ideas which is at the same time approachable from two outer directions: from the coastline on the south and from the savannah into which the forest thins towards the north. Of the two, it was the former which brought West Africa within the consciousness of Europe in the sixteenth century but it was no doubt the latter, the savannah, which had already linked Nigeria with the Nile as by a sort of transcontinental highway in previous centuries. This highway requires much further exploration, as do the significant trade-routes which branched from it northwards to the Mediterranean. The archaeology of the territories about Lake Chad, for example, is still a little-known quantity, in spite of its predictable importance. And it is more than likely that some part of the complex make-up of the art of Ife came from the east or north by or through this savannah zone. When the new Africa finds the moment and the mood for the discovery of its own past, here are matters which, properly understood, will provide a new chapter to world-history.

Meanwhile, Professor Willett and his colleagues, primarily as archaeologists, have pointed the way. The path is not an easy one. If the study of African art is not to degenerate into a theoretical and inexact typology, it must be based upon methodical excavation to which the developing techniques of modern science will be expected to contribute. A good beginning has been achieved in connection with the terracottas recovered with carbonized wood from the stratified deposits of the Nok alluvium where they have been extensively mined for tin. And, incidentally, the countryside in which these discoveries were made remains for the moment a culturally intact region of central Nigeria. If the art of wood-carving and clay modelling which their ancestors practised hereabouts two thousand years ago has deteriorated in the interval, the sense of rhythm and of theatre remains vividly amongst the present-day villagers; and the kaleidoscopic spectacle of tribal dancing interspersed with dramatic intervention, in the light and shade of the village-precincts, is a scene not lightly forgotten. In one way or another, the villagers are artists still at heart.

But this brings a final problem to those who value all this artistry. How long will the African tradition, whether in carving or painting or in semi-operatic folk-dance, retain its 'integrity' under modern pressures? And how far, indeed, can it rightfully expect to retain this integrity? The next twenty or thirty years may show the answer. Meanwhile the inborn art of Africa, like that of Asia, stands in peril of the mechanization which is too readily the accompaniment of the process commonly and optimistically designated as emergence. The moment is not too soon for the brief but knowledgeable stock-taking of past achievement which Professor Willett and his publishers here offer us at first hand.

MORTIMER WHEELER

Acknowledgements

THIS BOOK results from archaeological and art-historical work undertaken by the author since 1956. During this time he has received help in many ways from a large number of people, which he is very happy to be able to acknowledge. His interest in Ife was first engaged by William Fagg. It was encouraged by Kenneth Murray and Bernard and Catherine Fagg, who all gave him most generous access to their notes. His work was helped by many natural rulers, especially the Oni of Ife, Sir Adesoji Aderemi; Oba Akenzua II, of Benin; the Olowo of Owo, Sir Olateru Olagbegi II; the late Owa of Ijesha, Oba Adelupo Ogunmokun Biladu III, and by their chiefs, particularly the Ife chiefs Akogun, Jaran, Obalorun and Obawinrin, and Chief Akeredolu of Owo who was also a colleague in the Nigerian Department of Antiquities. Without the co-operation of the Department's labourers, workshop and office staffs, his work in Nigeria would have been impossible. Since leaving the Department he has continued to receive help, particularly from Messrs Ekpo Eyo, Simon Okeke, John Picton and Robert Soper, to all of whom, and to Mr Kenneth Murray, he is grateful for their willing help and permission to take photographs. He also wishes to thank Philip Allison, Philip Andrews, Edwin Ardener, Ulli Beier, R. E. Bradbury, Fr K. Carroll, Alan Dempster, Michael Egan, Professor Evans-Pritchard, Robin Farquharson, Douglas Fraser, Catherine Hall, Robin Hallett, Brian Harrison, R. Hoeppli, Kurt Krieger, Peter Lloyd, Raymond Mauny, Jonathan Miller, Peter Morton-Williams, Oliver Myers, John Omer-Cooper, James Packman, Andrew Shonfield, Doig Simmonds, Francis Speed, Robert Stanton, Robert Thompson, John Underwood, Joseph Webb, P. E. S. Whalley, J. Zwernemann and the White Fathers of the Oshogbo Diocese. For financial support he is grateful to the British Academy, the Leverhulme Trustees, the University of Manchester, the Warden and

Fellows of Nuffield College and the Yoruba Historical Research Scheme.

He is particularly indebted to Tom Cross who prepared the line drawings; to Michelle Treiman who compiled the index; to William Fagg for the photograph in Plate 99, and to Francis Speed for Plates 1, 12, 14, 16, 17, 18 and 29.

To Sir Mortimer Wheeler, however, he owes a gratitude for help and encouragement which he can never hope to acknowledge sufficiently.

Orthography

Yoruba words which may be familiar to the European reader have been spelled in the customary way, *e.g.*, Ibadan. Less familiar words which the reader may wish to look up in Abraham's *Dictionary* (Bibliography item 1) follow his orthography. In all cases, however, the dotted *s* has been spelled *sh*, whilst the dotted *o* has been ignored to simplify printing.

I

Something New Out of Africa

When European artists in the later nineteenth century began to appreciate the highly imaginative forms of African sculpture, they were greatly stimulated and refreshed, and under its influence set out upon a course of experiment in artistic form which completely revolutionized European art, liberating it from its nineteenth-century materialistic naturalism. In consequence, the freedom the African artist appeared to enjoy in expressing his own personal concepts of the world around him was considered to be the most important characteristic of African sculpture. The more abstracted a sculpture was from reality, the more typically African it was thought to be. It came as a tremendous surprise to the art world when, in 1938, a group of bronze sculptures of heads of life-size and of natural appearance were found during the digging of foundation trenches for a house in the middle of Ife. These sculptures were quite unlike the stereotype of African art which the connoisseurs had in their mind's eye. Who could possibly have made these heads? What a remarkable achievement this was, to model heads to look so like real people, but even more amazing, to have cast them in bronze! How could this have come about? To be sure, the people represented were, many of them, negroes, so the heads were probably made in Africa, not simply imported, but how could they have been made by Africans? They were so very different from any other work of African art, yet so very much like the general run of European sculpture. Those who could see no beauty in the abstract mode of much African sculpture had no difficulty in appreciating the beauty of these heads. Their appeal is immediate, even to those who have had little or no experience of African sculpture.

Plates 3–5, 7, I, II

In fact, these finds were not the first to be made in Ife. An incomplete face in terracotta[1] of about half life-size had been brought to Europe before 1910, by which date a plaster cast was already in the British Museum.[2] We do not know who brought this piece out of Africa, or where it was during the next half-century, but it is now in a private collection in America. It was probably taken from the Iwinrin Grove in Ife, where a large number of terracotta sculptures used to be kept; there is some evidence that there used to be many more pieces in this grove[3] than there were in 1934 when they were brought into the Palace in Ife for safe-keeping, and later transferred to the Museum. No one paid much attention to this piece until the German anthropologist, Leo Frobenius, visited Ife in 1910. He worked with phenomenal industry for he had only three weeks in Ife on his first visit and was brought back by the police to spend a further three weeks whilst his actions in Ife were investigated. His movements during this second spell were restricted, yet in this very limited time in the town he collected a great deal of information about the way of life of the people, about their traditions, their religion, and particularly about their antiquities. Indeed he collected a large number of ancient works of art, which he was forced to surrender, including a bronze head with a crown which had been found in the middle of the nineteenth century in the Olokun Grove outside the town to the north and had been kept there ever since, being dug up for the annual festivals, and reburied afterwards. However, he took back to Germany seven fine terracotta heads and a number of other important fragments, some of which are illustrated here. Frobenius made sweeping claims about his discoveries in articles in the German press, claiming that here in Ife he had found traces of a Greek colony on the Atlantic coast of Africa, founded in the thirteenth century BC and left without further Mediterranean influence after about 800 BC. He thought that Olokun, the sea-divinity of the Yoruba in whose Grove the head had been found, was the same god as the Greek Poseidon.[4]

Plates 22, 29, 30, 60, 63, 96, 102

Although anthropologists paid some attention to Frobenius, his discoveries appear to have been largely ignored by the art world. Yet during the years that followed, a number of accounts of Ife were published, notably in Talbot's four-volume work *The Peoples of Southern Nigeria*, which illustrated many of the stone-carvings, and in Hambly's *Culture Areas of Africa*, which illustrated eight terracotta sculptures not previously known. The art critics seem not to have seen these books, so that they were quite unprepared when, late in 1938, thirteen bronze heads were discovered at Wunmonije Compound, only a hundred yards from the back door of the palace.

Plates 11, 23, 28, 39, 73, 74

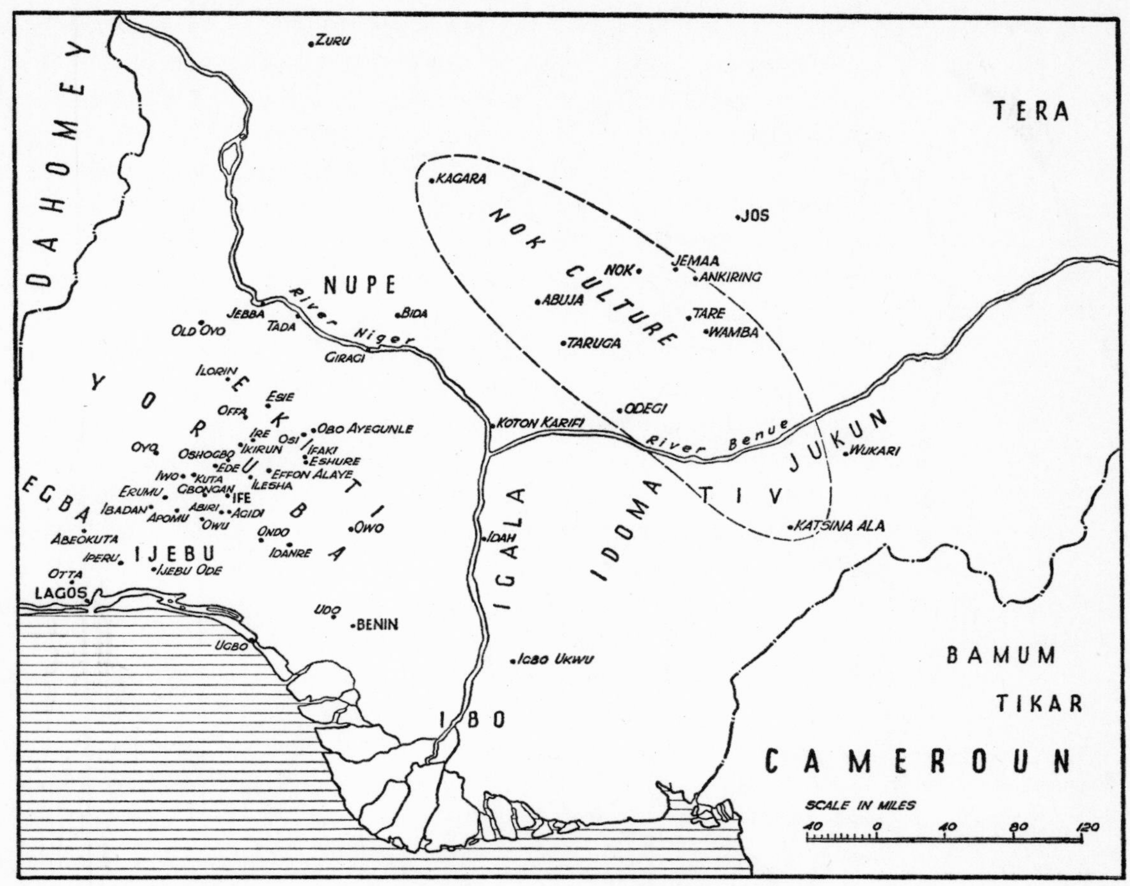

1 Part of West Africa showing places and cultures mentioned in the text. Small upright capitals indicate towns with major museums

Shortly afterwards, early in 1939, four more bronze heads were found together with the upper part of a male figure wearing a beaded crown, an elaborate beaded neck-ring, armlets, and necklaces. One of the heads was brought to Britain, where it was bought for the British Museum;[5] two others were bought by an American anthropologist, Professor W. R. Bascom, who was working in Ife at the time of the discoveries. He gave these two heads back to the Ife Museum when it was opened, so that now there is only one bronze head known to be outside Nigeria, namely, the one in the British Museum. The original 'Olokun' head described by Frobenius has disappeared; the head in the Ife Museum, which was supposed to be this one, has been found to be a copy made

Plate 7

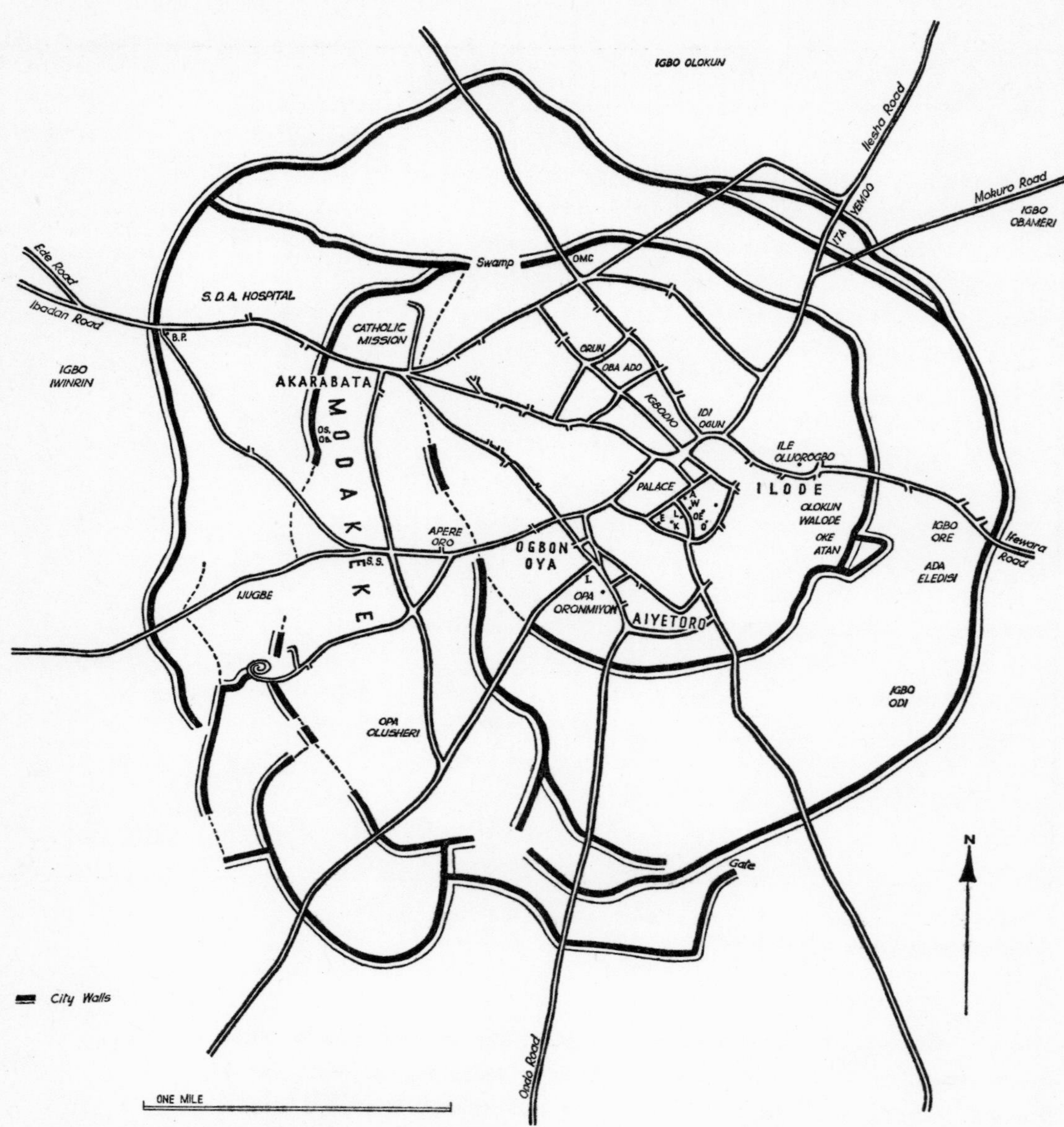

2 *Ife, showing the course of the city walls, plotted from air photographs and partial ground survey, and the principal sites mentioned in the text.* A: *Aro Ajin Compound;* B.P.: *B.P. Petrol station;* E: *Epinbodo;* I: *3 Iyekere Street;* K: *Kubolaje;* L: *Lafogido;* O: *Orishanla Temple;* OE: *Ogun Esa;* OMC: *Oronmiyon Memorial College;* Os. Ob.: *Osongongon Obamakin;* S.S.: *St Stephen's Church;* W: *Wunmonije Compound*

by a modern industrial casting technique, not by the traditional African method.[6]

Apart from the bronze head, the British Museum has a terracotta head, three fragments of terracotta sculpture, probably parts of the stool group, and a quartz stool. In addition to these, the terracotta face in private hands in America and the items brought back by Frobenius are the only known pieces from Ife outside Nigeria. The great bulk of the art of Ife is in consequence still in the town where it was made. It is the aim of this book to convey some idea of the range of styles, materials and subjects which compose this art, a great deal of which is now collected together in the Museum in the Palace, though much of it is still in use in shrines and groves in the town. Plates 76, 77

Scarcely a month ever passes without some new item turning up as new roads are cut or foundations are dug for new buildings. It is amazing how often these new discoveries are unlike pieces already known, so that the range of creation seems to have been unlimited. Our view of the art of Ife in consequence is much more complete now that we have more evidence to study than it was in 1938, when the bronze heads burst upon an unexpectant art world. Not only in Ife has our knowledge advanced, but since 1943 we have had increasing evidence from Northern Nigeria of a group of people whose culture straddles the Later Stone Age and the Early Iron Age, the bearers of the Nok Culture, who themselves possessed a rich sculptural tradition which was discovered and has been described by Bernard Fagg.[7] Long before the art of Ife became at all widely known, the bronzes and ivories of Benin had been famous, in fact ever since they were brought back to Britain after Admiral Rawson's expedition against Benin in 1897. The study of this very large series of sculptures began at once, but although the early works of Read and Dalton, Pitt-Rivers and von Luschan are still of fundamental importance, it is the studies of William Fagg over the last two decades which have made real sense of this prolific art centre.[8] From these studies, and from the study too of more recent sculpture, especially in Nigeria, principally by the same two brothers Fagg, we can now increasingly perceive the main threads from which the history of sculpture in West Africa is woven, and we can now attempt in this book to put the art of Ife into its historical perspective.[9]

II

The Bronzes from Wunmonije Compound

THE ARCHAEOLOGICAL PROBLEM

In 1938, when the group of bronzes was discovered in Wunmonije Compound, there was no Government Antiquities Service. The discovery, however, prompted the (then Colonial) Nigerian Government to issue in 1939 an order prohibiting the export of such antiquities from Nigeria, and this eventually led to the beginnings of a proper service in 1943. Four years later, an archaeologist was seconded to assist this work. If there had been an archaeologist in Nigeria in 1938 the site could have been excavated, but as it was, the house in whose foundations the bronzes had been discovered was completed and is still occupied. Such evidence as we have then comes in part from inquiries made in Ife by Kenneth Murray,[10] destined to become Nigeria's first Surveyor (later Director) of Antiquities, but at that time employed by the Ministry of Education, and from accounts published by W. R. Bascom,[11] who was conducting social anthropological research in Ife at the time. Even if it had been possible to excavate, there might not have been very much useful evidence recovered, for the usual method of building in Ife consists of digging a number of irregular holes, often one inside each area destined to become a room; water is poured into the loose earth in these 'borrow-pits', and the earth trodden into a thick paste. This may then be used to build a course of mud wall, about eighteen inches high, which is allowed to dry out for a day before the next is added; or more recently, the mud has been put into a rectangular mould, and then tipped out on the ground to dry in the sun; or, most advanced technique of all, smaller moulds are used, and after drying the bricks are fired in a kind of clamp. It was this last method which was used for the new building in Wunmonije Compound. The effect of preparing mud on the site in this way is, of course, to destroy completely the archaeological deposit. Where a site has been occupied for a long time, early occupation material has been dug up time and time again, and has been incorporated with ever younger remains into newer and newer walls—a process resembling that by which madeira is produced, in which there survives ever less and less wine of the original year. Although such wines are dated by the year of the original vintage, archaeological deposits have to be dated by the youngest item present, so that the value of the older items as evidence is totally destroyed. We are forced, therefore, to examine the bronzes themselves to see what they can tell us of their own history, and to look for possible analogies elsewhere.

THEIR NATURALISM

Plate 1

The head which was shown to Frobenius in the Olokun Grove and the mask, reputed to represent Obalufon and to have been kept in the Palace in Ife ever since it was made, are so similar to the bronzes found at Wunmonije Compound that they can all be considered together. The most striking characteristic of these sculptures is their naturalism. They look like real people. Yet they are also idealized, in that they do not seem to be attempts to portray accurately the idiosyncrasies of each individual, but rather to represent the subject as he would wish to appear, or wish to be remembered. Moreover, however naturalistic we may consider a work of art to be, it remains a composition of conventions, of stylized ways of representing the different parts. It is because one artist learns these conventions from another, and because in the course of his life he develops new ones of his own, that it is possible to study the history of art.[12] Now in these Ife bronzes, some of the conventions are less naturalistic to our way of looking than the overall effect. Most conspicuously, the eyes are not a natural shape, the angle at which they are set in the head varies considerably, and there is little sense of the anatomical structure which composes the globular eye in a round socket. The eyes indeed vary in form from very long, narrow ones to short, wide-open ones, with many intermediate forms; they comprise not less than three different conventions. The ears too are highly stylized, so that the most common shape of ear found among Nigerians nowadays is not at all clearly represented on these bronzes,[13] although the characteristic small lobe, scarcely, if at all, detached from the skin of the jaw, is clearly represented on some heads. The stylizations of the ears vary considerably, as can be seen from Figs. 31a and 31b, the former of which shows the extreme of idealization, whilst the second is much truer to life. Again, several types of ear can be distinguished, and these too probably represent the concepts of different artists, though since ears are the most variable part of

Plate 4

the body (and have in consequence been generally neglected by physical anthropologists), it is quite possible that they are based on observed variations.[14]

The mouths too have their stylizations: the lips are often slightly apart with a horizontal slit between them which passes right through the casting; a number of them have a triangular cavity formed in each corner of the mouth which seems to hint, as William Fagg has pointed out,[15] at the form of protuberant lip we see in later Yoruba sculptures.

Plates 106, 109; *Fig. 3*

These conventionalized features are most important in establishing the origin of the art style, for, once given the idea of naturalistic representation, since human beings resemble each other, the works of naturalistic art will similarly resemble each other in a general way. It is this fact which led Frobenius to postulate a Greek, and Flinders Petrie an Egyptian origin for them.[16] But, in fact, these art traditions have conventions of their own, quite different from those of the Ife bronzes. Indeed, the origin of the art of Ife deserves to be considered, not simply from the evidence of the bronzes which, although most impressive, are numerically only a small proportion of the output, but principally from the terracotta sculptures, which are not only more numerous but also far more varied, both in subject-matter and in style.

THE SMALL HOLES

Of these twenty bronzes we have mentioned, no less than sixteen are life-size. The half-length figure is about one-third of life-size, whilst the crowned head in the British Museum is about three-quarters and another example of a crowned head is two-thirds of life-size, as also is the head found by Frobenius. These smaller heads have their crowns cast integrally. The remainder are without crowns; indeed, they are without hair too. Where the hair should be, we find a relatively smooth area edged with small holes. Sometimes this area stands proud of the surrounding surface, sometimes it is recessed, and in one case there is no clear step at all. Evidently the holes were intended for the attachment of something which covered the top of the head. The smaller heads are represented with crowns, as are other bronzes to be described later. Now, most of these crowns follow the hair-line, with a piece cut away over the ears, whilst behind the head the edge of the crown may either sweep round in a continuous curve, or else come down only a little way before being cut off horizontally. The holes round the life-size heads fall

Plates 5, 7

Plates 3, 4, I, II

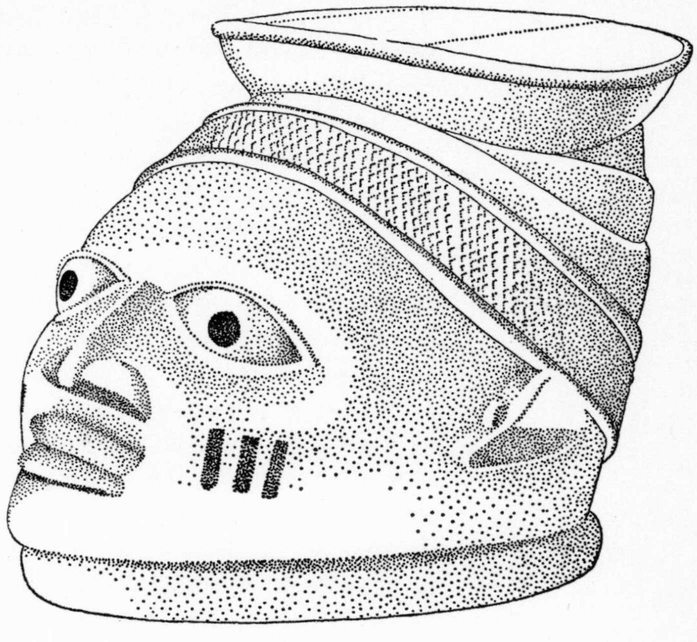

3 Wooden mask of the Gelede *society, from Otta in Yorubaland, used in ceremonies intended to placate witches (*see Bibl. 16g)

into two patterns which correspond exactly to these two shapes of crown. It would seem likely, therefore, that the heads originally had real crowns attached, and, after the face had been modelled, the size of the top of the head was adjusted to fit the pre-existing crown by building up or cutting back the wax as necessary. The heads which were modelled on too small a scale to carry real crowns had crowns cast integrally with them.[17] On one of the heads there is a nail in one of the holes over the temple which had evidently been used to secure the crown, whilst another head has a piece of thread through the holes. Plate II

All the life-size heads have these holes above the top of the face. Similar holes around the lips and the jaw are found on fourteen of the heads, outlining the area where a man's beard grows, but they stop at the bottom of the ears, instead of continuing up to join the hair of the head. When these heads were cleaned, a number of small black glass beads[18] were found stuck to them, and indeed to this day two heads still have a bead jammed in one of the holes. It seems likely that these beads were strung from the holes round the mouth and jaw to represent hair, but William Fagg[19] has suggested another Plates I, II possible explanation, that they may have been a real beadwork veil, paralleling the real beaded crown, intended to hide the wearer's mouth in public. The fact that three of the heads were crowned, as are also the majority of the terracotta sculptures, suggests that these are representations of Onis or divine kings of Ife. Nowhere is the divinity that doth hedge a king more noticeable than in Africa. Typically the divine king may be supposed not to require food, and there are often beliefs that it is dangerous for him to open his mouth in public. For example, Johnson remarks that the King of Oyo generally holds the *iru kere*, the cowtail fly-whisk which is his symbol of office, 'in front of his mouth when speaking, for it is considered bad form to see him open his mouth in public'.[20] In Ife, the Oni used only to appear in public on two occasions in the year, the feasts of Orishanla and of Ogun, and then he wore a crown with a fringe of beads covering his face. During this century, the Oni has appeared increasingly in public, but even the Oni Ademiluyi, who died in 1931, used to cover his mouth with a fan when he as much as took kola[21] in public. Nevertheless, the more obvious explanation—that these were originally for a representation of hair—is not to be positively excluded. Very possibly, the skin of an animal, with its hair intact, was sewn on, or else loose hair was woven into a suitable fringe. Wooden sculptures are still commonly decorated in both these ways in Africa, whilst fringes of vegetable fibre to represent hair are very common. Although small black beads were certainly strung from these holes at one time, this may well have been done when the heads were refurbished, as we shall see shortly.

Plate 71

It is strange that none of the bronzes and scarcely any of the terracotta sculptures show eyebrows, although these are a detail which is often omitted from modern African sculpture. It is quite possible that they were painted on, for most of the bronze heads have some traces of paint, if only in the whites of the eyes. Some, however, have red paint on the neck, and Head 6 has lines of red and black forming 'spectacles' round the eyes. Probably this represents a decoration for some festival, in the same way that the modern priests of the god Orishanla paint themselves for the Itapa festival.

Plate I

Plate 69

THE STRIATIONS

Twelve of these bronzes have striations on the face, and the half figure even has them on the abdomen. In seven cases the lips are left smooth, and in five cases the lower lip only is striated. The most obvious interpretation is that these lines are tribal marks, but in this case it is odd that eight of the bronzes should lack them. Moreover, two heads[22] are very similar indeed—almost identical in fact—but one, a failed casting which the bronzesmith made several attempts at saving before apparently deciding to try again, has striations whilst the successful casting does not. If these represent the same person, then it is odd to show his tribal marks on one portrait and not on the other, unless indeed everyone bore them so that they could be considered irrelevant. Again, William Fagg[23] has suggested too that it may be intended to give the effect of a face seen through a fringe of beads hanging from the crown. The heads with cast crowns give colour to this, since they are all striated, although the more recent discoveries at Ita Yemoo contradict it. In any case the crownless heads could certainly have had real fringes on their real crowns. Again, the visual effect of the striations, when the heads are viewed from a distance where the lines themselves are not noticed, is to break up the highlights so that they do not shine so much and, at the same time, to lighten the shadows. This effect is not entirely lost even on photographs, as a comparison of Plates 4 and 5 will show. The striated head looks less shiny, less metalic, and much more delicately modelled. This technical explanation is attractive, but if this was the intended purpose it is difficult to understand why the arms of the half-figure were left unstriated and why so many heads were left without these marks. None of these explanations is completely satisfactory. The idea that they were tribal marks is the least unsatisfactory, despite the fact that it raises the further problem that the Yoruba no longer use a tribal mark like this. It is, however, a little similar to facial marks found on bronzes at Igbo Ukwu in the Eastern Region of Nigeria where some Ibo groups still make a pattern of close set lines over the forehead and temples—the *itchi* scarification. Moreover, as we shall shortly see, other sculptures at Ife in terracotta show recognizable tribal marks, so we may cautiously accept them as possibly representing an ancient form of tribal mark which is no longer used in south-western Nigeria, though the Tera of north-eastern Nigeria, who do not seem to be related in any way to the Yoruba, still use a closely similar mark.

Plate 71

Plates 6, 9, 10

Plate 103

Plates 13, 31

Plate 34

THE PURPOSE OF THE LIFE-SIZE BRONZE HEADS

All these heads have quite large holes in the neck, usually with chamfered edges, evidently intended to permit attachment to something else. Indeed the head in Plate 5 and the one in the British Museum have each an iron nail still in position in one hole. It seems very likely that they were attached to carved wooden bodies. Of course, no wood survives, and we are forced to look for analogies among modern practices in related cultures.

A close examination of the Wunmonije heads, however, affords us further evidence. Three have received quite violent crushing, presumably from a collapsing building, and most show signs of recent damage from sharp digging tools which have made cuts which still look quite fresh. This damage evidently results from their accidental digging-up in 1938; the crushing was probably caused by the collapse of the shrine which housed them, as a result of which their location was forgotten and all memory of their function lost. Yet there is evidence of even more damage, similar to the cuts received when they were found but quite heavily patinated. It looks as if they had been dug up a long time before the building at Wunmonije Compound collapsed on them. Only one of these heads (not counting for the moment the mask, which is unique) has been found elsewhere; this is the one which, according to Frobenius, was dug up in the Olokun Grove, during the nineteenth century.

Now the Olokun Grove covers a very large area—about half a square mile—just outside the town on the north side. It has now been largely cleared and planted with cocoa, but it still retains its sacred shrines and its pits. It is in fact riddled with pits, a number of which were excavated by Frobenius, who decided that they had probably been dug as burial chambers;[24] it seems to have been from these pits that he obtained the terracotta heads now in Berlin, and he reports finding with them glass-making crucibles and beads. The beads and crucible fragments coated with glass in a rich variety of colours—pale transparent greenish blue, brilliant peacock-blue, rich dark red, olive-brown, dark green, turquoise—are still to be picked up there in quantity. Olokun, to whom the grove is dedicated, is the divinity of the sea, and also of wealth, possibly because wealth came (eventually) from over the sea. However, here in Ife, the grove itself is full of wealth—beads and glass droppings—which have led to a minor industry of mining this material for re-exploitation by drilling to make new beads. In the course of this mining, it seems likely that the crucibles, and some of the terracotta sculptures, now found in relatively recent shrines in the city, were discovered. It seems that all knowledge of the purpose of these crucibles had already been lost, for they were not only used as containers for beads as in one shrine excavated at Ita Yemoo, but in the Grove of Oduduwa, the divinity credited with the creation of the world, one is said to have been his drum. This seems too to have been the way that the fragments of terracotta sculpture excavated by Bernard Fagg in 1953 came to be in the grove known as Olokun Walode: the Olokun Grove of the Walode family. Here only a few inches below the surface was found a fragmentary face. It is in a remarkably unweathered condition whereas a small head with enormous ears[25] found with it is noticeably eroded. Close by were found individual fragments from a variety of terracotta sculptures: the leg of a bushcow, the left thighs of two different kneeling figures, two hands holding a bowl, a right hand holding a matchet, a fragment of a right foot of about two-thirds of life-size, and a dozen other pieces, apparently all from different sculptures. Clearly, these are oddments collected together after finding in different places. There lay with them a fragment of a glass-making crucible, and a complete one is kept by the Walode family (together with a terracotta head) for use in the worship of Olokun in this grove. This suggests that some, if not all, of these fragments probably came from the Olokun Grove. Further confirmation is provided by one of the hymns which they sing during the festival, which begins:

Plate 31

Lokun Lokun gbera nile o
Oshin erupe gbera 'le o, omo omi
Olokun dan owo
Yeye dana omo.

'God of beads rise out of the earth
Oshin (a chief) of earth rise up out of the earth, children of water (*i.e.*, the water in the pits in the Olokun Grove where beads are found after rain)
Olokun has wealth,
Mother gives children.'[26]

This seems to imply a close connection between the Grove of Olokun Walode and the main Grove of Olokun, the source of beads, crucibles and other riches. Some inches below the terracotta fragments was a very worn patch of potsherd pavement[27] which had evidently become covered with earth before the fragments were placed in the grove.

It is quite possible that the bronzes from Wunmonije Compound were found in the same way, perhaps in these grave pits in the Olokun Grove, but possibly from other places around the town where they had been in use at a former time. If they were buried in the Olokun Grove, or some similar place, we have to consider how they could have got there.

It is common practice in any hot climate to bury the corpse as soon as possible after death, for reasons of hygiene. The funeral ceremony proper is held later, perhaps delayed by only a few days, perhaps by months or even years, depending on the degree of elaboration of the ceremonies, and whether the survivors find it necessary to save up in order to afford the expense. One particularly interesting and elaborate version of a funeral ceremony is performed in Owo, where it is called *ako*. It was last performed in 1944 by the King of Owo (the Olowo) in memory of his mother, Queen Olashubude. On this occasion the Olowo distributed five sheep, fourteen cows, eighty goats and 1,835 pounded yams. The central feature of Plate 2 the ceremony, however, was a life-size wooden effigy of the deceased which was dressed in cotton, woven into narrow strips of a special design in black and white reserved for these occasions. The figure was set up in the Palace where the mourners came to pay their last respects. Then it was carried in procession through the town to visit many shrines and eventually buried, the special cloth being divided among the bereaved who wore it as a sign that they had performed this ceremony. One cannot help feeling that this may have been how the Ife bronze heads were mounted in use. The use of wooden figures for these *ako* ceremonies, however, is a recent innovation. It was introduced by the carver Ogunmola Olujere who died about 1935, when he was believed to be about eighty years old. Already before 1910 the innovation was being copied by another carver, Ologan, so the change was probably adopted around the turn of the century. Before this time the *ako* figures had been made of straw or wickerwork. Similar ceremonies, known by the same name, are conducted in Benin too, where the figure is made of red cloth, with the nose formed over a piece of wood sewn inside. Carried upright with a supporter holding each arm, the figure looks remarkably alive in its chief's beads, despite its stylization.[28] *Ako* is found also at Onitsha, an Ibo town on the River Niger, which has been greatly influenced in its chieftaincy organization by Benin. Owo too, although a Yoruba town, shows clear signs of Benin influence, so it is likely that *ako* is of Benin origin.[29] However, it is only the most striking example of an institution which is found widely in the Nigerian forests. In Ife itself, for example, when a hunter dies, second burial figures are set up by the roadside and left to decay.[30] It is not unreasonable, then, to suppose that the bronze heads from Ife may well have been used in some similar way as the top of commemorative figures used in second burial ceremonies.

How closely these rituals resembled those of the present day we have no means of knowing, but a comparison of their social function in Benin and Owo reveals that the Owo practice has become an ostentatious display of affection for the deceased which does as much to enhance the prestige of the survivors who pay for it as it does to ensure the well-being of the deceased in the after-life. Dr R. E. Bradbury has studied the phenomenon in Benin, where the figure is prepared only for certain narrowly prescribed chiefs. In the ceremony the effigy wears the beads which constitute the insignia of the chiefly office, while the successor to the title accompanies the effigy stripped to the waist as a mourner. The next time the successor appears in public is at his installation, when he wears the self-same insignia. The purpose of the ceremony is to indicate that though the individual chief is dead the chieftaincy is immortal. Such ideas which distinguish between the mortal holder of the office and the eternal *dignitas* of the office itself are widespread: they have been studied in medieval Europe by Kantorowitz,[31] whilst the most familiar expression of this continuity of office despite the change of occupant is the well-known phrase: 'The king is dead; long live the king!'

The life-size bronze heads in Ife were probably used on wooden effigies to symbolize the *dignitas* of the kingship. To this cause is to be attributed the dignified serenity of their expression, which many of the terracotta sculptures do not share. Such a use also explains why the life-size heads have no crowns—they wore real ones—whereas real crowns would not have fitted the small heads, which had to have crowns modelled on them. Since these smaller heads, too, have holes in the neck, they were probably used in the same way.[32]

It is likely then that these bronze heads were buried once after some kind of second burial ceremony, and then found, most probably one by one, and assembled in a shrine in the Palace. The Palace was enlarged during the reign of Odidi Rogbeshin, which is said to have covered most of the eighteenth century, and apparently reduced again in the reign of Lajodogun who may have reigned early in the nineteenth century.[33] It seems possible that the heads were brought together into a special shrine in the Palace, which must have collapsed and been forgotten already by the time that the area of the Palace was reduced, otherwise these bronzes would hardly have been left outside. It seems possible that the small black beads which were found on the heads were attached to them at this time, and indeed we have the thread still in position on some of them. One piece

Plate II

from over the forehead of Head 11 was found to be probably of linen, and therefore likely to be an imported thread.[34] Smaller threads from Head 7 were also found to be 'somewhat similar in appearance to flax', whilst samples from a fragment of a head which came to light among the belongings of a man who had died in Ado Ekiti in 1964 were very much finer, but too small to be identified.[35] On the other hand, Head 4 retains a nail on the left temple which suggests that the crowns were originally fixed in this way,[36] and that thread was a later device for attaching beads. The antiquity attributed to these beads by van der Sleen's identification suggests that they may have been retrieved from the decayed crown and re-applied with thread, to decorate the heads when they were brought together in the Palace.[37]

FAMILY RESEMBLANCES

Although the naturalism of these heads is stylized to a considerable degree, and the features are idealized, they are nevertheless quite distinctive in their character. Indeed, as John Underwood pointed out one day when he was making a film of these heads in the Ife Museum, one could quite easily arrange them in what appear to be groups of brothers. There certainly seem to be family resemblances between these different groups of heads as if they had all come from three or four families. Leon Underwood considered these to represent different racial types.[38] If they are indeed funeral effigies, as has been suggested, then it is entirely reasonable that they should bear family resemblances to each other, for there are nowadays four ruling families in Ife, all descended from one person, the Oni Lajamisan, to whose reign we cannot yet assign dates. The Yoruba nowadays expect, when a child is born, to be able to recognize the ancestor who is reincarnated. It is possible that some such ideas are reflected in the family similarities of these bronzes: that they represent recurrent facial types within the royal family.

It is not entirely inconceivable that the differences should represent the hands of different sculptors, but the skill that is shown in all these heads belies the implication that the artists were only capable of representing one type of head each. Yet we can see in these heads traces of individual sculptors. One group, for example, shows quite clearly very elongated eyes which are associated with a characteristic type of ear. These heads have almost certainly been made by one person. The methods of the modern Yoruba craftsmen in Ekiti, where the master-carver blocks out the main forms of the carving whilst allowing his apprentices to sculpt the details, often makes it difficult to establish with any precision who has worked on a particular carving.[39] It is even more difficult to do this in naturalistic art where the stylizations characteristic of the sculptor are relatively slighter and more difficult to detect. Nevertheless, the variety in these heads is such that it seems unlikely that all these bronzes have been made by one person. When we consider the terracotta sculptures, their numbers alone, as well as the great variety in their styles, gives the lie to the suggestion that the whole corpus of Ife sculpture was made by one individual.

THE 'OBALUFON' MASK

Plate I

One of these life-size bronzes, however, is quite distinct from the remainder. It is the mask reputed to be of Obalufon II, who is placed in the king lists of Ife next but one to Odudua, who created the world. It is reputed to have been kept in the Omirin chamber in the Palace ever since it was made, and is thus possibly the only example of the Ife bronzesmiths' work not to have been lost and found again. Obalufon is credited with having introduced bronze-casting to Ife, so it is easy to understand how his name should have come to be attached to the only known example of the craft. Unlike the other bronzes, this is a true mask intended to be worn over the face, with slits below the eyes so that the wearer could just see out.[40] It carries holes round the hair-line, like many of the other heads, but it also has pairs of holes round the edge which are clearly intended for the attachment of cloth or vegetable fibre to hide the body of the wearer, as is normal in African face masks.[41] It is rather heavy ($12\frac{3}{4}$ lb) to have been used as a dance mask over the face, although if a firm head-dress had been attached, it might not have been intolerable to wear; indeed, many wooden masks currently used in Ekiti weigh more than half a hundredweight. In the course of Yoruba funerals nowadays an *egungun* masquerader takes it upon himself to speak as the voice of the deceased, to reassure the living that he has been satisfied with his burial. Among the Bini, one of the bereaved family is chosen to represent the dead man, although he is not allowed to speak;[42] moreover, his mouth is not allowed to be seen. It is possible that this mask was used in such a funeral ceremony, and that the holes in the face may have carried a veil to hide the mouth.[43]

THE 'LAFOGIDO' BUST
Plate 7

The remaining bronze from the Wunmonije find is the upper half of a broken figure which was given the name of the Oni Lafogido, because, according to the Oni of Ife in 1957, he was the great-great-grandfather of the Oni Wunmonije in whose compound it was found. He reigned for a short time immediately before Abeweila, during the fifth decade of the nineteenth century, and is supposed to be buried in an open space bearing his name near Wunmonije Compound. Clearly, this name has no significance in interpreting the bronze sculpture itself, but it is at least more attractive than referring to it by its catalogue number. The main significance of this figure was first pointed out by William Fagg, who observed that the head appeared to have been about a quarter of the overall height of the figure, a proportion which is nowhere found in Egyptian, Classical or Medieval European art, but which is characteristic of African art.[44] He believed that this feature alone was sufficient reason for believing that the art style was essentially African. Subsequent discoveries have proved him right.

III

The Bronzes from Ita Yemoo

THE GREATEST archaeological discoveries seem often to be made by accident. In a country like Nigeria where tens of millions of people are turning the soil as they cultivate their farms or dig foundations for their houses, it is only to be expected that they will make more spectacular discoveries than will a handful of archaeologists. So it was that on Friday, 22nd November 1957, workmen levelling ground beside the road to Ilesha, ready to build a splendid modern headquarters for the Ife Co-operative Produce Marketing Union, were surprised when one of them struck with his pick something buried in the ground. There was a sharp crack and at his feet lay what appeared to be a green lemon, encrusted with red laterite. He picked it up. It was a head with a strange head-dress. Another look through the soil and the simpler head-dress of a similar figure came to light. The bodies were soon found and the hard laterite rubbed off them. One face, however, was missing, and a careful search at the time failed to find it. Nor could four months of sieving of the disturbed earth by workmen of the Department of Antiquities succeed in finding it. The casting around the face where the pick had struck was only a sixteenth of an inch thick, and after pouring the bronze had been left to cool slowly inside the mould, with the result that the crystals composing the metal had been able to grow large, till they were as long as the thickness of the casting. As a result, the sharp blow shattered the face into its constituent crystals. If only the bronzesmith had been less patient and had hurriedly chilled the mould with cold water in his eagerness to see whether his casting had succeeded, we might have had his sculpture complete. His patience probably indicates the confidence he had in his own skill. When we look at what survives of his casting we can recognize his virtuosity and acknowledge that his self-confidence was entirely justified. Plates 10, III

It represents a pair of royal figures, apparently an Oni and his queen, with arms and legs intertwined in a way utterly unparalleled

so far in the rest of Ife sculpture. They are, as ever, portrayed in a convincingly naturalistic manner, which successfully disguises the fact that the man's leg would need an extra joint in the middle of his shin to be able to put his foot in the position shown. As for the meaning of their posture, we can hardly even guess. The serene composure of the woman's face gives us no clue as to whether she enjoys or merely endures the man's proximity. To suggest that it may be a ritual gesture of obscure significance, is to say nothing at all. It is interesting to notice that the woman's wrapper is drawn up to her armpits, as seems often to be the case in Ife art, whereas it is not usual in later African sculpture. The man's wrapper too is unusually arranged, for it is drawn through between his legs. This is found to
Plate 8
be the case also in the seated figure from Tada, whilst it is also found occasionally in modern Yoruba sculptures.[45] The most significant characteristic, however, is that here, in the first full-length bronze figure ever found in Ife, we have confirmation of William Fagg's
Plate 7
observation that the head of the broken figure must have been about a quarter of the overall height.

The workmen continued to level the ground, and soon found a
Plates IV, V
pair of bronze staffs with human heads, one wearing a rope gag, and an object they called an ash-tray. The staffs are circular at the top just below the head and oval at the bottom; they are quite heavy, but it is not clear whether they are of solid metal or whether a core has been left inside, as seems much more likely. In 1949, the head of a similar staff to these two was discovered in Wunmonije Compound.[46]
Plate 9
The 'ash-tray' is a very curious object and evidently a ceremonial vessel of some kind. It has the form of a round stone or terracotta stool with an elaborate loop supported on a rectangular four-legged stool. The surface decoration is a herring-bone pattern and suggests
Plate 76
that these are terracotta stools like the example illustrated. On top of the stool is curled a royal figure wearing a crown with a tier of flanges which, so the Oni of Ife informs me, distinguishes her as a queen. She supports herself with her left arm on the handle of the stool, with her head raised, and a staff in her right hand of the same type as the pair found with it just mentioned. Within the curve of her spine there is a circular vessel, apparently a pot.

A little farther away, the workmen found next day an elaborate pot containing three more bronzes. A figure like the broken one
Plate 6
from Wunmonije Compound, but this time complete, and a pair of

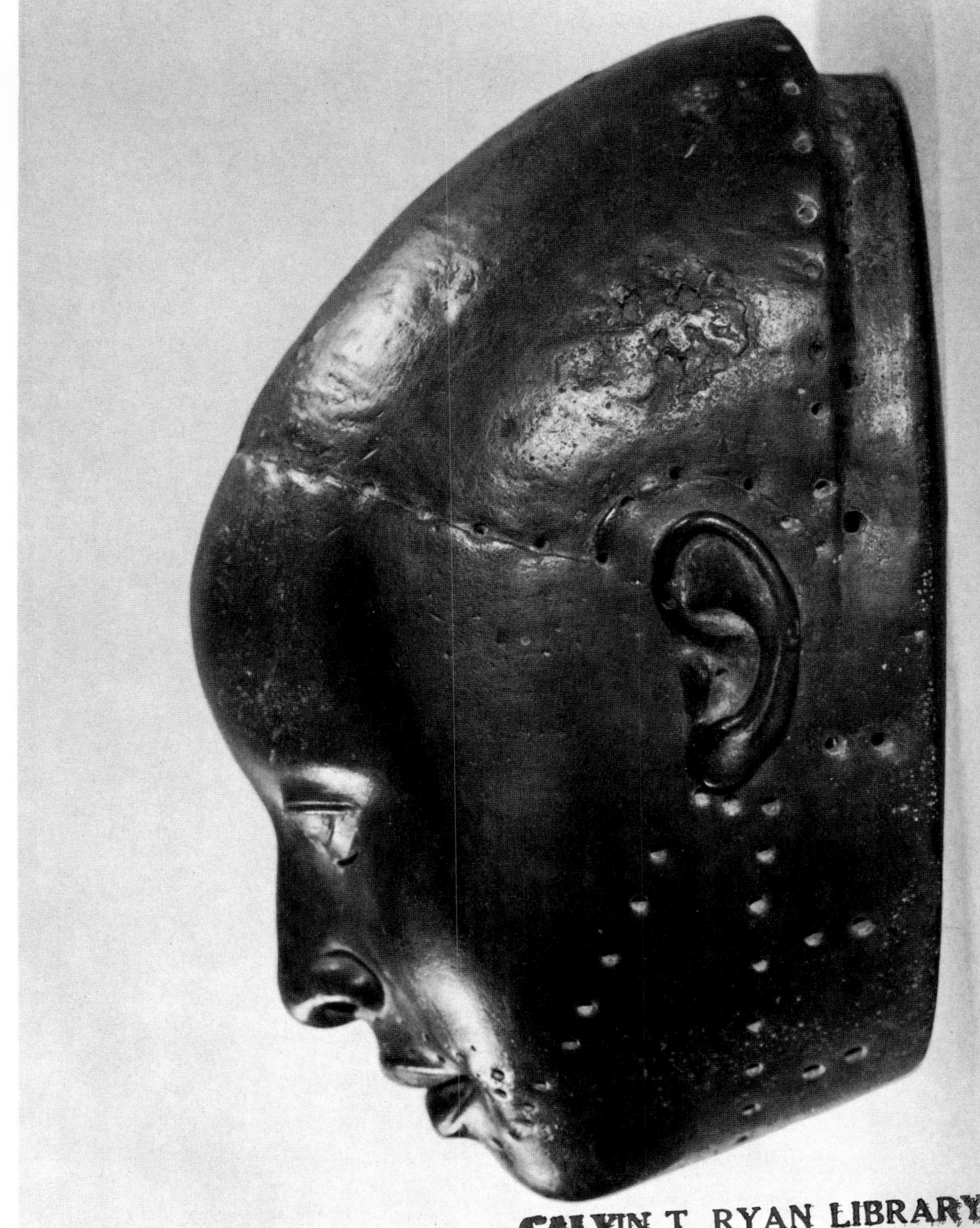

1 This, the only true mask from Ife, is said to represent Obalufon II, also known as Alaiyemore, who is supposed to have been the nephew of Oronmiyon and thus the third Oni of Ife from the creation. He is credited with the introduction of bronze-casting into Ife. Over the ear the irregular mark of a casting sprue can be seen

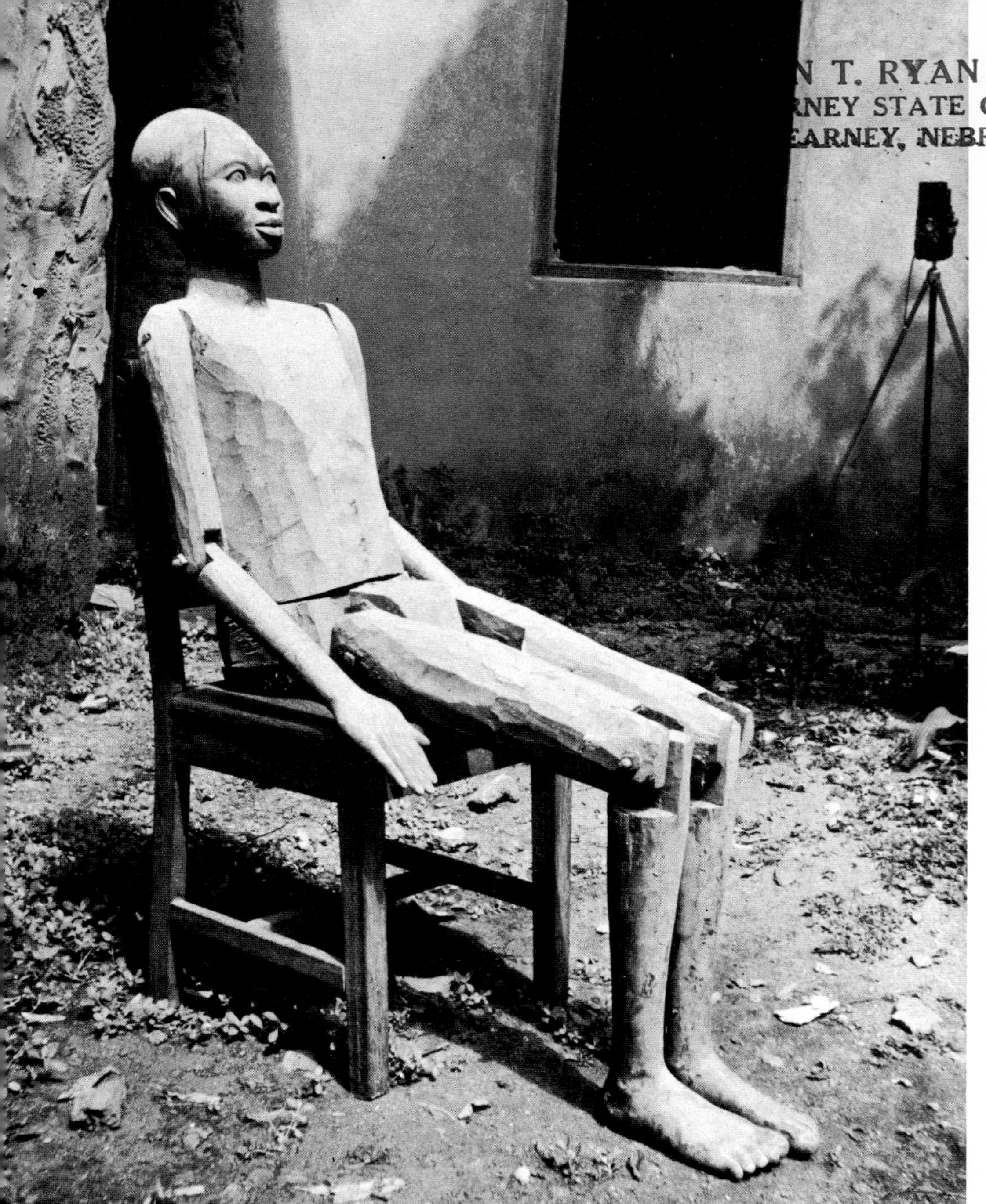

2 Life-size wooden figure from Owo, representing Queen Olashubude, the mother of the present king of Owo, who died in 1944. This type of figure, intended to be an accurate representation of the deceased, is used in the second burial ceremonies, which take place some time after the interment. This figure was carved by Lamuren, but was not considered to resemble the deceased sufficiently closely, so Ogunleye Ologan was commissioned to make a second figure which was buried. The one illustrated has been kept in the Palace ever since. In use the figure is clothed so that only the naturalistic head, hands and feet are seen. The life-size bronze heads from Ife may have been fitted to similar bodies, for use in this way

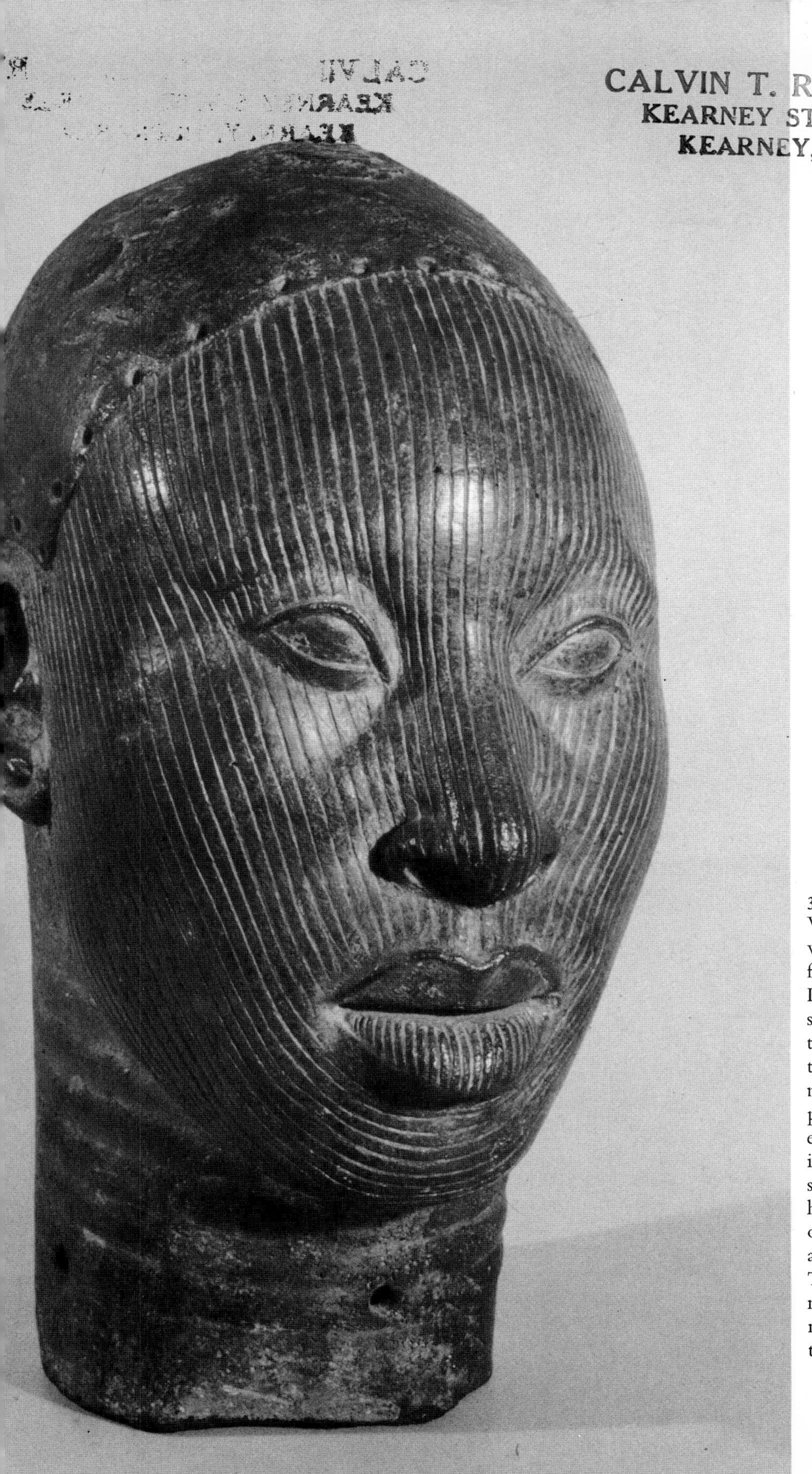

3 Bronze head from Wunmonije Compound with the finely striated face commonly found in Ife sculpture. White paint survives in the corners of the eyes, and there are traces of red paint on the neck. One of four iron pegs can be seen above the ear near the top of the casting. In the neck can be seen two of the four nail-holes by which it was originally attached, probably to a wooden body. The grooves round the neck are considered to be marks of beauty among the modern Yoruba

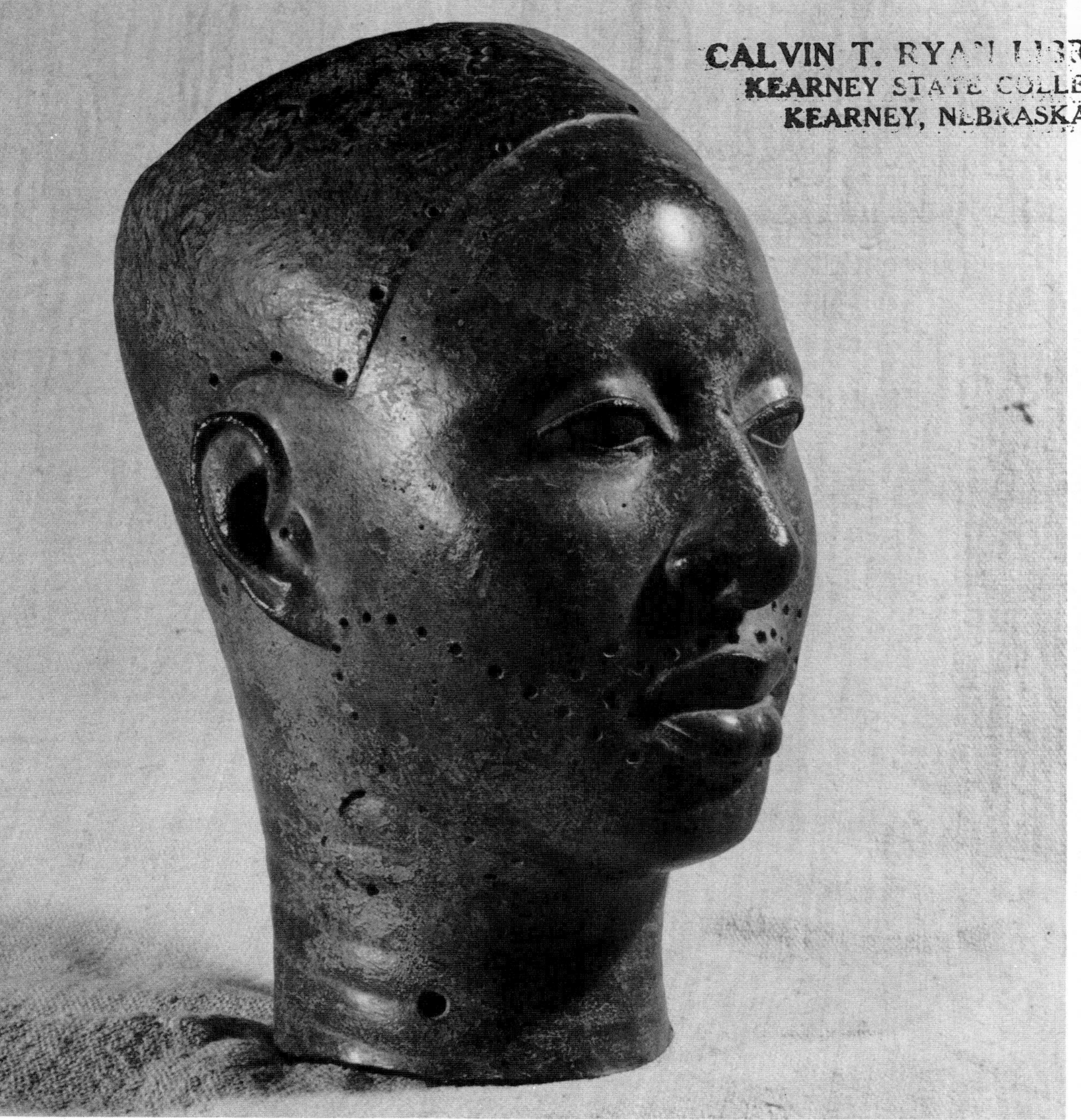

4 Bronze head found at Wunmonije Compound. This and one other are very similar in style, both having large round holes in the top of the head, and, round the mouth and hair, widely spaced holes of greater size than those on the other heads. Both castings are very thin at the back of the head; indeed there is a large hole in the back of this one where the core and the mould came so close together that the metal could not run between them, probably due to inadequate fixing of the core

5 Crowned bronze head found at Wunmonije Compound, one of three, all smaller than life size. The top of the crest has broken from this one, which, artistically, is probably the best of the three. Traces of red paint survive on the crown, while the hole in the front of the neck still retains the iron nail by which it was formerly attached, probably to a wooden body. This head and another were bought at the time of their discovery by Bascom, who took them to America. When the Ife Museum was opened he returned them as a gift

6, 7 Two bronze figures of an Oni or King of Ife. One example, *left*, was found at Ita Yemoo in 1957. This is the only undamaged standing figure we have from Ife, and not only shows the regalia worn in the Classical Period, but also helps us to interpret the hundreds of fragments of similar figures in terracotta which survive from sites all over Ife. The objects in his hands are his symbols of authority. The upper part of a similar bronze figure, *above*, was found at Wunmonije Compound. Many of the beads are picked out with red paint. The bow-like ornaments on the chest are thought to be badges of office, comparable in function, though not in shape, to those worn by chiefs in Ife today (Plate 69). This piece was given the name 'Lafogido' some time after its discovery in 1938, because the Oni Lafogido was buried near Wunmonije Compound

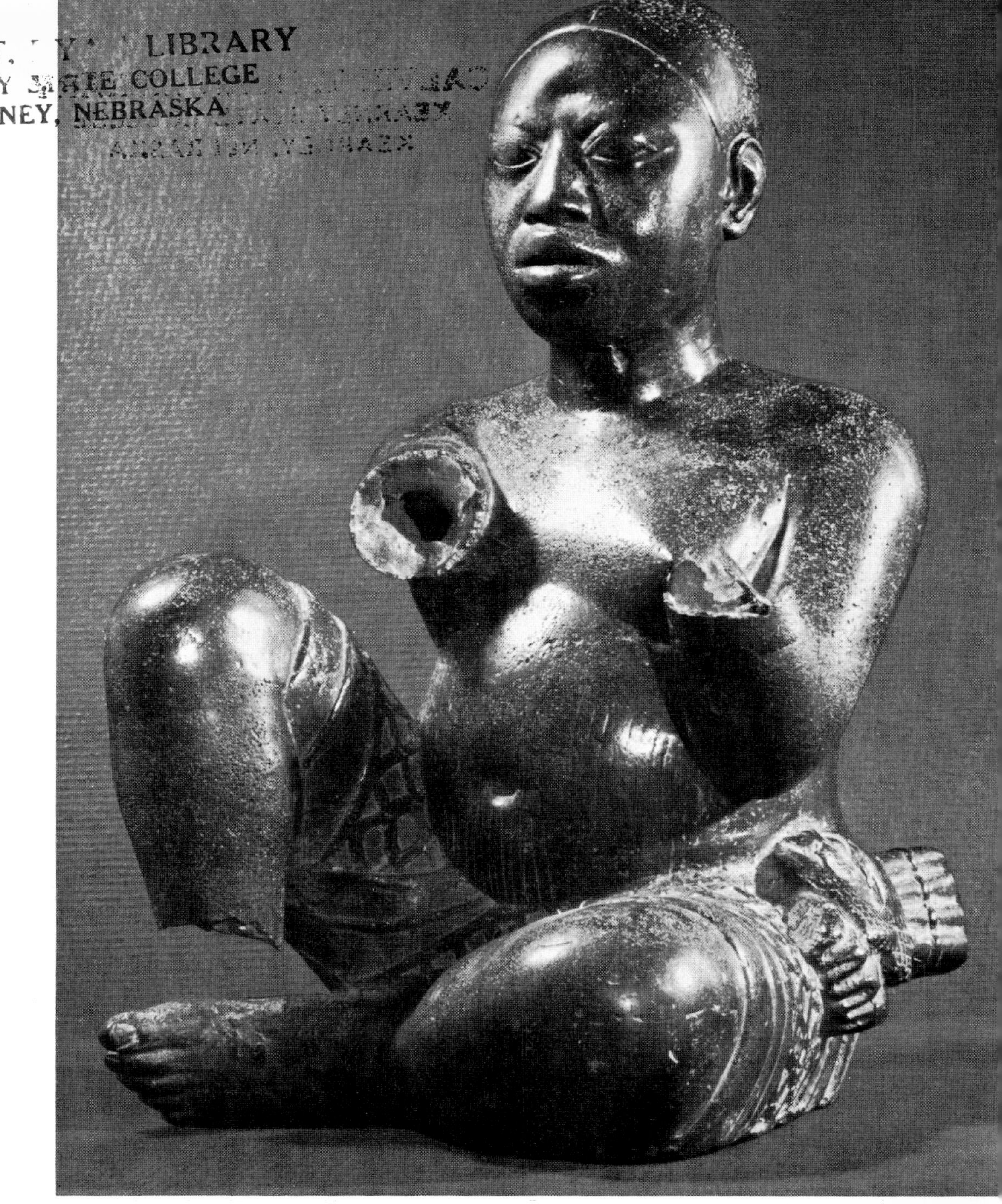

8 Seated bronze figure from the Nupe village of Tada on the River Niger. Although evidently of Ife manufacture, this piece is so far unparalleled there except for the terracotta shown in Plate 39. Despite the damage it has suffered, it is clearly the finest work of Ife bronze-casting so far discovered

9 Vessel in the form of a queen curled round a pot, and lying on a round stool of characteristic Ife shape, with an elaborate loop supported on a four-legged stool. The decoration of the stools may be derived from painted or incised decoration on wooden prototypes. In her hand she carries a staff with a human head like those found with this piece (Plates IV, V). The edges of the stools are heavily encrusted with red paint, as are her beads and clothing, whilst the crown is painted black

10 Pair of bronze figures found at Ita Yemoo in 1957. (The rear view of this pair is seen in Plate III.) He holds similar symbols of authority to those which appear in Plate 6, but has his forefingers hooked round each other in a gesture which was probably significant at the time but at the meaning of which we can now scarcely guess. (During the Olojo festival in honour of Ogun, the divinity of iron, the Oni and Chief Oshogun link their little fingers together at one point.) The thinness of this casting can be seen in the broken edges round the man's face

11 A very well preserved terracotta head of life size said to represent the usurper Lajuwa, who seized the throne of Ife after the death of the Oni Aworokolokin. This sculpture is reputed to have been kept in the palace since his day, but as there is still earth inside it, it seems likely to have been buried and recovered at some time in the past. Nevertheless, its excellent condition shows that it has been well cared for, apart from some abrasion on the left side on which it seems to have been regularly laid and moved about. The hat appears to be of basketwork edged with beads, whilst there is a hole through the hair over the forehead, presumably intended to hold a crest

12 Terracotta head probably representing an attendant, excavated at Ita Yemoo in 1958. Fragments of this head were among the first pieces to be discovered in excavating this shrine which had been disturbed in digging earth to make into bricks to build a house. The house was afterwards demolished, the bricks opened and a great deal of terracotta recovered, including a piece of this head. It has a wider mouth and broader, flatter nose than the example in Plate VIII, and the eyes are more conventionally modelled. Although the head is unstriated there are striations on the lower lip, whereas in the bronzes this feature is only found accompanying striations. It occurs on three of the four heads found on this shrine. (Plates VII, IX)

13, 14 Terracotta heads from the shrine of Olokun at Obaluru, near Ife in a variant of the Ife style not so far represented elsewhere. Both are modelled on globular bases, in this resembling the Nok sculpture shown in Plate XII. The facial markings are represented as wide cross-hatched bands edged with straight lines. Similar bands run from the eyes to the ears, and across the bridge of the nose. Nowadays Ife people usually do not have tribal markings, but when they do, a band of cross-hatchings between the eye and the ear is characteristic. The pattern on these faces must therefore represent tribal markings and it seems likely that the straight striations which are more usual in Ife sculpture are also tribal marks, even though no similar marks are found within about five hundred miles of Ife

15 Terracotta head found in digging mud for walls inside a house which was being built in Akarabata, Ife, in 1960. The long neck suggests that this may have been modelled as a head, not as part of a larger sculpture. It probably represents a woman, as the bandeau with three rosettes belongs to a group of head ornaments which seem to be worn only by heads with delicate features. In the centre of two of the rosettes are iron nails

16 A terracotta head, evidently in the Ife style, still venerated in a shrine at Ikirun, thirty miles to the north of Ife, where it was discovered by Phillip Allison in 1961. The high shine and dark colour are due to the remains of blood poured over it from sacrifices. For its size this head has the longest neck known. The elaborate group of pendants below the right ear is another unique feature. (Other photographs of this head are in *Bibl. 4 c*)

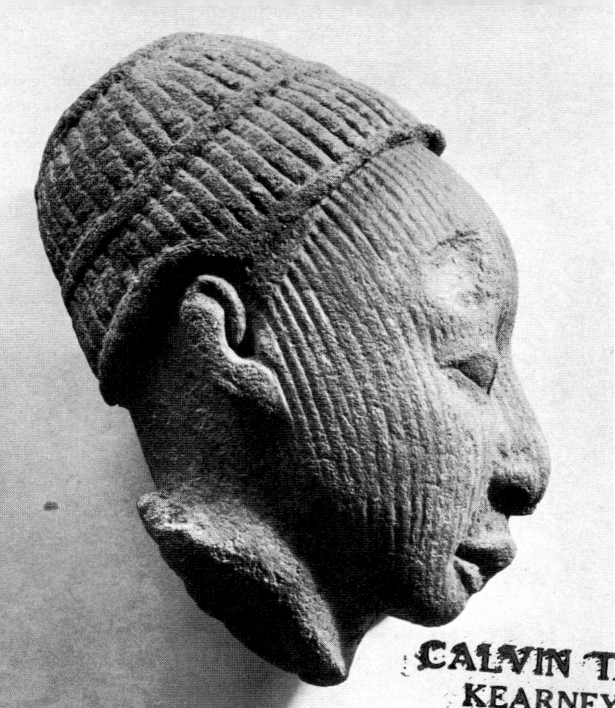

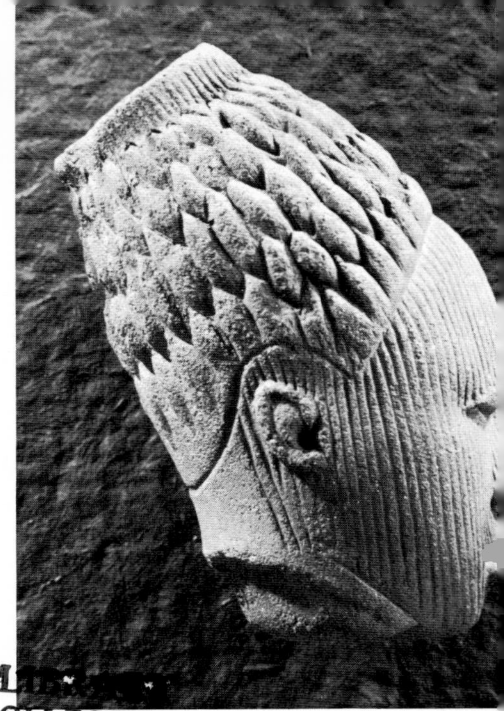

17–20 Four terracotta heads, all from figures. The head, *above left*, was found near St Stephen's Church, Modakeke; that *above right*, was found eroding from the ground at Otutu Compound, Ife, in 1957. The modelling of this head is most delicate, and the hair or head-dress is without parallel. There are still faint traces of red paint in the grooves of the face. The small head, *below left*, was found in 1962 by a small boy who left it at the museum without saying where in Ife he had found it. A head of an old man, *below right*, with moustache and beard, although rather damaged is still recognizable as a skilful and lively sculpture. As on the preceding, the hair is receding and the mouth open; the brows are furrowed rather like the bronze head in Plate VI. It was found at Okesokun Compound, Ife

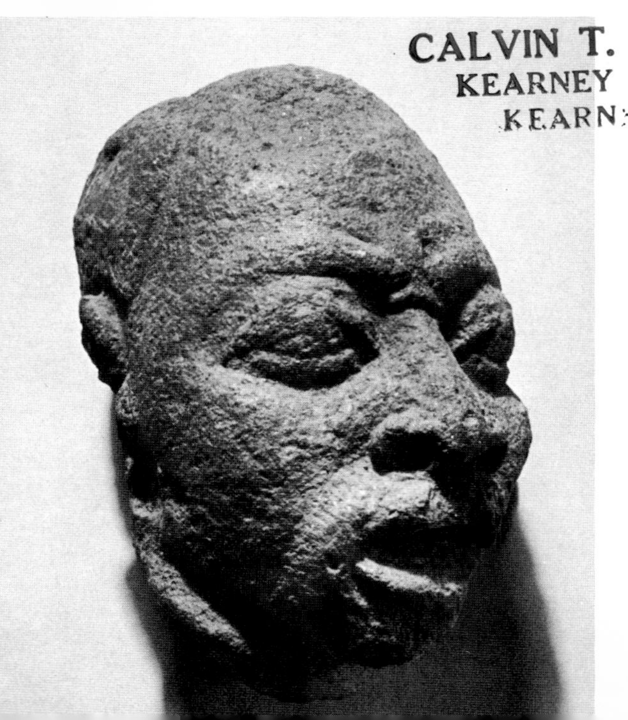

21 Terracotta head, broken from a figure, said to represent Osongongon Obamakin, and previously kept hidden beneath a pot (for it was not supposed to see the sun) in the grove of the same name. The transverse ridges of the hair have been decorated by impressing a finger nail

22 Terracotta head with raised weals. This and Plate 23 are the only two heads with raised as opposed to incised lines. The beaded collar indicates clearly that this head has been broken from a figure. It was found by Frobenius in 1910, apparently in the Olokun Grove. The treatment of the hair as separate curls has been found only on two heads (*see* Plate 29) but in the present example the tips of the curls have been broken off in most cases. Down the centre the hair was dressed into a continuous crest, which has been broken away

ovoid mace-heads each decorated with a pair of human heads. The smaller of them has two small heads facing opposite ways, one with a striated face; the other mace-head is very much more skilfully modelled and seems unlikely to be by the same sculptor. This has a young man's head facing one way and an old man's head the other. Plate VI
It is very unusual in African art to have representations of people in any recognizable stage of life: they are usually at some indeterminate prime, but here we have a deliberate contrast between youth and age. Old men appear also in terracotta. All four of the heads on these Plates 19, 20
two maces wear rope gags whose significance can best be understood by reference to a piece of pot which was later found in excavations Plate 64
near by. This represents a decapitated male figure with a rope gag in his mouth. Evidently these figures were intended to represent sacrificial victims, and inquiry conducted by Peter Morton-Williams in Ife revealed that such victims used to be gagged so that they could not cry out a curse upon the executioner, for such a curse would prove fatal.

The full-length figure is closely similar to the broken one from Plate 6
Wunmonije Compound and afforded yet more evidence of African proportions and therefore of African workmanship. It is, moreover, the type specimen of most of the standing figures in terracotta on whatever scale and, since the large terracotta sculptures are naturally always broken it is a great help to have one complete figure in bronze to help us to interpret the scores of terracotta fragments. He holds in his right hand a staff called *ashe* which is a symbol of authority. Nowadays a Yoruba ruler carries a beaded cowtail fly-whisk as his symbol, and this object evidently corresponds to it. In the other hand, he carries a horn which is a further sign of authority and said to be tremendously powerful. Horns filled with medicine are still used as an instrument of cursing among the Yoruba.[47] He wears a heavy collar round his neck and elaborate bracelets and anklets of beads. There are rings on the second toe of each foot, as is also seen more clearly on the terracotta foot in Plate 54. His chest is covered with bead necklaces over which there hangs from a thin string of beads round the neck, a badge in the form of a double bow. Nowadays chiefs in Ife wear, hung round their necks in a similar way, Plate 69
badges made of beads, but they are of a different shape from those of the ancient sculptures, although it seems very likely that they serve the same purpose as badges of office. The crown of this figure

is one of the simpler types, a cap made of beads with a motif on the front consisting of a shallow cone at the base with a plaited section which rises above it to a pointed knob on top. It has occasionally been suggested that these motifs are phallic, but this has been refuted by Dittmar.[48] As is usual on all the male figures from Ife the chest is bare, apart from the beads; a cloth is worn round the waist with a tuck over the right hip and an elaborate sash tied on the left. Traces of red and black paint remain on this bronze as on many of the others, both the life-size heads and these smaller figures from Ita Yemoo. Originally they must have presented a very vivid appearance.

These bronzes from Ita Yemoo are obviously quite different in purpose from the life-size heads of Wunmonije Compound, although the full-length figure of an Oni evidently corresponds to the broken figure from that compound. Five of the six heads on the staffs and maces represent gagged victims of human sacrifice. It therefore seems likely that these particular objects were intended for use in some cult or ritual which involved the sacrifice of human lives. We have, of course, little knowledge of which cults did and did not require such sacrifice, although we do know that the cults of Oduduwa and Orishanla did, whilst a spot outside the Palace in Enuwa Square in Ife is still pointed out as the place where criminals used to be executed by the same method. It is conceivable that the staffs were used in the course of human sacrifice, perhaps for clubbing the victim before the execution in much the same way as animals, which are now used instead of people in various Ife cults, are struck repeatedly with wands before their head is struck off with one sharp blow from a curved sword (*ada*).

Plates 6, 7

The royal figures on the other hand are much more difficult to interpret. It is possible that they commemorate deceased Onis, but it is perhaps more likely that they are symbolic objects used as shrine furniture in a cult of the royal ancestors, rather than sculptures commemorating an individual Oni or his queen.

Artistically these smaller sculptures from Ita Yemoo are more vigorously modelled than the large heads. It is possible that they were made by different artists, or perhaps the fact that they are intended for a different purpose has permitted a greater freedom of expression for the artist. The need to symbolize the dignity of the king would account for the relative lack of expression in the life-size heads.

THE SEATED FIGURE AT TADA

The most important work of Ife bronze-casting, however, a seated male figure, was not found buried at Ife but is still in use in the Nupe village of Tada on the River Niger, where it is one of seven bronzes said to have been brought from Idah by the Nupe founder-hero Tsoede in the sixteenth century. (These are discussed in Chapter XII.) The priest in charge of them believed that this particular one represented Tsoede himself. It has been particularly associated with the fertility of the people, of their crops and of the fish in the River Niger on which they live, and it used to be taken down to the river every week to be washed and cleaned with gravel. For this reason its features have become smoothed over, and both hands and a foot lost completely. The figure wears a wrapper with a section passed between the legs, resembling in this one of the Ita Yemoo figures. The relief decoration on the cloth is unusual, as is the elaboration of the hip-knot, although a fragment of a similar one has been found in terracotta which may be from the stool from the Iwinrin Grove, Ife. William Fagg has suggested that this bronze, too, may have been intended to sit on a similar stool since the missing foot would have projected below the bottom of the sculpture (*Bibl.* 50 h). The bold asymmetry of the posture of this sculpture, which is not common in African art, though it occurs in other pieces from Ife and Nok, implies a lively imagination on the part of the sculptor, and makes one wonder whether other works of equal importance might one day be discovered.

Plate 8

Plate 10

Plate 76

IV

The Technique of Lost Wax Bronze-casting

THE USUAL TECHNIQUE for casting bronze in West Africa is known as the lost wax or *cire perdue* process. This was the technique by which all the bronze-castings from Ife were made. The first step is to prepare a model in clay which forms the core of the object to be cast, and is slightly smaller all over than the finished object. The core is then covered with beeswax, or in some cases a latex prepared from a cactus.[49] This covering represents what will finally appear as bronze, and it is finished very carefully to represent the sculpture it is intended to cast. Where the finished object will have delicate projections, like the rising motifs on the front of the crowns of three of the Wunmonije heads, a piece of iron wire is inserted into the core and covered with wax which is sculpted to the final shape. At this same stage, in order to keep the core from moving inside the mould, iron pegs are inserted through the wax into the core and left to project.[50] When the modelling is completed, a wax (or latex) cup is made which is fixed above the top of the object to be cast, and wide legs are attached to join the bottom of the cup to the upper part of the wax model. Narrower strips are also attached higher up the cup and higher up the edge of the bronze head. The wider pieces, known as runners, are to form channels for the metal to run down into the space at present occupied by the wax model; the risers are to allow the air which the metal will displace to pass from inside the final mould, and to escape from the top of the cup without causing too much bubbling and splashing of the metal, which would be dangerous. The whole of this object is then enveloped in clay; first of all a very fine mixture, to give a detailed impression of the wax, is applied, and when this is dry, successive layers of thicker clay are added on the outside so that the whole wax object is enveloped in a strong mould of clay. This may well be bound round with iron bands, since the weight of the liquid metal inside may be sufficient to burst the mould during casting. The upper part of the clay cup is not

Fig. 4

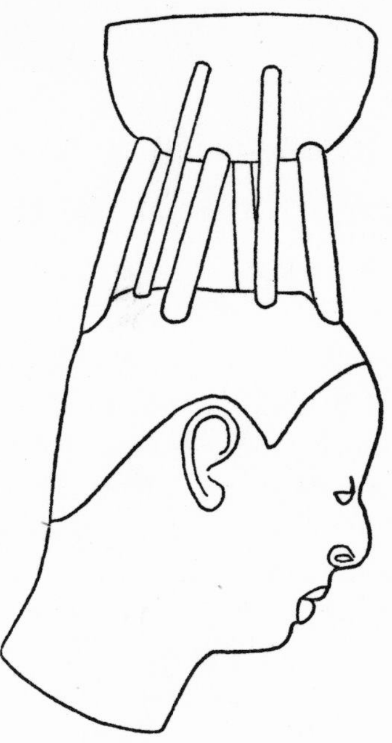

4 Wax model of an Ife head before being covered with clay. After baking the parts shown exist only as cavities in the mould. The cup at the top acts as a funnel for the molten metal, leading it through the four broader passages (runners) to the main part of the mould. As the metal rises to fill the mould the air is drawn out and escapes through four narrower passages (risers), two of which have been omitted on the far side in order to clarify the drawing

covered with this investment. When it is dry, the whole mould is baked in a fire to melt the wax, which is poured off usually into a bowl of water so that it can be recovered and re-used, and the mould is returned to the fire and baked thoroughly hard so that all the remaining traces of wax are baked out. The metal has meanwhile been prepared in a crucible which has also been standing in a similar fire or a different part of the same fire, so that the metal itself and the mould are heated to the same temperature. If they were not of the same temperature, there would be a serious risk that the mould would crack when it was struck by the hot metal, or alternatively that the metal itself would be chilled and would cease to flow evenly through the mould causing a failure. The pouring has to be done with great care and smoothness to ensure an even flow of metal through the mould. The runners are placed in a position which is intended to ensure this, whilst the risers are also placed in the best position to allow the air which is being pushed out by the metal to escape from the top. The metal is poured in until it can be seen that the risers are partly full.

Fig. 4 In the case of Head 9 at Ife, which is the basis of the diagram, the metal in the crucible was not sufficient to make a complete casting and it had to be topped up from another crucible. As a result, the metal fused only at the front of the head, where the hot metal was first poured in. The metal continued round the head and completed the casting, but there is a crack around the level at which the metal had cooled. This line must originally have been horizontal, and it shows that the head was tilted forwards and inclined a little to one side when the metal was being poured in. When the casting was finished, it was put aside to cool, and must have been left a considerable time, because in every Ife casting the crystals of the metal are of large size. When cool, the mould is removed, and the casting jets (the metal which filled the runners and risers) are cut off with a chisel, as are the projecting iron pegs. This leaves a certain amount of roughness on the surface. In the case of the Ife heads, these eight patches would be hidden by the crown which covered this part of the head. In Benin, where heads of similar size were made later by the same technique, nothing was used to cover the top of the head, so these were cast upside-down so that the marks caused by the removal of the jets were hidden underneath the finished casting. In the case of Plate 5 the Ife heads with crowns, the jets were arranged so that they were on the edge of the crown or even partly inside it, so that they did not spoil the carefully worked surface. Most of the heads from Ife have holes in the top, either square or round, apparently to economize in metal, though they do offer the technical advantage that the core and the investment could be joined together helping the iron pins to keep the core in place, whilst also allowing a greater area of the core to have access to the outside air, so that when the hot metal is poured in any air which is still inside the core can easily escape without passing through the metal and thereby possibly producing bubbling.[51] Despite these precautions, success was not inevitable. There is a hole in one head where a bubble of air was trapped. Several were found to have serious faults when the mould was opened and had to be saved by burning-in; that is, the faulty part is made good with wax, to which new runners and risers are attached, and it is reinvested in clay. The great difficulty is to get the fresh metal to fuse on to the original. In the Ife pieces this was usually done successfully, but some of the Tsoede bronzes (p. 172) have repairs which are loose and which rattle.

The surface of a casting produced by the lost wax process depends on the fineness of the inner layer of the investment. The finer the mud which is used for this the smoother will the surface be. Nevertheless, some finishing work was necessary, for some of the bronzes appear to have been rubbed down to produce a very smooth finish indeed. The modern copy of the so-called Olokun head discovered by Frobenius was cast by the modern sand-casting technique in which both the core and the outer mould are made of special casting sand. This sandy surface was reproduced in the metal which consequently has a distinctly rough granular surface quite unlike all the genuine Ife bronzes.[52]

THE COMPOSITION OF THE METALS

Bronze is an alloy consisting principally of copper with at least 5 per cent of tin. Now the Obalufon mask and four of the life-size heads are all of more or less pure copper, with less than 1 per cent of all other elements combined. The remaining Ife castings never have more than 3·6 per cent of tin and usually less than 2 per cent, whilst the zinc content of the Wunmonije heads ranges from 9 to 15 per cent, and the lead content from 4 to 16 per cent. The Ita Yemoo castings have a slightly different composition—zinc varies between 1·8 and 6·7 per cent, lead from 1 to 6·7 per cent, and tin from 0·3 to 3·6 per cent, but even when the tin content is as high as 3·6 per cent, the lead and zinc together outweigh it.[53] It follows then that none of the Ife 'bronzes' are bronze at all. They are either coppers or brasses, but since the term bronze is usually applied to any artistic metal-casting composed mainly of copper this term will continue to be used in this book. Moreover, it would bring in a false sense of accuracy to use it of the Ife castings alone, since very few other copper-alloy castings have been analyzed. We do know that some of the Benin pieces are of brass whilst others are of bronze. If one were to distinguish brass from bronze in Ife, it would be difficult to tell whether, when one said bronze of a Benin piece, one meant that it certainly was bronze or that one was using the term loosely because the object had not been analyzed.

SOURCES OF THE METALS

It had been hoped that the analysis of the metals used in ancient bronzes, not only in Africa but in Europe and all the rest of the world, would allow us to make deductions about the sources of the ores of which they are composed, for no ores are completely pure: most of them have small quantities of other elements included. Mauny has suggested that the site of Takedda or Azelik, which is known to have been an active copper mine in the Middle Ages, was the source from which the copper for these Ife bronze-castings came.[54] This, however, does not appear to be the case. Trace elements which have been identified in Ife bronzes have not been found in the ore from Azelik, and conversely trace elements that were found in the Azelik ores have not been found in the analyses of the Ife bronzes. The ores seem indeed to have come from more than one source, for some of the castings are of nearly pure copper, whilst others approximate to the proportions of orichalcum, a natural mixed ore found on the southern edge of the Sahara and probably also in Nigeria.[55] Others again seem to represent a mixture of equal parts of these two ores, whilst it is also very likely that bronzes were remelted and the metals mixed. Whether we shall ever know with certainty the sources from which the copper came is difficult to tell. However, we do know that the copper from the mine at Takedda was described in 1353 by Ibn Battuta as being exported southwards into Northern Nigeria, so that it is not unlikely that some of this Takedda ore eventually found its way even farther south. There may well have been many other centres of mining at this time, but we have relatively few accounts of travellers in the Middle Ages in the interior of West Africa. A later traveller, Macgregor Laird (1832–4), refers to copper being traded down the Benue Valley from the east, whilst Barth (1849–55) met caravans of copper, again in the Benue Valley, which had been mined in Darfur. These might have been following old-established routes. Commercial quantities of tin, of course, are still exploited in the Plateau area of Northern Nigeria, and smaller quantities of lead and zinc are mined in Eastern Nigeria, whilst copper has been found, though it has never been exploited on a commercial scale. It is likely that in the Middle Ages quite small quantities of ore were worth exploiting, and it may be that a large number of small deposits were used and possibly even worked out entirely in the Middle Ages, so that we may never be able to trace the precise source of some of these metals. But we can at least hope that by continuing analyses we may find out more and more about the technique and possibly about the sources of the metals from which these bronzes were made.

V

The Terracotta Sculptures of Ife

THE SCULPTURES in terracotta from ancient Ife are far more numerous than the bronzes and far more varied in subject matter, style and size. Artistically they conform for the most part to the same canon: they are essentially naturalistic representations, although there are several sculptures which are not naturalistic. Many of the terracotta sculptures represent human beings of nearly life-size. They must have been extremely impressive to see when they were whole, but now, unfortunately, since they are fragile, we have very few pieces which can be completely reconstructed. In many cases the heads have survived in reasonably good condition, perhaps because their roughly spherical shape is mechanically strong, but for our interpretations of the rest of the sculpture we are forced to rely on fragmentary pieces which we can compare with the bronzes.

'LAJUWA'
Plate 11

The first terracotta sculpture from Ife to become known was the head known as Lajuwa, which was said to have been kept in the Palace ever since it was made. It is of life-size but was never part of a larger sculpture. First published by the Oni of Ife in 1937,[56] it is said to have been made in commemoration of Lajuwa, the Chamberlain to the Oni Aworokolokin, who, when his master died, hid his body and pretended that the Oni was still alive by wearing the regalia himself. It will be remembered that the Oni wore a crown fringed with beads so that such a deception could quite easily be carried out, particularly as the Oni used only to be seen normally in a dark chamber by a few inner chiefs. It is alleged that the rightful successor, on discovering this deceit, had Lajuwa executed. It seems odd, if this story has any truth in it, that Lajuwa should have been commemorated by a terracotta head in this way and that he should be considered the patron of the Palace servants. However, although the head is said always to have been kept in the Palace, there is soil still adhering to the inside which suggests that it has at some time been buried and rediscovered just like the bronzes, and that the

Plate 71

attribution is probably recent. The condition of this sculpture, however, is quite remarkable for it has still managed to retain a very smooth surface despite the fact that the nose has been broken. Stylistically it is almost identical with the Wunmonije bronzes and could well have been made by one of the same artists.

Plates 16, 27, 68

This sculpture may be taken as typical of a whole series of human heads in terracotta, though in most cases the sculptures were originally of full-length figures ranging in scale from almost life-size down to small figurines varying between about six and twelve inches in height. The majority of these human figures wear elaborate costumes which appear to represent the regalia of an Oni or of a queen, but in many cases much simpler garments are worn, and many of the figures are without any head-dress at all, though many of these have very

Plates 27, 29, 30

elaborate hair-styles, in some cases with iron nails inserted into the terracotta in the centre of the curl. One or two wear the distinctive

Plate 60

hair-style of court messengers (*emese*) whose half-shaved head can be seen in the two attendants in Plate 71.

ANIMALS

The animal figures in many cases represent creatures which have been sacrificed. These were probably intended to serve as a permanent reminder of such offerings, since the real heads would not remain

Plates 41, 43–45

indefinitely on the shrine.[57] Many of these terracotta sculptures show the heads of rams on platters; they resemble very closely the heads which one can still see displayed in shrines on the occasion of the annual festival. It is interesting to note in this connection that in Benin there are wooden ram-heads which are placed on the shrine of male ancestors, and cocks of wood and bronze which are placed on the shrine of the queen mother: rams and cocks are the particular sacrifices offered at these altars.[58] Other animals represented in Ife

Plates 42, 50

include a dog from Osongongon Obamakin and the figure of an ape from the same shrine. This is probably not a sacrificial victim, although the dog could well have been. Particularly notable are an

Plates 47, 48, 51

owl and a chameleon, both of which were found casually, not in shrines, in Ife. These are both extremely lively representations and show very clearly the artistic capacity of the Ife terracotta sculptors.

Plate 49

Another find of great interest is the head of an elephant, which was found in the Lafogido area just behind the Palace in the centre of the town in 1963. It was eroding from the ground so that the top has been worn away. It is decorated all over with a herring-bone design and wears an elaborate crown. There are a number of other examples

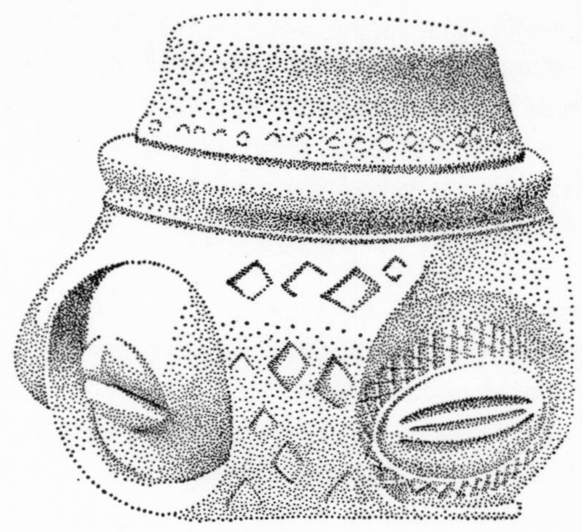

5 Partly reconstructed sculpture from the grove of Obameri, Ife. cf. *Plate 67*

of this elaborate style of terracotta sculpture: one, the head of a ram with serpents round the eyes, is still in use in one of the Ife groves, whilst a damaged head of a ram was taken to Berlin by Frobenius;[59] a small fragment in the same style is in the Ife Museum, whilst another in a similar style was excavated by Bernard Fagg at Olokun Walode. An animal with a rope round its neck appears to be from the side of a larger sculpture, probably that of a kneeling figure who was holding the tether. There are fragments of two other such sculptures from Osongongon Obamakin in which a kneeling figure has an animal at its side. There are also some small fragments of a sculpture of a leopard in terracotta. Bernard Fagg excavated at Olokun Walode the leg of a bushcow, whilst a similar leg from the writer's excavations at Ita Yemoo was identified as that of a dwarf goat. There is also from Kubolaje a small head of a bird, somewhat damaged.

Plate 46

THE VARIETY OF STYLES

The freely imaginative sculpture includes such highly stylized heads as those illustrated in Plate 61 and the naturalistic but mysterious head illustrated in Plate 67 and Fig. 5. Fig. 35 shows a fragment from Kubolaje which is part of a monstrous head with snakes emerging from the nostrils, although it is possible that they are fishes rather than snakes, for another fragment which may be from the same sculpture bears the head of a fish. There are also a pair of massive ears and a horn adorned with a small human figure, which may belong to the same sculpture. This motif appears in many other forms of sculpture in Nigeria. Yet another example of highly

Plate 90; *Figs. 36, 37*

Plate 102

imaginative representation was collected by Frobenius. Here the naturalistic head of a man on one side is balanced by a very stylized ornamental representation of an owl backing him on the other. From the mouth of both there emerges an object (now damaged on both sides) from which hangs a loop consisting of three elements on one side and four on the other, but evidently corresponding on the two sides. It would appear that we are intended to consider the owl and the man to be equivalent, but what precise significance we are supposed to attach to the sculpture is at present unknown and is possibly beyond discovery.[60]

SUB-STYLES: THE IWINRIN GROVE

Although the sculptures just described are stylized to varying degrees, the great majority are in a style of idealized naturalism which is entirely comparable to that of the bronzes. Nevertheless, there are within this general naturalistic style a number of sub-styles, some of which appear to be related to different cults. The terracotta sculptures of the Iwinrin Grove, for example, are highly naturalistic, and all the surviving heads appear to be striated. The great majority of the figures from this grove are about life-size, though some very fine sculpture is on a smaller scale. This grove has produced more terracotta sculpture than any of the others and must have been tremendously impressive when all these figures were standing complete in the dark shadows of the high forest.[61] The stool group is especially remarkable for it had a human figure of two-thirds of life-size seated upon it, and it appears to have been flanked by other figures of life-size; a fragment of one of which is illustrated, from which it will be seen that the hands hold garments. It is not clear to which figure these garments belong, but it is not impossible that they represent the robes of the central figure sitting on the stool, although the stool group is on its own base and the flanking figures, judged by the surviving feet, were also on independent rectangular bases. Whether this group was sculptured as one piece or as several is not of great importance, since the stools and central figure alone represent a tremendous technical achievement, for this whole sculpture must have been built up from sections of unfired clay; a task which must have taken a considerable length of time. When the whole construction was completed and had been allowed to dry out in the sun, it would have to be fired in an open wood fire, for there is no evidence whatever of the use of a kiln in Ife. The resulting terracotta is of an even colour and shows that the sculptors were able to control a very

Plates 23, 25, 27, 28, 39, 76

Plate 76

Plate 36

large fire with great skill, a skill probably at least as great as that required to cast a life-size bronze head, although it is these heads which have caused amazement to art historians not acquainted with African technology.

ITA YEMOO AND OBAMERI
Plates 12, 65, VII–IX

The sculptures from Ita Yemoo are very similar in general character to those from the Iwinrin Grove, but none of them is striated. They too represent both royal figures with crowns and figures without crowns who presumably are attendants. The Grove of Obameri, which is close to Ita Yemoo, was recently excavated by Oliver Myers. He found a group of sculptures in another very similar style, including one striated and five unstriated heads. The paste of these Obameri sculptures is rather grittier than that of the Ita Yemoo pieces; most of them have also been more eroded, with the result that they look less refined than those from Ita Yemoo, but the arms, the legs and the beadwork on both the limbs and the body are very similar indeed in treatment. The terracottas from Igbo Obameri,[62] however, show more variety in their conception, for example Plate 67, and a very simplified and stylized head which is quite clearly derived from the form of Plate 61, *right*. The Ita Yemoo pieces, in comparison, are not so varied, but whereas these come from a group of shrines which have long been abandoned but which contain whole figures, the Igbo Obameri material appears to consist of a collection of heterogeneous fragments of terracotta sculptures, none of which form complete figures, brought together at random apparently in the eighteenth century, for a radiocarbon date of AD 1730 ± 100 has just been obtained from associated charcoal by the University of Michigan (No. M-1686. *J.A.H.* VII, 1966, p. 496).

OSONGONGON OBAMAKIN

Another grove with its own characteristic sub-style is that of Osongongon Obamakin, which is close to the Iwinrin Grove. This has produced a great range of terracotta sculpture much of which is in a highly micaceous paste. There is the head of Osongongon Obamakin himself, which is about half life-size and is sculptured in a naturalistic style, though it has not received a very refined treatment; there is also a conical head. The head of a dog and a legless animal have already been mentioned, as has the kneeling figure with an animal. The most remarkable group of terracotta sculptures from this grove, however, represent diseases; for example, an unfortunate victim of elephantiasis of the scrotum. Various forms of elephantiasis are quite common in tropical Africa, and this particular form, which

Plate 21

Plates 42, 46, 61

Plate 40

6 Top of a pottery bottle stopper showing anacephaly; excavated in the grove of Osongongon Obamakin, Ife

is so intimately associated with the idea of procreation and the progeny of the victim, has called for special ritual treatments in many African societies. Bascom reports that even in modern Ife such a condition requires the services of the priest of the *Oro* or bull-roarer cult when the victim dies. This priest removes the scrotum and performs a ceremony which ensures that other members of the family will not suffer from the same disease. *Oro* apparently performs no other function at funerals, so this condition is evidently regarded as special in some way.[63] Similarly, Talbot also refers to special practices among tribes in Eastern Nigeria, where the affected scrotum is removed and given separate burial, whilst in some cases the body is not buried at all but thrown into the 'bad bush'. He also gives evidence that this condition was sometimes considered to be a punishment for sin.[64] In this terracotta sculpture the figure is evidently manacled, but whether there is any connection between this fact and his clinical condition we do not know.

Fig. 6 A small terracotta stopper excavated in this grove by Bernard Fagg appears to represent a condition known as anacephaly, in which the bones of the vault of the skull fail to ossify, and the brain

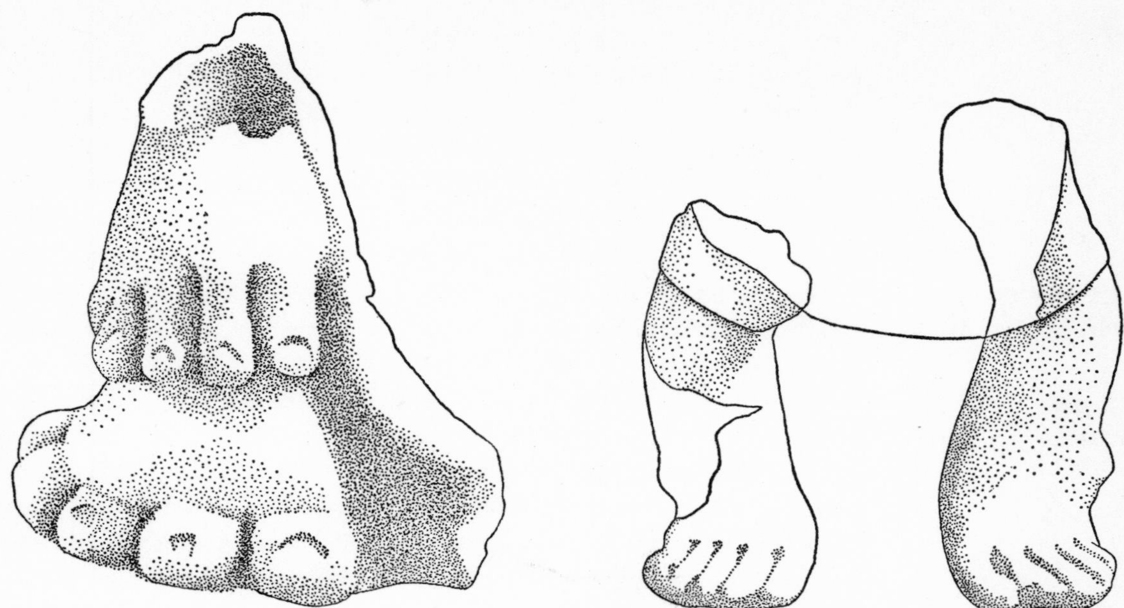

7, 8 A number of the terracotta sculptures represent various diseases. Left, *a right hand and foot from a terracotta sculpture of a victim of elephantiasis, perhaps from the grove of Osongongon Obamakin, Ife.* Right, *partly reconstructed legs of a terracotta figure with rickets, of uncertain provenance in Ife*

and the eyes are protected only by a membrane. The unfortunate baby usually dies with a few days. Yet another fragment shows a hand and a foot both swollen, presumably from another representation of elephantiasis; this is only one of several sculptures showing this condition.[65] This same grove also produced a ritual pot with a relief decoration of considerable interest. It shows, for example, *edan*, the bronze staffs associated with the Ogboni society,[66] a human figure lying on his back with his hands tied together, a leopard, a ritual staff with curled projections down each side of a type which may be related to staffs currently in use in Ife, a drum, an object with two skulls at its base which defies certain interpretation, a snake, an axe and two human figures both headless, one perhaps because the pot itself is damaged at this point, but the other with its hands fastened behind the back—yet another sacrificial victim. Also from this grove is an interesting stone sculpture representing a calabash with a cord round its neck; the opening at the top appears to be filled with a ball of some fibrous material, which suggests that it contains palm wine.[67] The great majority, then, of the pieces from this grove can be easily distinguished from the sculpture in other groves. One fragment of

Fig. 7

an elaborately beaded neck, painted in a brilliant red, which was found in the course of Fagg's excavations, is, however, rather more like the Iwinrin style but is not identical with it. It is possible to pick out pieces of unknown provenance which match closely in form, style and paste these sculptures from Osongongon Obamakin, but we cannot necessarily be sure that this is where they originated.

KUBOLAJE
Fig. 34

The shrine of Kubolaje, which is in the middle of the town, produced a series of small figurines in a naturalistic style,[68] together with the fragments of a monstrous head already described.

ABIRI
Plate 24

The site at Abiri, ten miles from Ife, has produced three terracotta heads (two of them striated) in a naturalistic style which can hardly be distinguished from that of the Iwinrin Grove. One has a hat with a narrow brim, whilst another has a very elaborate head-band with three bell-like objects hanging over the forehead and another hanging behind.[69] This is rather similar to the head-dress of one of the figures in the Iwinrin Grove.[70] In the same naturalistic style is the terracotta head of a ram. There is also a fragmentary coiled-up snake, apparently a puff adder, and an arm from a human figure with ornamental metal bangles represented on the wrist, but the most striking objects from this site are four highly stylized terracotta heads. There are three of the type illustrated in Plate 61, *right*, whilst the fourth is conical and somewhat resembles Plate 61, *left*, but is more highly stylized. The first three have a point rising from the centre of the head and a ring of points around the edge, presumably representing a crown. The eyes and mouth are quite clearly, though very roughly, indicated. It is very interesting to have both these styles occurring on the same site and evidently in association with each other. There is no evidence whatever to suggest that these are not all contemporaneous so that we have evidently two strands of art represented, one the classical naturalism and alongside it this very highly stylized way of representing human heads. The head from Osongongon Obamakin indeed shows features of both these strands combined in one sculpture, for although the head is conical, the features are naturalistic.

Plate 45

Plate 61.

OGBON OYA

In 1935 a site was discovered just behind the palace in the Ogbon Oya quarter of Ife. This produced a fragmentary terracotta head in the naturalistic style and a head in the stylized manner just described from Abiri, but in this case with eyes and lips modelled in a way much closer to that of the naturalistic heads, although the nose was indicated simply by two small impressed points. It resembles very much the piece illustrated in Plate 61, *right centre*. More unusual, however, than these heads are the fragmentary remains of a group of stands of which there appear to be parts of four surviving, which are remarkable for having on the side a lug shaped like a shell. It is very difficult to understand how these can have been used, but they appear to have formed flat bases with the lug projecting upwards to prevent a figure from slipping. A similar piece has since been discovered on the site at Lagere.

OBALURU

Plate 13

One shrine which is still in use, that for Olokun at Obaluru just outside Ife, contains two heads in a sub-style unparalleled elsewhere. The striations on the face are more widely separated than is usual in Ife sculpture, whilst the alternate spaces between are finely cross-hatched; in addition there are horizontal bands of similar striations with cross-hatching between the eyes and the ears as well as over the bridge of the nose. These marks closely resemble in the way they are made, though not in the extent of their distribution, tribal marks still used in Ife today, where a band of cross-hatching is commonly found horizontally between the ear and the eye. These two heads are remarkable also in being modelled on top of globular bases.

LAGERE

Plate 57

Plate 58

In April 1958 a group of terracotta sculptures was found in the Lagere district of Ife at a point just outside the Seventh Day Adventist Mission Hospital on the west side. These are all made in a very distinctive paste which is rich in mica and extremely friable, the surface having frequently flaked off. At least five figures are represented. One of them is of life-size; a foot and both arms with hands have survived, whilst there are three fragments of very decorative tassels, bells and crotals, which probably belong to the same figure. The beadwork on the arms is rather different in style from most of the Ife sculptures in that the globular beads are much more prominent than usual. There is also part of a figure of about half life-size the arms of which are illustrated. The smaller piece is split in the centre revealing an iron armature inside it to give support to the terracotta when it was being built up from moist clay. There are parts of another figure of half natural size of a female torso with striations on the body, and the left breast and arm surviving. In addition there is a headless kneeling figure of about a quarter life-size apparently male, with a striated torso, crossed baldricks of beads, a heavy collar round the neck, and three strings of beads round the waist from which hang crotals behind and an unusual pubic apron in front. There are also two small heads on the same scale which do not belong to this body, and the fragment of a base with a shell-like lug which has been mentioned earlier (p. 65). The tassel, bells and crotals represented here have been found on no other Ife sculptures, whilst the decoration of cross-hatching to form lozenges with a dot in the centre of each, which is found on the bells and on the apron,

Plate 89

is only paralleled elsewhere in Ife sculpture in the small bronze figure from Benin. These features are characteristic of this Lagere sub-style, which is also rather more stylized in character than the classical Ife sculpture exemplified at the Iwinrin Grove and Ita Yemoo. Although still highly skilled as sculpture, the technique of these pieces from Lagere, both in preparing the paste and in firing it, seems to be poorer than that of the classical sculptures, whilst the metal bracelet

Plate 58

represented as worn by one figure appears to be similar to a type which is still freely available in white metal in the markets of the Sudan. It is difficult not to consider these pieces to be rather later than the Classical Period of Ife art represented by the Iwinrin and Ita Yemoo sub-styles.

ONDO ROAD

Another very distinctive sub-style is represented by a group of pieces found in 1955 on a cocoa farm, fourteen miles from Ife

Plates 55, 56; *Fig. 9*

towards Ondo. Three of the pieces, a sculpture representing a striated head, a headless male figure and a very stylized human figure, are illustrated. The other finds consisted of a female torso with the breasts bare, lacking head and legs, the upper part of a male torso rather similar to Plate 56 and a very stylized head in the general style of

Plate **61**

those from Abiri but with only three points on the crown. All these are in a paste of very poor quality and have been poorly fired; it is distinct from, and inferior to, that of the sculptures from Lagere. Moreover, in this group we have examples of the two distinct elements: the naturalistic and the stylized modes, which are to be seen also at Abiri and at Osongongon Obamakin. These sculptures from the Ondo Road are evidently all of a piece, and yet it is very difficult to consider them as being anything other than late, probably

Plate 55

a good deal later than the sculptures from Lagere. The striated head is very stylized in its general form, while the lips are flat and protrude

Plates 106, 109, 110

in a way which reminds us of later Yoruba sculpture, as do the stylized ear and the bulging eyes which are quite unlike the Classical Ife sculptures. Examples of these characteristics can be seen in other

Fig. 9

pieces of Ife sculpture but the very stylized human figure is quite

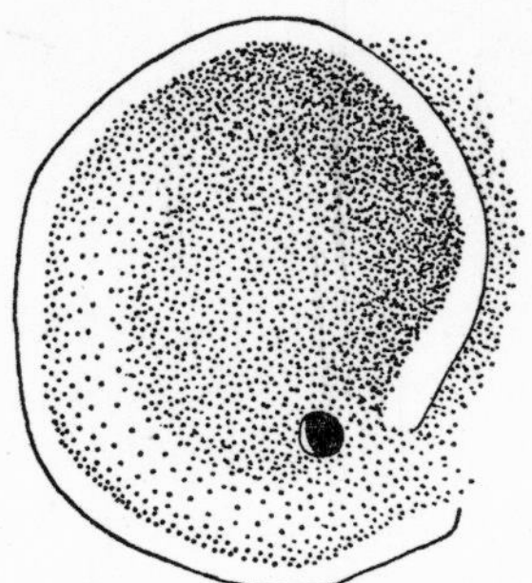

10 Ear of the late terracotta head from near Ife shown in Plate 59

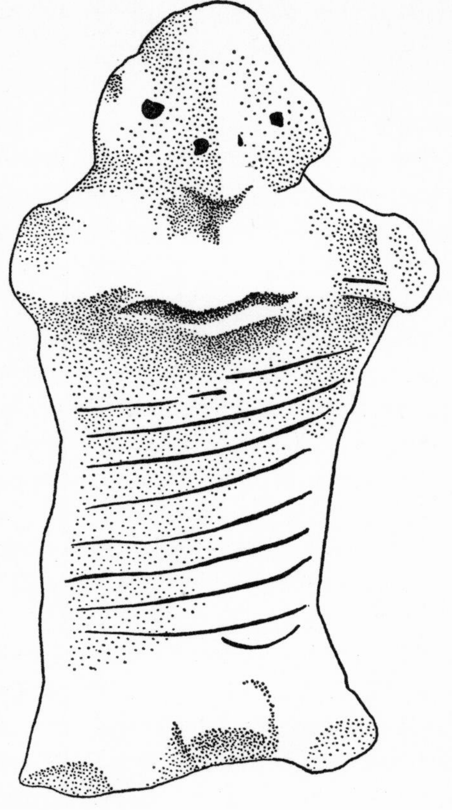

9 Crude terracotta figure found near Ife with the pieces illustrated in Plates 55 and 56

without parallel in Ife, though in general character it reminds one a little of the Sao terracottas from sites excavated by Lebeuf around Lake Chad. This one nondescript piece from Ife cannot be considered evidence of contact between these two areas.[71]

MOKURO STREAM

Plate 55; *Fig. 11*

Another fragmentary terracotta sculpture, also probably of late date, survives in four pieces, the head, the two arms with the adjacent parts of the body, and the left foot. The discovery was made by two Hausa goldminers who were panning the gravels of a stream about three miles from Ife up the Mokuro Road. The head retains the striations from the naturalistic art of the classical period, but is itself very stylized: the lips protrude and are very thin, whilst the ears are curious. The representation of eyebrows is an unusual feature in Ife sculpture and the hat, rather resembling that of a sailor, is also odd. The body fragments are extremely conventional, whilst the

Fig. 10

Fig. 11

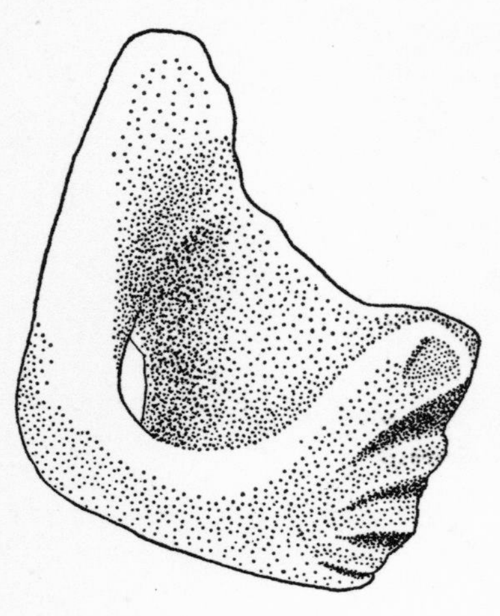
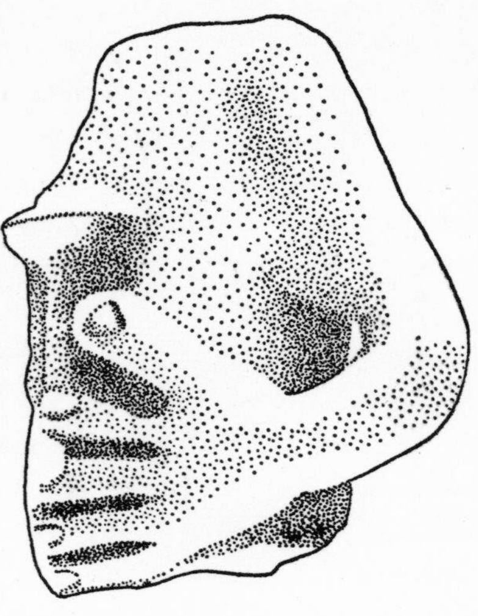

11 Fragments of the body and arms of a terracotta figure found near the Mokuro Road, Ife. The head is shown in Plate 59 and a detail of one of its ears in Fig. 10

feet are similar in character and are very square, with the heels projecting backwards—probably to give the figure some stability. Despite the presumed lateness of its style it is extremely well fired.

OTHER LATE PIECES

Plate 60

One of the heads collected by Frobenius also appears to be a late piece, although it is fairly naturalistic and appears to represent an *emese* or court messenger with half his head shaved. It has very oddly represented eyes, which bulge curiously, and it too has eyebrows shown. The nose and lips are rather abraded so that one cannot say very much about them, but the ear is very highly stylized. The head projects from the neck at an odd angle; normally the head of an Ife sculpture is balanced on top of the neck as it is in a real person, but this head leaves the neck at an angle of about forty-five degrees.

Fig. 12

Plate 62

There are also three gagged terracotta heads representing victims for human sacrifice. As these appear all to have been modelled as heads not as parts of whole figures, it is likely that, like the ram and

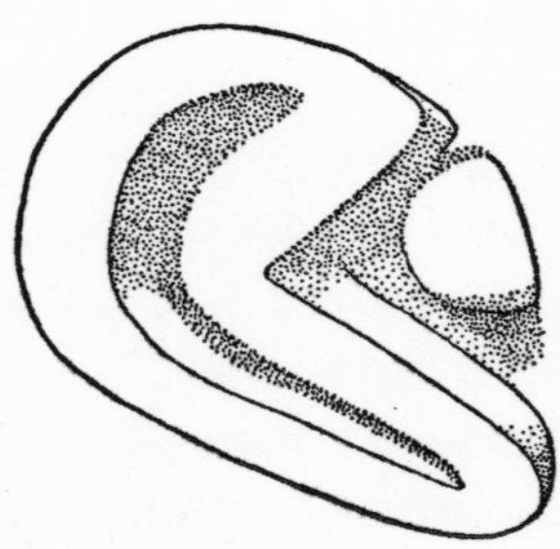

12 Ear from the Post-Classical Ife terracotta head illustrated in Plate 60

other animal heads, they were intended as commemorations of executed victims. The head in the centre, which was excavated in 1953 by Bernard Fagg in the grove of Osongongon Obamakin, is moderately naturalistic, as is the one on the right, which may also be from the same grove. They are both in a similar micaceous paste and clearly similar in style. The ears show some stylization and the lips are protrusive, but they are not much removed from the classical Ife style. The head on the left, found on the Ilesha road opposite Ita Yemoo in 1958, is very much different although clearly related in subject matter. The whole head is treated in a far more stylized manner: the ears have become little more than hooks; eyebrows are represented; there are keeloid bosses between the ear and the eye which are evidently a tribal mark which has not previously been seen on any of the Ife sculptures; the lips protrude very markedly and are themselves quite flat and lacking in naturalistic modelling, and the nose itself is highly stylized; the oval eyes are very reminiscent of modern Yoruba wood-carving, as indeed are the forms of the ears and lips. Plates 106, 109, 110; *Fig. 3*

The last few groups of terracotta sculpture which have been described, have been considered to be late principally on stylistic grounds. It is not easy to distinguish, of course, which end is which when one places antiquities in a typological series, but external evidence does lend some support to the idea that certain features are recent; *e.g.*, the bracelets on the Lagere sculptures constitute external evidence, whilst the general tendency towards bulging eyes, stylized ears, flat horizontal protruding lips all show progress towards the modern Yoruba sculptural style.

There are many terracotta sculptures which have been discovered in other parts of Ife which can be assigned to one or other of the various sub-styles, but in many cases each individual find is without any close parallel. This great variety complicates the problem of attempting to distinguish the individual hands of the sculptors, but the fact that there are so many styles and that they vary so much, and that they appear to show a development through time, does suggest that many sculptors were involved and that the art continued for some considerable period. How long that time was and when it was, we leave for later discussion. Among these casual finds we must point out one or two characteristics. One is the tribal marks which appear on some of them. We have already discussed the question of whether or not the striations on the heads are to be considered tribal marks, but there are a group of heads which undoubtedly bear tribal marks. One head, for example, has a tribal mark which is nowadays found among the Beni Nupe who are said to have acquired it from the Yoruba.[72] Another version of this same mark is found on a head from Gidiogbo Compound, whilst a number of other examples have marks of similar design but are represented by much finer lines. It is very possible that these are an ancient Ife mark.[73]

Plate 31

Plate 32

LIMBS AND BODIES

Plate 39

The bodies of some Ife figures are treated in a naturalistic manner, but the limbs are more often highly stylized. The arms are often hidden by a profusion of bracelets, so that this fact is often disguised, but Plate 37 shows an arm represented without beads in a smooth stylized manner, whilst Plate 38 shows an even more stylized representation, though this figure is probably itself not as naturalistic as many of the Ife sculptures. The legs too are often treated in a very simplified and stylized form, which again is hidden by either the skirt or the beaded anklets. The feet, although stylized, are modelled with considerable delicacy, particularly the toes and the toe-nails, whilst the second toe very frequently wears a ring. A fragment of a foot on a base from Wunmonije Compound has toes which are quite realistic in appearance, but the upper part of the foot rises steeply and can hardly be considered naturalistic. A foot from Ita Yemoo, however, is rather more naturalistic, though it is still idealized to the point of stylization. It is noticeable that the first of these feet is from a figure which stood originally on a plinth; this was not always the case at Ife, but was more usual than not. It also bears traces of paint: probably all the terracotta sculptures were originally painted.

Plate 54

Plate 52

THE TECHNIQUE OF TERRACOTTA SCULPTURE

Terracotta is sculpture made from clay by techniques which are closely similar to those by which domestic pottery is made. In Ife a great variety of pottery clays seems to have been available, many of which were used both for domestic pottery and for sculpture. In the case of the sculptures from the Iwinrin Grove the paste is particularly coarse and contains quite large pieces of amorphous quartz. In other cases there is a considerable amount of mica included.[74] The main problem in building a terracotta sculpture is to keep the clay moist whilst additional pieces are added to it. Normally in building up a domestic pot the lower part is first moulded and allowed to dry leather-hard, the edge is trimmed, moistened and a large sausage of clay is applied to build up the shoulder of the pot. If necessary the process is repeated to build up the rim on the leather-hard shoulder. Terracotta sculpture has to be built up in much the same way, beginning with the base and building upwards, but the Ife sculptures are so big that there is considerable risk of collapse, so many of them have iron armatures inside at their weakest points to help to support them. They appear to have been built in separate sections; the stool group, for example, appears to have had all the parts of the stool made separately and to have been luted together in the leather-hard state. The body, however, would have had to be built up on top of the completed stool, and this must have presented a considerable problem, especially as no iron armature was used in this case.

Plate 76

The way in which many of the terracotta sculptures have broken teaches us something of the way in which they were made. For example, in the course of excavating one of the shrines at Ita Yemoo, the writer discovered many detached fragments of headgear—rosette decorations and motifs intended to be on the front of the crown—which had evidently been made separately, perhaps even in a mould, and then pressed on to the basic clay of the main sculpture. A head with a mass of curls has had each curl separately made and then attached to the head, which has been tooled at the appropriate point to give a key for its attachment. The inner surface of many of the terracotta sculptures reveals the method by which they were built up from separate sausages of clay. One ram-head was built up in a series of loops of clay beginning at the neck, with a final strip running from the nose to the top of the head inserted in the centre. It has been suggested that the whole of these heads may have been made in moulds,[75] but if that were so the pressure required to push the clay into the mould would have had to be applied on the inside, and as a result these separate sausages would have been pushed together much more. As it is, this particular piece shows quite clearly the undeformed shape of the sausages on the inside as if the whole thing had been built up very delicately and then all the work done on the outside of the head. Indeed, the form of the ear suggests that it has been worked with sharp tools to cut away the part that was not required. This would have been done after the head had dried to a leather-hard state.[76] It is very probable that it was in this state that the final details such as the striations on the faces were applied, but

Plate 29

Plate 43

I Face of a life-size bronze head found at Wunmonije Compound, Ife. Traces of red and black paint can be seen forming spectacles round the eyes, and some of the red paint which forms a broad band round the neck is also visible. The top of the head has been built up to fit the crown which it was intended to carry

II The largest of all the bronze heads found at Wunmonije Compound, this has traces of white paint in the eyes, and a band of red paint round the neck. The area covered by the crown shows signs of cutting away round the edge to recess it below the level of the face to make the crown fit better. This would have been done on the wax model before investment. Inside this head some thread still remains which has been identified as being probably of linen. The ears are modelled in a highly idealized form (*see Fig. 31a*), but are cut away behind in a more naturalistic manner than on the other bronzes, most of which have ears which are triangular in horizontal section

III Pair of bronze figures from Ita Yemoo, representing an Oni and his queen, seen from the rear. On the king's left hip are two monkey skulls and another charm. The queen's flanged crown was, like her hair, painted black. The large beads on his crown, the beads round both their necks, and the wrappers they both wear were painted red. The three oval vents in the back were to permit the core (which can still be seen inside the casting) to be united with the clay investment, so that the gases generated inside the core during casting could escape without bubbling through the metal and ruining the sculpture. Technically this is the most difficult and the most proficiently executed of all the Ife bronze castings. In parts it is scarcely $\frac{1}{16}$ of an inch thick. Plate 10 shows the front view

IV–VI Some of the finest sculpture is found on the smallest bronzes. The head of the bronze staff, *above left*, was found at Ita Yemoo in 1957. It has what appear to be diagonal tribal marks on the cheeks. The eye-brow ridges are strongly modelled, as are the thick protruding lips and hooked nose. The shape of the head itself, as is usual at Ife, is much foreshortened. The lobes of the ears are pierced for earrings, which are nowadays worn only by women, though they might formerly have been worn by men also. The features are very strongly modelled and the beard and receding hair well indicated though there appears to be no moustache. A photograph showing the full length of both these staffs will be found in *Bibl. 119 d, pl. VIa.* The head of another staff, *right*, is the pair to the example *left* and was found with it. The rope gag indicates that he is intended for sacrifice. *Below left* is a detail of the head of an old man from a mace-head also found at Ita Yemoo in 1957. In general, African art represents people in their prime, but two or three pieces at Ife are exceptional in showing old men. This particular mace-head is egg-shaped and carries two heads back to back, both of them gagged, the one not shown appearing particularly youthful in contrast to this one. The heavy ridges over the eyebrows, and the emphasis which the sunken cheeks give to the cheek bones, make this sculpture outstanding in the whole corpus of Ife art in which the idealized forms tend usually to show an observance of the surface appearance rather than any obvious understanding of the bony structures which give form to the face from within. A finger lies against the lip, and Chief Akeredolu tells me that some Yoruba believe that people who die a violent death place a finger to their lips as they expire. The rope gag shows that this man was expecting a violent end, for it indicates that he was to be decapitated as a human sacrifice. Photographs of the whole mace-head and its companion piece appear in *Bibl. 119 c, Figs. 1, 2; and d, pl. V a, b*

I

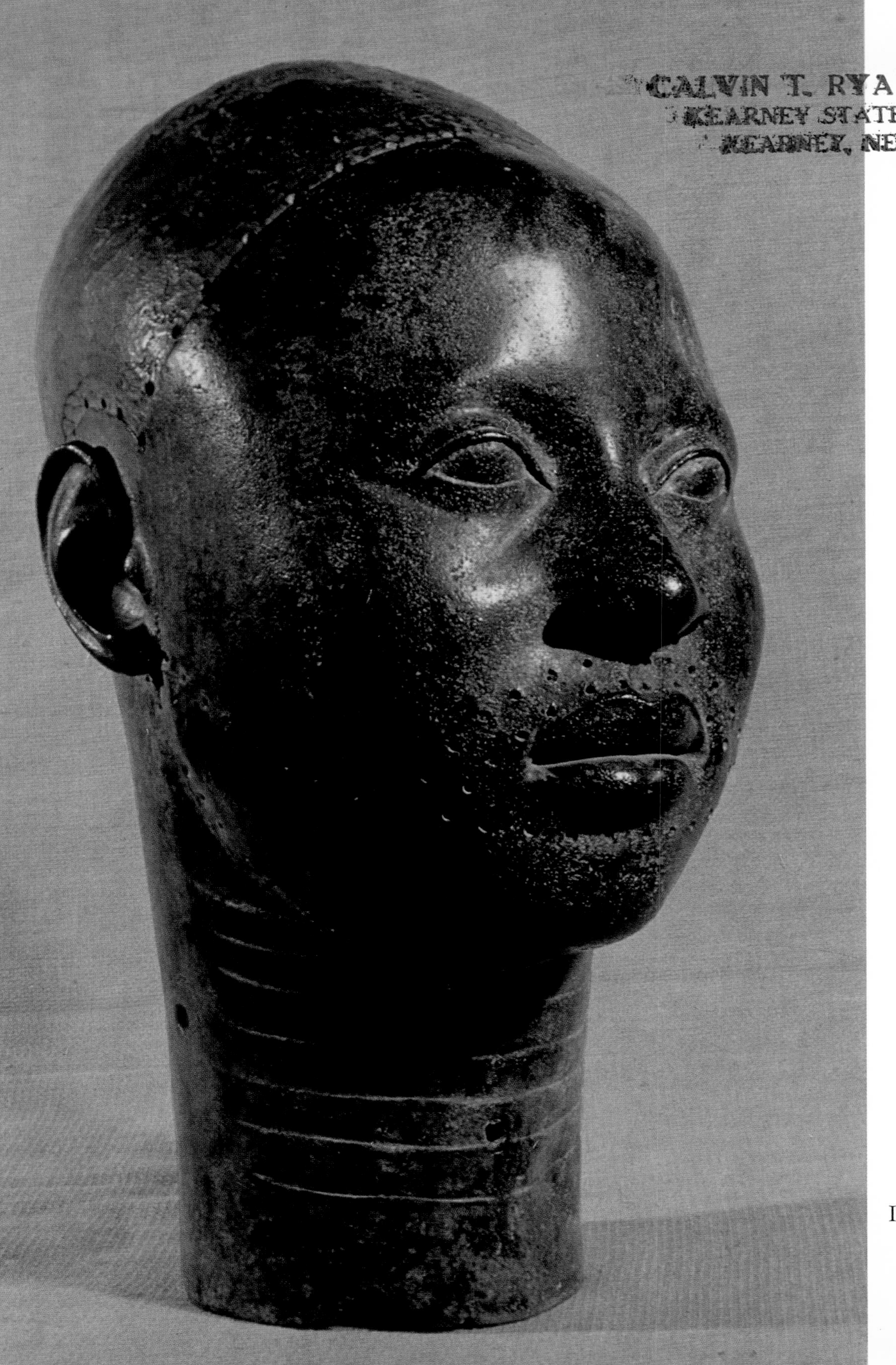

II

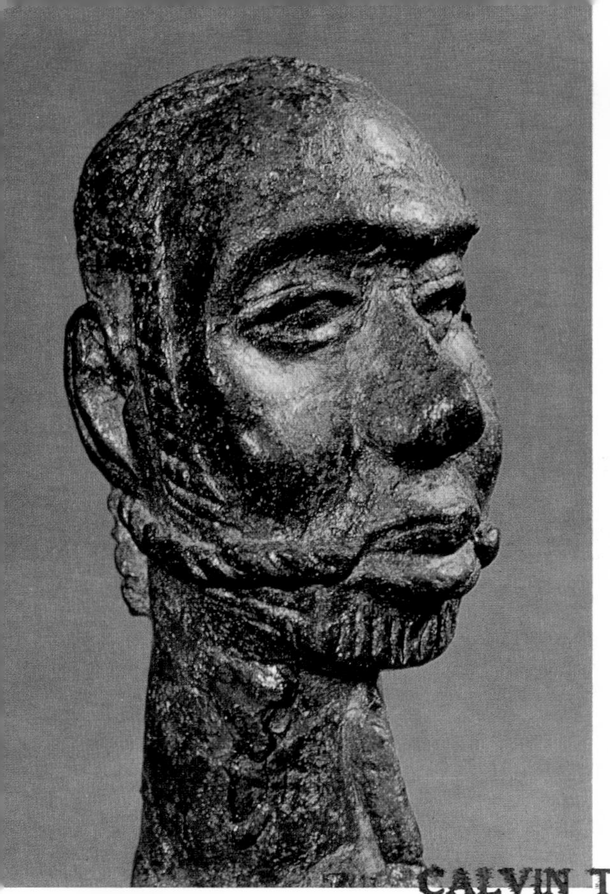

IV V

VI

the very smooth surface of many heads suggests that they may sometimes have been wetted again to soften the lines of the surface and to hide some of the marks of cutting.

The internal surface of the terracotta sculptures does not always show the sausages from which they were constructed, but usually it is quite rough and not at all carefully finished. This distinguishes the technique of terracotta sculpture from that of domestic pottery, for here the pottery is invariably well smoothed inside and out. The only exception is in the case of certain offering pots which are used only in shrines. These were probably regarded as associated with the terracottas and made by the same people. This distinction of technique implies that, since the domestic pottery in the whole of Africa is normally made by the women of the community, the terracotta sculptures are likely to have been made by the men in Ife. This idea is further supported by the fact that the casting of bronze is everywhere a man's business, and the naturalistic sculptures in terracotta are so clearly related to the bronzes. The skill required in manufacturing many of the terracotta sculptures of large size is comparable to that required for bronze-casting on a similar scale. Indeed the dominant problem in both is that of controlling a large fire to produce the required effects. The terracotta sculptures would have been fired in a simple wood fire built up all round the figures once they had dried out thoroughly. It is interesting to observe on the larger sculptures (which, of course, are hollow, although some of the very small ones are solid) that vents have been left to allow the air to escape freely from inside, otherwise the sculpture would have collapsed during firing from the pressure of the air inside. The small terracotta sculptures may well have been placed inside a pot to protect them in the fire, but it seems hardly possible for the large figures to have been enclosed in any way. There is no evidence at all for the use of any kind of kiln in Yorubaland, and indeed the only thing which resembles one at all in current use is the clamp in which bricks are fired, and this appears to be a very recent introduction and is certainly of European origin.

The great majority of the terracotta sculptures are very well fired, but there are a number which are poorly fired and made of a very inferior paste. On stylistic grounds these have been considered to be relatively late, and it appears that as the style changed so also the skill in preparing and firing the clay gradually declined. The only sign of anything remotely resembling terracotta sculpture still carried out in Ife is the manufacture of ritual vessels with faces on them, which are made by the women to a reasonable though not distinguished quality, and also the manufacture of mud figures of an extremely crude character called *shigidi*. These latter, however, are never fired but simply allowed to dry in the sun and are solid. They are much more comparable in technique to the sculptures from Ilesha (p. 179).

VI

The Stone Sculptures of Ife

COLUMNS

THE MOST STRIKING stone monument in Ife is the one called the Opa Oronmiyon or Staff of Oronyon. This stone column, about seventeen feet high, is made of granite-gneiss and is decorated with iron nails with spiral heads, a form of decoration which is found on a number of figure sculptures from Ife and elsewhere. This *opa* is said to be the walking-stick or fighting club of the great warrior Oronmiyon, who was the son of Ogun the God of Iron (but see the caption to Plate 73). The fragmentary remains of two similar staffs still stand at Idi Ogun, the main shrine for Ogun in the middle of the town, whilst other staffs in Ife vary in size and height from about four feet upwards. One in the Ore Grove was originally about twelve feet in height, quite slender, and with a rounded tip, whereas a second is 3 feet 6 inches high and sharply pointed.[77] Another in the Grove of Obameri is flat and thin in section; one at the Grove of the Temple of Ijugbe is simply an unworked column of triangular section; whilst that at the shrine of Ogun Esa is also triangular and almost six feet high.[78] The Opa Olusheri is of similar height but a rounded rectangle in section. The most striking example of all, however, is called the Ada (or sword of) Eledisi; this is unique and is about five feet in height, and has its upper part curved rather like a hockey stick. Most of these stone monoliths are associated with the cult of Ogun, the father of Oronmiyon. It is common to find a shrine for Ogun in groves to other gods, just as it is usual to have also a shrine for Eshu, the divine trickster, who needs always to be placated.

Plate 73

Plates 74, 75

FIGURES

Another group of stone sculptures consists of figures both human and animal. The main group is in the Ore Grove where there are two stone figures, the larger of which is commonly called Idena.[79] Recently a group of stone-carvings of similar type, one evidently a copy of the Idena figure, has been discovered at Eshure in Ekiti by a geologist, Alan Dempster.[80] One of these has all over its body

Plate 74

Plate 75

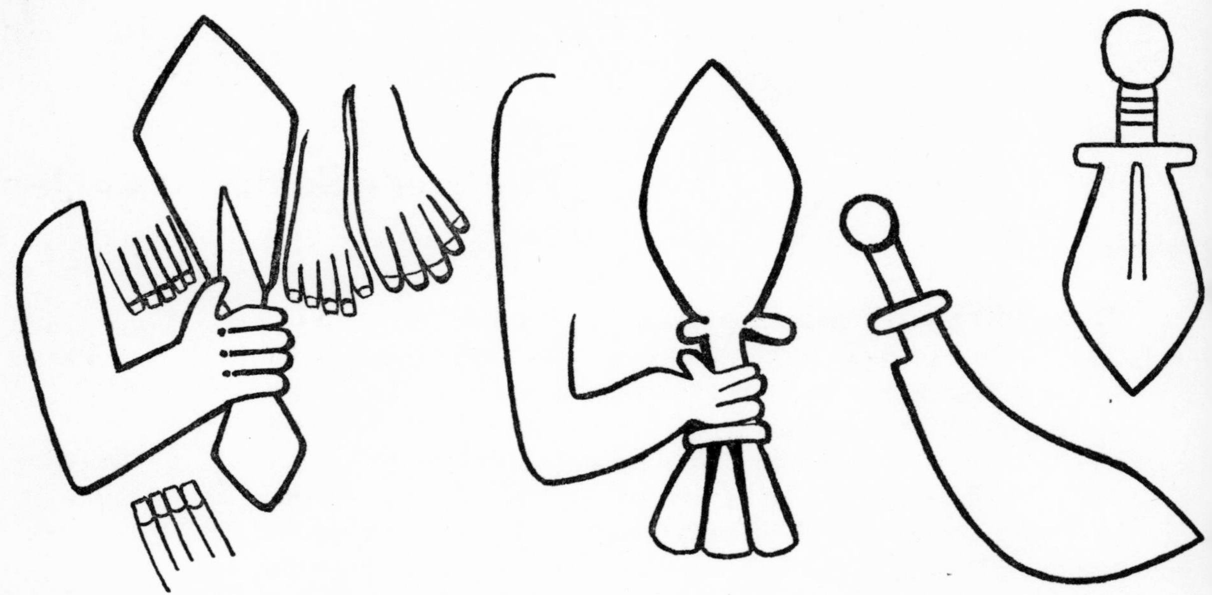

13 Low relief sculptures in stone from Agidi, nine miles south of Ife

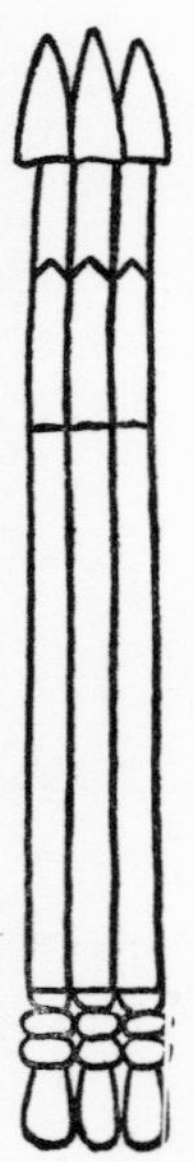

Plate 73 spiral-headed iron nails like those on the Opa Oronmiyon. Originally the hair of the Idena figure was similarly decorated, though only the shafts of the nails survive. It will be recalled that iron nails

Plate 30 were used to decorate some of the terracotta pieces, notably the 'Mia' head. The close similarity between the Idena figure and one of the figures at Eshure, together with the similarity of these iron nails and the fact that at Eshure too there is a stone column comparable to those from Ife, suggests that here we have an extension of the Ife culture, or at any rate of the stone sculpture of Ife, out into Ekiti about a hundred miles away from Ife to the east, whilst to the west a similar stone column still stands at Erumu, not far away from the site of Kuta, where there are two stone stools related to those found in Ife (p. 82).

The writer's excavations in the Ore Grove in 1957 discovered a stone sculpture probably of a snake or perhaps a fish with spiral-headed iron nails similar to those just described forming its eyes and nostrils.[81] A

Plate 72 similar piece with relief sculpture on it has been known for a long time in the shrine of Ogun Ladin which is inside the Palace in Ife. It evidently represents a mudfish, for it has the characteristic barbels over the nostrils. One stone sculpture recently discovered in Ife in digging the foundations of a house is in a style similar to that of the large group of figures at Esie which will be described later (p. 177), whilst a large number of stone figures and heads have been found in various parts of the town, some of them apparently unskillful copies of well-known Ife pieces, whilst others, in a variety of styles, are evidently relatively recent in date. They are often very crude and frequently carved in a soft talc schist, whereas the stone favoured in this principal period of stone sculpture was granite-gneiss.

Another group of stone-carvings at Agidi's farm, near the village of Agidi, nine miles down the Ondo road, are in a style not otherwise known. They are low-relief carvings and have motifs which are in some cases entirely their own: hands holding swords; swords alone; groups of spears; but some subjects they share with Ife, notably the decapitated corpse with the hands tied behind the back, although this is found also in Benin and Ijebu bronze-castings. One carving has been interpreted as a Muslim prayer-board, and this has been taken to indicate a late date for the carvings, since Islam seems only to have become influential in the Ife district late in the nineteenth

BAS-RELIEFS

Fig. 13

century. Whilst it is true that the carvings do not appear to be as old as the Classical Period of Ife art, this interpretation appears to be mistaken, for the single knob of a Muslim prayer-board is quite different in shape and it is not the kind of object one would be likely to find represented in a pagan grove. The line engraved inside it suggests that it is a shallow tray, probably one for Ifa divination. Such an object is clearly more in keeping with the paganism of the grove. The equipment used in Ifa divination is not represented in the art of the Classical Period, which implies that Ifa may not be an original Ife cult and also supports a post-Classical date for the Agidi reliefs.

STOOLS
Plate 77

Plates 9, 76

The most remarkable stone sculptures, however, are the quartz stools of very elaborate form, the best example of which is in the British Museum. These stone stools cannot be studied in isolation, for the similar representations in terracotta and in bronze have to be considered. Bernard and William Fagg have studied the majority of these stools, and have proposed a hypothesis for their origin and development which has been confirmed as more evidence has come to light.[82] They suggest that the prototype of these stools was the wooden box which is used still in Ife where it is known as *apere*, the name which is applied also to these stone stools, and in Benin, where it was frequently represented on the bronze plaques.[83] In Ife and Benin these boxes are used for containing ritual objects and also as stools. In Benin, indeed, on certain ceremonies of the divine kingship 'gifts from Ife' are brought to the Oba in one of these boxes.[84] When used for the cult of Ifa they are frequently painted with vertical bands of white paint composed of separate small motifs, including circles and dots. This appears to be the origin of the decoration of two stone stools at Kuta.[85] The form of these stools is closely similar to that of the wooden boxes, namely, the upper and lower parts are both flanged and the central column is of a wide diameter. A recent discovery in Ife is a fragment of the central column of a stool of this type represented in terracotta, with a diameter of 19 inches; the decoration appears to represent a metal strip set with glass bosses, and in the Iwinrin Grove, where the most famous of these terracotta sculptures was found, five glass bosses were discovered, each of them set in a piece of decayed bronze strip. Presumably, the terracotta fragment we have is from a representation of a wooden box decorated thus with bronze and glass. Probably there

Fig. 14

Plate 76

14 Fragment from the column of a terracotta stool found opposite the Ife Museum

was at one time one of these boxes in the Iwinrin Grove, but the wooden parts have decayed. Once this stylization had begun, the development is clear: the column is made narrow, the loop which joins the two pieces of the box which originally was only a strip of bark or leather becomes elaborated into the same form as the stool itself and is decorated in the same way. This is seen in Plate 76. Copies of this model could then be made in bronze. At the same time, stone stools of this type were being made in quartz, which must have taken a great deal of patience, since quartz has a very coarse crystalline structure which does not break in any easily predictable form. It would be necessary to grind the stone away, using a paste of coarse sand and water applied with strips of soft wood.

Plate 9

Plate 77

The mouldings on these stone stools are undercut, a form which one would not expect to find in stone or wood sculpture. Underwood[86] suggested that the idea of this elaborate stool was produced by a bronzesmith modelling in wax, but since we can trace the whole development from an original wooden prototype it is perhaps rather to be considered that the plastic nature of the terracotta material allowed this elaboration of the mouldings, which was then copied in stone.

It is interesting to note that wherever the quartz stools occur there is usually a four-legged stool to support them, just as is represented in the terracotta group from the Iwinrin Grove and in the bronze group from Ita Yemoo. This is true, for example, of all the stools illustrated in Plates 77, 78 and 79. They seem always to have been used in pairs.

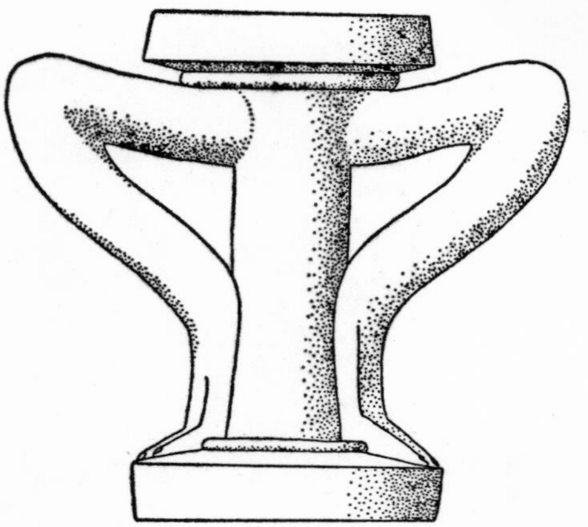

15 Reconstruction of an unusual stone stool from Aro Ajin Compound, Ife

A unique stool survives only as two separate fragments, with the springs of the loop showing on both pieces: it has two loops ending *Fig. 15* in feet which are carved on the base as can be seen in the reconstruction of this stool. The material from which it is carved is much softer than the other stools, and it may well be that this is relatively late. The single-looped stools are also represented in soft stone and these too are probably later than the Classical Period.[87]

23 Terracotta head from the Iwinrin Grove, Ife, perhaps originally from a figure, with raised weals on the face. The Oni of Ife, Sir Adesoji Aderemi, tells me that it used to be the custom for members of the Royal Family to paint their faces with an extract of blister beetles (*Cantharidae*) for certain festivals. This would certainly have raised weals like this, but probably not such neat ones. It was a painful experience which is no longer practised. The widely flaring nostrils should be compared with the fragment illustrated in *Fig. 40*, but the lips have received a very different treatment

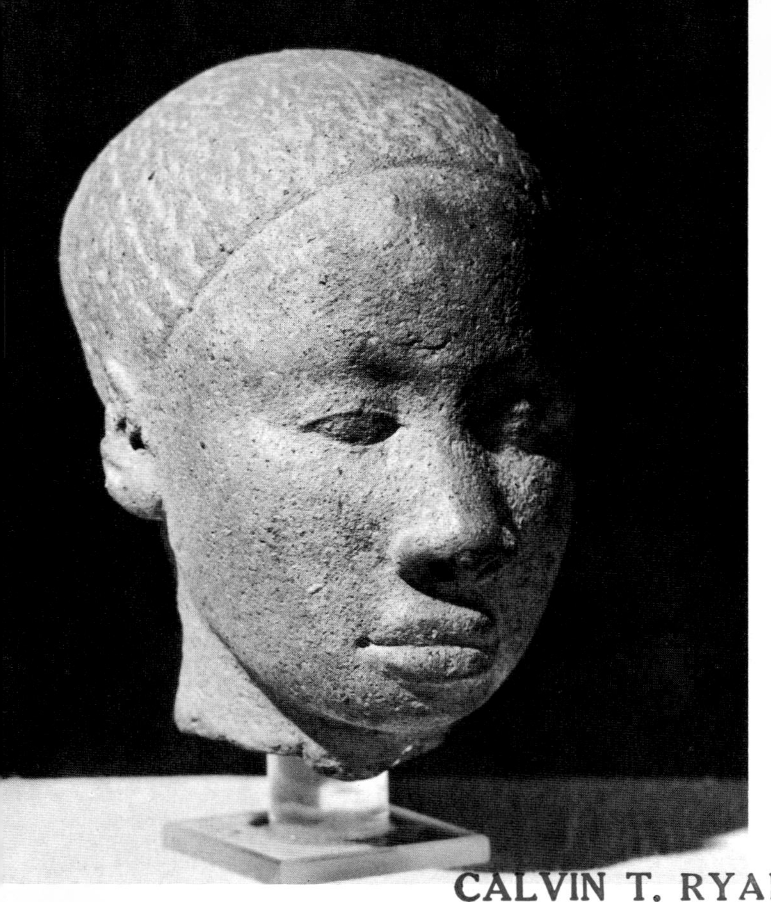

24, 25 *Left*, a smooth-faced and youthful looking terracotta head found at Abiri, ten miles from Ife, in 1947 whilst digging earth to puddle for house building. This head comes from a figure, for the overlap of the clay of the body and the neck can easily be seen on the original. One of the pieces illustrated in Plate 61 was found at the same time, together with Plate 45. *Below left*, a terracotta head broken from a larger sculpture from Iwinrin Grove. The decoration of the cap shows groups of three bands of cross-hatched decoration radiating from the crown, perhaps representing swathes of cloth, overlying the horizontal beads which form the cap itself. There are two holes over the forehead, one appearing as a black shadow in the photograph, and one in a smooth shallow pit farther back. They probably formed a double attachment for a single crest. Red paint survives on the face and cap, whilst black paint on the upper lip may have represented a moustache

26 Terracotta head broken from a figure, brought into the Palace in Ife in 1949, but unfortunately no record was made of where it was found, though *Bibl. 49 e* describes it as 'from a farm site close to Ife'. It is in very fresh condition. The beadwork cap has a hole over the forehead where a crest was originally fitted, so that it must have resembled the crown in Plate 10 or those in Plates 6 and 7. Many of the terracotta heads have similar small holes where crests have been lost. In the course of excavations at Ita Yemoo a large number of detached crests came to light, in a great variety of designs >

27 Terracotta head probably of a young woman, from the Iwinrin Grove. The long neck of this head is characteristic of a series of terracotta heads which were intended to be free standing. The lines round the neck, which are found also on many of the bronzes, are considered in modern Ife to be a feature of great beauty. The hair is dressed into fifteen transverse ridges, a style seen on some other heads but never with the delicacy achieved in this example

28 Terracotta face, probably of a queen, from the Iwinrin Grove, Ife. Now very much eroded, this face appears originally to have been striated. The crown was of the type shown in Plate IX, but with the projecting tiers composed of feathers. This is probably from a figure of about three-quarters of life size

29 Terracotta head found by Frobenius in 1910 in the Olokun Grove, Ife. This appears to come from a figure, and has not only an unusual hair style (*cf.* Plate 22) but has raised dots resembling keeloid scarifications along the eyebrows, a feature not found on other Ife heads. The curls appear to have been modelled (or moulded) separately, and applied to the head, the surface of which was tooled to give tooth for their attachment, as can be seen above the ear in this view

30 Face, probably from a whole figure, found by Frobenius in 1910 and referred to by him as 'Mia'. The representation of the hair as rings with iron nails in the centre is unusual and resembles a fragment from the Iwinrin Grove which may well be from the same sculpture. The unweathered surface below the mouth shows a lack of delicacy which is paralleled on the corresponding area of the bronze heads

32–35 The small terracotta head from a figure, *above left*, with faint 'cat's whisker' tribal marks at the corners of the mouth and ears pierced for earrings, was found at Opa Compound, Ife in 1961, and bears a striking resemblance to a young Ife man of today, *above right*. *Below left*, Umoru Gol, a Tera from north-eastern Nigeria, who worked with the Department of Antiquities in Ife, has scarification which closely resembles that of the Ife heads, such as that from a terracotta figure, *below right*, found in 1963 near the inner town wall at Oke Aton, Ilode, Ife. The hair is dressed into a disc on top of the head and two plaits sweep round from above the right ear to meet below the left

31 Fragment of a head, originally from a larger sculpture in terracotta, excavated by Bernard Fagg in the grove of Olokun Walode in Ife in 1953. This is one of the most delicate pieces of sculpture surviving in Ife; despite its broken condition it has been very little eroded by the elements. The tribal marks are nowadays characteristic of the Nupe, not the Yoruba, but there seem to have been considerable changes in tribal markings since the Classical Period of Ife art, and the Southern Nupe are said to have taken this mark from the Yoruba (*Bibl. 89, p. 22*)

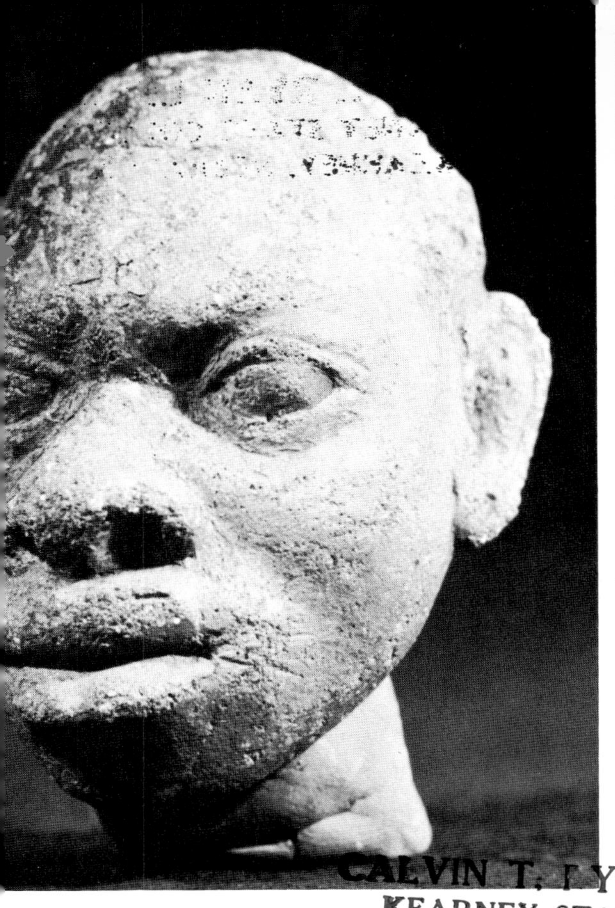

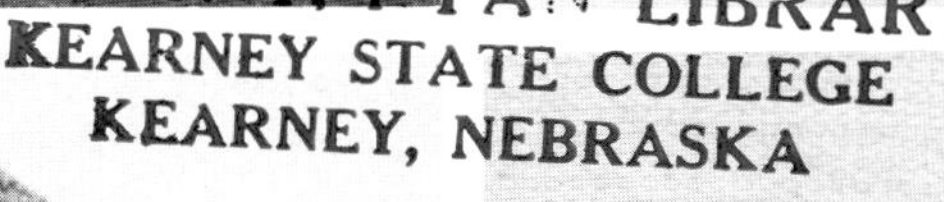

36 Right hand and forearm of a life size figure in terracotta, holding the folded end of a garment. Although rather eroded, the elaborate bracelets can be identified. From the wrist up there are four bracelets of mixed beads, overlain by a coiled bracelet encircling the wrist nearly twice. This was probably of bronze, cast in a design which includes human skulls. Next to this is a smooth bracelet of triangular section, representing an original in stone, glass or ivory. Then there are three bracelets with elements ridged alternately longitudinally and transversely, and finally three bracelets composed of cylindrical and spherical beads.

Comparison with other fragments found with it in the Iwinrin Grove suggests that the garment may be a cloak hanging from the shoulder, but the angle at which it is held suggests that the hand and the garment may belong to different figures in one elaborate terracotta group. There are many pieces of life size figures from this grove, most of them with coarse, white grits in the paste, apparently each standing on its own rectangular base. It is possible that the cloak belongs to the figure seated on the stool in Plate 76, and that he was flanked on each side by life size figures. Such a group of figures would have formed a single sculpture about five feet in height, of a similar width, and two feet six inches in depth. Its firing in an open wood fire would have been a unique achievement. The firing even of single figures on such a scale is remarkable enough

37, 38 Two fragments of terracotta human figures. *Above*, a right arm excavated by the author in the Iwinrin Grove in 1959. In contrast to the heads, the limbs are usually treated in a stylized manner as in this example. *Below*, the left arm of a pot-bellied individual, rather crudely modelled. Two other fragments bearing snakes in relief appear to belong to this figure, which must originally have presented a grotesque appearance

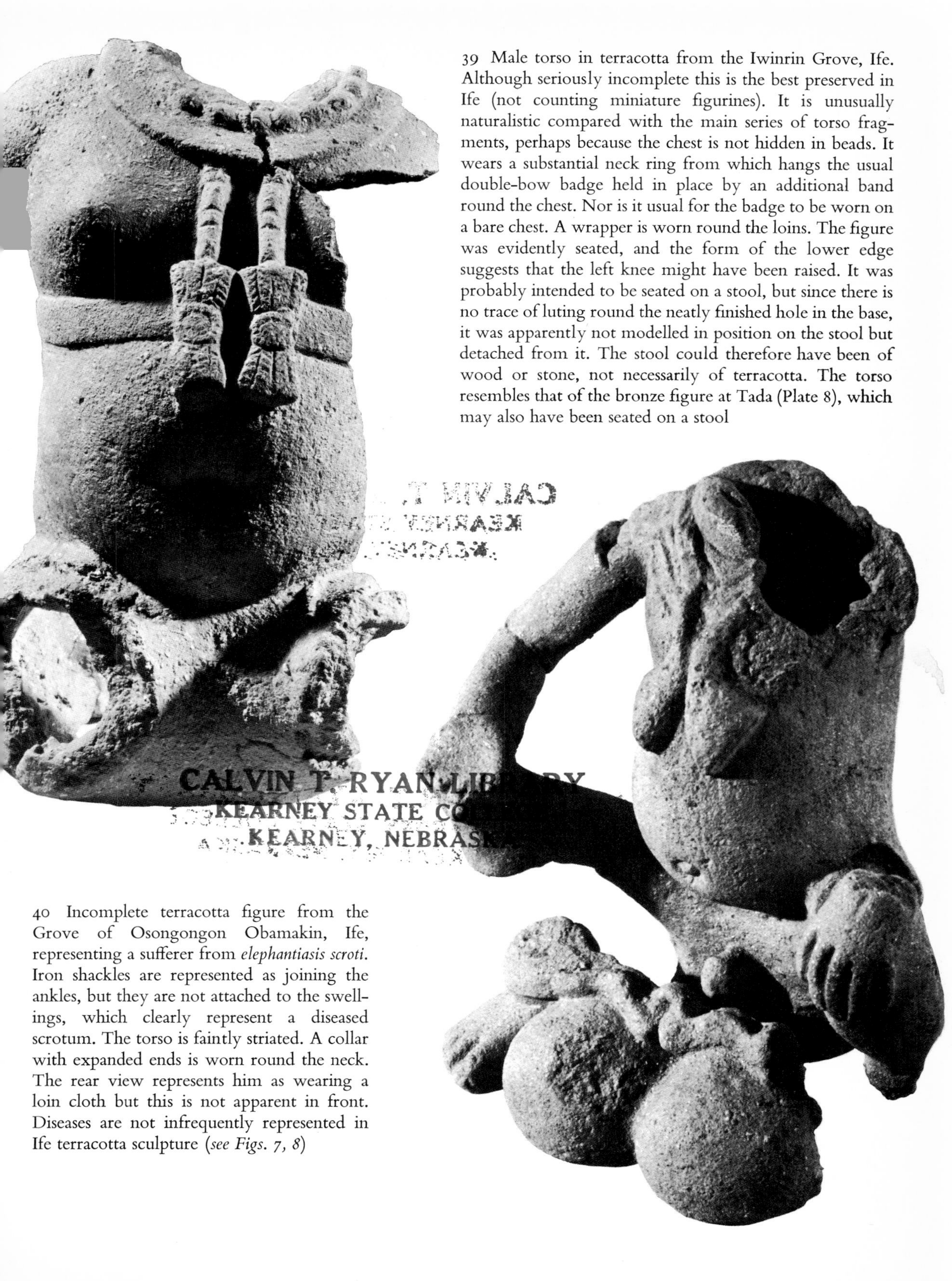

39 Male torso in terracotta from the Iwinrin Grove, Ife. Although seriously incomplete this is the best preserved in Ife (not counting miniature figurines). It is unusually naturalistic compared with the main series of torso fragments, perhaps because the chest is not hidden in beads. It wears a substantial neck ring from which hangs the usual double-bow badge held in place by an additional band round the chest. Nor is it usual for the badge to be worn on a bare chest. A wrapper is worn round the loins. The figure was evidently seated, and the form of the lower edge suggests that the left knee might have been raised. It was probably intended to be seated on a stool, but since there is no trace of luting round the neatly finished hole in the base, it was apparently not modelled in position on the stool but detached from it. The stool could therefore have been of wood or stone, not necessarily of terracotta. The torso resembles that of the bronze figure at Tada (Plate 8), which may also have been seated on a stool

40 Incomplete terracotta figure from the Grove of Osongongon Obamakin, Ife, representing a sufferer from *elephantiasis scroti*. Iron shackles are represented as joining the ankles, but they are not attached to the swellings, which clearly represent a diseased scrotum. The torso is faintly striated. A collar with expanded ends is worn round the neck. The rear view represents him as wearing a loin cloth but this is not apparent in front. Diseases are not infrequently represented in Ife terracotta sculpture (*see Figs. 7, 8*)

41–45 Animal heads in terracotta. The head of a dog, *opposite centre*, was excavated by Kenneth Murray in 1943 in the grove of Osongongon Obamakin. The others represent decapitated heads of sacrificed rams and were probably intended to act as permanent offerings on the shrine when the real object was not available, a usage comparable to the candle burning before the image of a saint to remind him of the prayer said when it was first lit. The first example *opposite*, from Oshogbo, shows a tethering rope round the horns. The third head comes from a shrine to Obalufon in the Palace in Ife. The ears resemble those of a Nok head (Plate 80, *Fig. 23*). The last example, *opposite below*, was found with a massive bronze neck-ring, in digging the grave of Samuel Oki in St Philip's churchyard, Aiyetoro, Ife. The head lying on a platter, *right*, was found at Abiri in 1947

46 Terracotta sculpture of a tethered animal, perhaps a sheep or a goat, from the grove of Osongongon Obamakin, Ife. The legs are missing, and the condition of the side away from the camera shows that it was attached to a larger sculpture, probably a human figure holding the tether; other fragmentary sculptures of such groups suggest that the figure was probably kneeling

47–50 Three terracottas of animals from Ife. The owl, *above*, was found in Olumobi Compound, Igbodo Street. *Below left*, an elephant head excavated at Lafogido, in 1963, rests on a flat base decorated with beads and feathers. This resembles the collars worn by some of the royal figures and the elaborate crested head-dress further suggests that some royal symbolism was intended. As in several other pieces, herring-bone incision has been used to give a decorative effect. *Below right* is an ape excavated at the Osongongon Obamakin Grove in 1953 by John Goodwin

51 The Ife terracotta sculptors produced some very lively animal figures. This chameleon on a hollow base was found in 1961 when a hole was being dug for an underground tank at the B.P. petrol filling station on the Ibadan Road, Ife

52, 53 *Left,* fragment of a left foot and plinth in terracotta found at Wunmonije Compound in 1961. It is unusual for the feet of Ife sculptures to have separate plinths, though modern Yoruba twin figures are sometimes carved in this way, especially in Abeokuta. The ring on the second toe is often represented at Ife. The foot which is about one third to half of life size carries the remains of red paint, whilst the toe nails and plinth were originally painted white. The very steep rise of the instep is an unusual feature. A terracotta foot, *right,* with massive beaded anklets was found in the Big Paddock at Nok. This short, broad foot with square-cut toes is typical of the sculptures of the Nok culture. It is paralleled at Ife only in the stone sculptures of the Ore Grove

54 The fragments, *right,* are of a naturalistic but idealized left foot excavated at Ita Yemoo in 1958. The careful modelling of the toenails is characteristic of the Ife sculptures

VII

Finding out about Ancient Ife

ART STILL IN SHRINES

IFE SCULPTURE has come to light in a variety of ways. In many cases ancient objects of art are used in the rituals in the shrines and temples of modern Ife. It was a great thrill to discover during the annual festival of Itapa in the Temple of Orishanla that an ancient terracotta head was still being used in worship. The Ogun Ladin shrine has not only the stone mudfish, but a quartz cylinder with holes drilled in the end and a strange pear-shaped droplet of wrought iron weighing well over a hundredweight, a remarkable example of blacksmiths' skill, since it must have been built up from small fragments of wrought iron. Another shrine, Epinbodo, had until recently a pair of stone stools, both broken: one in granite is of the cylindrical-column type, the second, in quartz, originally had four legs.

Plates 69, 70, 72

Plate 79

Antiquities from many of the groves like the Iwinrin Grove were brought into the Palace for safe-keeping as long as thirty years ago, and this process of bringing them together has continued ever since, being helped very much now by the existence of the museum, for in the groves in the forest these objects are not very safe. More recently the stone-carvings in the Ore Grove were brought into the museum for greater safety. Some of the shrines use more recent sculptures. A small shrine for Obalufon in the centre of the town has a very ugly modern stone-carving. The Grove of Igbodio, the premier grove in Ife, being as it is the centre where Oduduwa created the world and where he is still worshipped, has two mud sculptures which seem to be only of nineteenth-century date.

Plate 108

EXCAVATION

Other pieces have been found by excavation. The excavations in the groves of Olokun Walode conducted by Bernard Fagg in 1953 and of Obameri by Oliver Myers in 1964 have revealed fragments of sculptures, none of them complete, brought together in these shrines at some time in the eighteenth or nineteenth centuries (p. 61). The writer's excavations at Ita Yemoo have produced evidence of different types of shrines. The first, excavated in 1959, contained the remains of seven terracotta sculptures, which appeared to have been complete and in position at the time the site was abandoned, for they had been weathered and eroded for some time before the building collapsed upon them. A second shrine on the same site excavated in 1962–3 had contained dismantled sculptures. These were the remains of two figures of about three-quarters of life-size which appear to have already been broken when they were placed together in the shrine. Their positions were so jumbled that they could hardly have arrived at such disorder if they had been originally complete and had merely been smashed by the collapse of the building.

Plate 65

ABANDONMENT OF SITES

The date at which these sites were abandoned is difficult to establish. We hope that we shall be able to obtain scientifically determined dates in due course, which will help to establish the chronology of Ife history, not least by putting on a firm basis the date when these terracotta sculptures and bronze-castings were made. We do know from historical traditions that the town of Ife was abandoned twice in the nineteenth century, once in the middle around 1850 to 1854, and then again about 1878 to 1894. Both abandonments resulted from war between the Ifes and the Modakekes. The Modakekes were refugees from the area around Old Oyo, the political capital of the Yoruba empire, which had collapsed about 1837. They were pursued by the Fulani right down into the southern part of Yorubaland where they had settled in the Origbo district to the west of Ife. They were brought into Ife by Oni Adegunle Abeweila who was sympathetic to them. They did not manage to remain at peace with the Ifes, however, and on these two occasions successfully drove them out of the town. The return of the Ifes in 1894 was achieved to ensure that the ancestral shrines of all the Yoruba people should not be allowed to fall into neglect, and an adjudication was given that the Ifes should return and the Modakekes should leave Ife to them. This was not implemented until March 1909, shortly before Frobenius visited the town, when he found the Modakeke area in complete ruin. It was here that he made many of his most interesting discoveries, for he was not prevented from wandering freely around this part of the town. Many of the shrines in Modakeke, however, are much older than the advent of the Oyos. The Opa Olusheri (p. 79), for example, was handed over to the ancestor of the priest now in charge of it by the Oni Abeweila, who asked him to continue the worship of it, so that these are true Ife shrines even though they are served now by Modakeke people. It was only in 1922 that the Modakeke began to drift back.

There must have been earlier disturbances. The eighteenth century as well as the nineteenth were times of great upheaval in Yorubaland, and it may well be that the abandonment of these sites in Ife was earlier than either of the nineteenth-century evacuations, particularly as the town wall runs across the site of Ita Yemoo cutting through the remains of buildings which must already have been abandoned at the time the wall was built. This wall, built by Abeweila a little before 1850, is earlier than either of these nineteenth-century abandonments of the town, so that it would seem likely that the abandonment of these shrines was still earlier, but it is not yet possible without radiocarbon or thermo-luminescent dates to say how much earlier it was.

CASUAL FINDS

The other main source of discovery of Ife antiquities, of course, is by casual finds. There has, since 1956, been an archaeologist resident more or less continuously in Ife, and the museum was there three years before that. This has stimulated the reporting of discoveries which would otherwise have gone unnoticed. At the 1952–3 census 111,000 people were found to be living in Ife, but there are undoubtedly more than this now, who are nearly all agriculturalists spending most of their time either turning the soil on their farms or digging foundations to build their own houses. As a result, a continuous flow of antiquities is being discovered from all over the town. Indeed one could well believe that it is practically impossible to dig a hole in Ife of any size without discovering the remains of an earlier civilization. It is difficult to avoid concluding that Ife has been there for many centuries since the antiquities discovered are so very numerous and so very varied.

THE EXTENT OF IFE INFLUENCE

The discovery of antiquities of Ife type is not restricted to the town of Ife. A number of sites have been mentioned which are a few miles from Ife, *e.g.*, Abiri and Agidi, but there are others farther afield. A terracotta ram's head was found at Oshogbo, thirty miles to the north, and a human head is still worshipped at Ikirun still farther north, whilst a terracotta hand holding a staff was found in Ijebu-Ode, seventy miles to the south-west, though this piece is not in the Classical Ife style. Stone sculptures at Erumu, Eshure and Kuta have already been mentioned, whilst fragments of glass-making

Plate 41

Plate 16

crucibles have been found at Ede. One of the most characteristic features of Ife architecture, pavements made of broken potsherds, have been found at Benin, Owo, Ifaki, Ikerin and Ede, in Dahomey at Ketu and Dassa Zoumé and in the Kabrais district of Togo. The cultural influence of Ife was evidently widely spread, as we might expect from the tradition that Ife was the point from which the Yoruba originally spread soon after the creation of the world.

Plate 66

LIFE IN ANCIENT IFE

European visitors to Ife frequently ask how it could have been possible for people living in mud houses with grass roofs to have made such beautiful objects as the bronze and terracotta sculptures which are exhibited in the museum. This is a very ethnocentric view, for we must remember that in the Middle Ages England itself was an agricultural country with essentially a peasant population living in mud huts with grass roofs (we call them wattle-and-daub and thatch, but there is no real difference), and yet they produced some of the finest art that has ever been produced in Europe.[88] In the Middle Ages, there must have been very little difference between the ordinary people of Europe and of Africa. Indeed, the earliest travellers' accounts of Africa suggest that they were not themselves conscious of any difference of standing between themselves and these strangers: they regarded the Africans as equals. It is only after the age of mechanization and mass production that one gets any appreciable difference in the standard of living between the vast area of Africa and the more industrialized Western world.

ARCHITECTURE

The houses in which the ancient Ifes lived, of course, have collapsed and are extremely difficult to recover in excavation, because they are made by the process described earlier (p. 18), of puddling the collapsed building with water and re-erecting it in continuous courses of mud. This technique of building does not require the use of foundation trenches. As a result, the walls themselves are almost impossible to detect. Fortunately, however, the houses in Ife were paved inside with layers of potsherds laid on edge, often arranged in very decorative patterns. Sometimes these are revealed in present-day roads and footpaths, and have proved to be extremely durable. One pavement beside the lorry park has been regularly driven over by mammy-wagons for years, and stands up to it very well. In some cases these seem to have been pavements under verandas around open courtyards. In others, they were the pavement of the small courtyard itself, known as an impluvium (*akodi*). This is the traditional method of building houses in Yorubaland so that the opening in the roof is over the centre of the room and allows light to enter and, of course, the rain as well, which is then collected either in a tank nowadays or formerly in large water-pots. The pavement from St David's, on the Roman Catholic Mission site in Ife, had the neck of a pot as a stand for a water-pot, and a pottery drain-pipe to conduct the surplus water away. A near-by pavement had an old grinding stone, worn out completely, so that there was a hole through the centre, set on edge beside the pavement to conduct the water through the wall whilst protecting it from erosion. The pavements vary considerably in style. Sometimes they are simple straight rows of potsherds laid side by side; in other instances such lines alternate with lines of white quartz pebbles; occasionally the rows of pottery are set in herring-bone style, or the lines of potsherds intersect to form rectangular spaces which are filled with quartz pebbles. From the plans of pavements like this we are gradually learning something about the architecture of ancient Ife. The doors were of wood, hinged by means of an iron loop attached to the wall above and passing round a tab on the door, whilst a similar tab at the bottom corner turned in a cup-shaped stone, two of which were found close to pavements at the St David's site.

Figs. 16, 17

Plate 66

CRAFTS AND COSTUME

The bronze and terracotta sculptures show evidence of other crafts. The clothing worn by the figures is evidently of cloth with hems sewn round, whilst in some cases embroidery is represented. Both the types of loom currently used in Yorubaland, the broad loom on which women weave wide cloth and the narrow loom used by men to make narrow strips which are sewn together to make wide pieces, seem to have been in use, for most of the figures wear sashes which were probably woven on narrow looms. The figures are also conspicuously bedecked with beads which can be interpreted both from the paint that has been applied to them and from the shape in which they are modelled. Many of them appear to be red stone beads of a variety of shapes, whilst others are evidently intended to represent blue glass beads. Both kinds are found in the excavations. In addition, there are a great variety of bracelets, some smooth ones of glass, metal or ivory; more elaborate ones are quite certainly of metal, some having expanded trumpet ends; others have openwork decoration; many of them are sculptured to represent human and animal heads as well as motifs of an abstract nature. Many of the

Plate 36

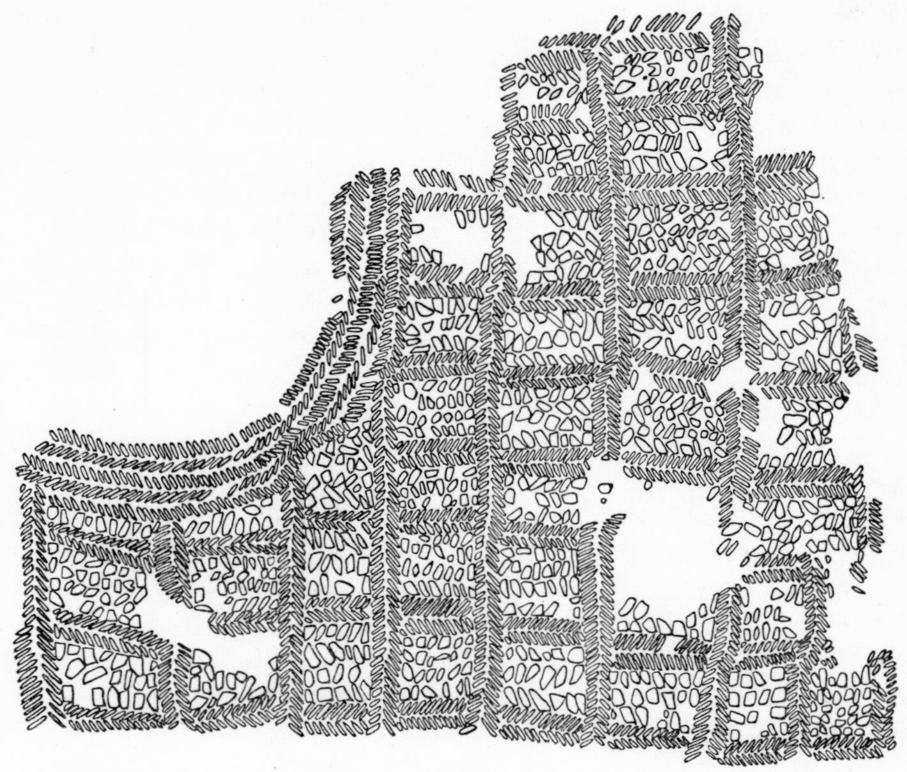

16, 17 Detail and plan of the potsherd pavement excavated at the Roman Catholic Mission, Ife, shown in Plate 66. The drainpipe is shown on the left and the pot-stand in the centre of the plan

figures wear caps and badges which appear to be made from small beads. The chiefs in Plate 69 wear beaded badges on their chests probably comparable to those worn by the figures which have been described earlier, although their embroidered caps are not closely parallel in the sculptures. Around their necks, these chiefs are wearing beads; two of them have long beads of blue glass known as *segi*. The manufacture of glass beads in Ife appears to have been a major industry. All over the town, one finds fragments of crucibles used in the process: pots made of a white paste, usually rather thick and coated with glass both inside and out. Some scores of fragments of these crucibles were found in the course of the excavations at Ita Yemoo, whilst a complete one was used to store beads on the shrine with seven terracotta figures. A lump of fused beads which were

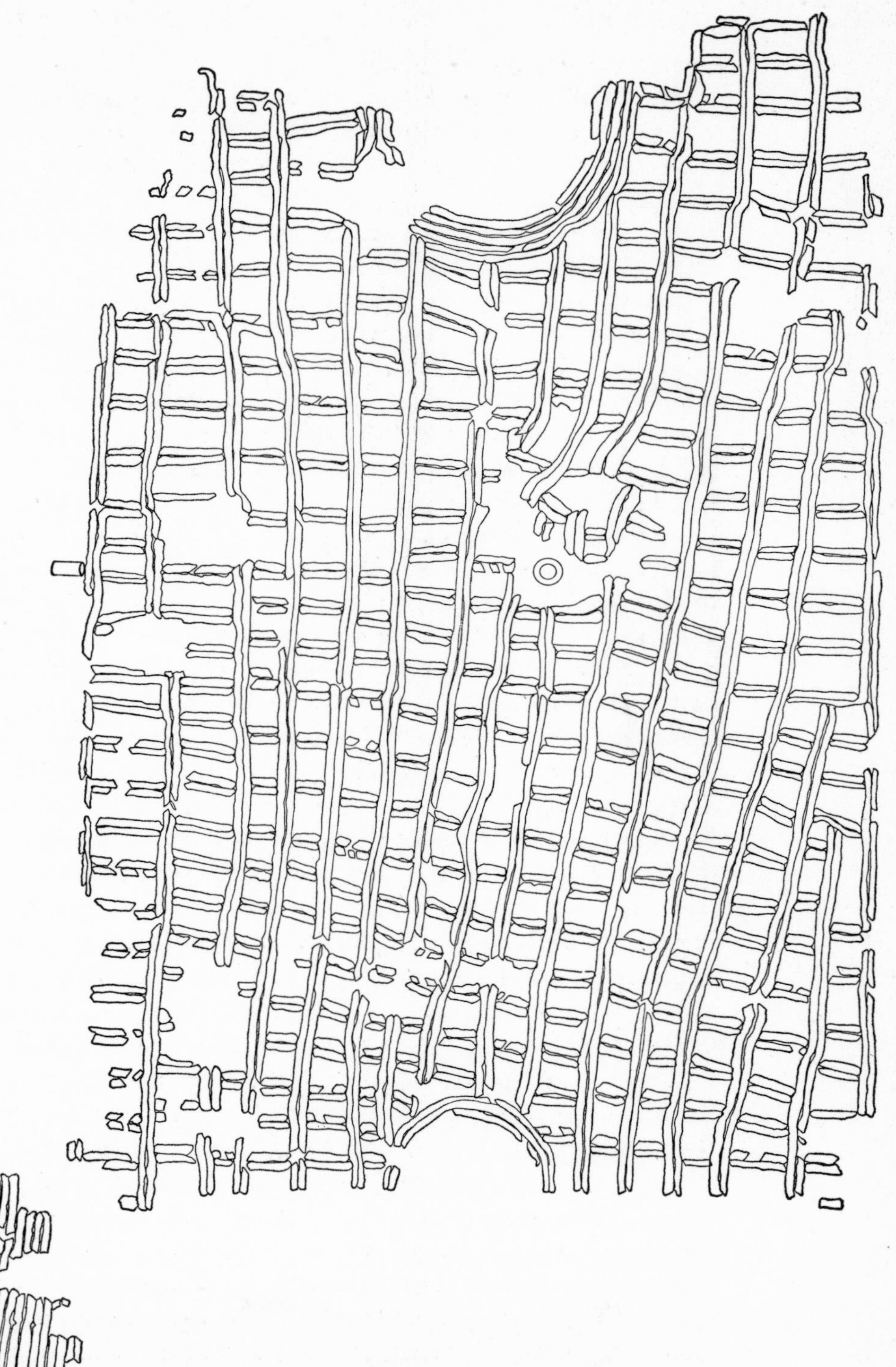

being re-melted in one of these crucibles was bought by one of the Lander brothers in the market at Old Oyo on 15th May 1830. He was told that 'it was dug from the earth in a country called Iffie where according to their traditions their first parents were created and from whence all Africa has been peopled'.[89] Lander did not know precisely what this material was. He thought it was some form of mineral and resembled, he said, a rough mosaic work. Unfortunately this piece probably went to the bottom of the Niger when their boat sank some time later. Evidently the nature of these glass objects from the Olokun Grove was already unknown in 1830, whilst the drum of Oduduwa (p. 25), associating one of these crucibles with the god who created the world, suggests that the glass industry had probably ceased to function some centuries earlier.

FOOD

One of the difficulties in investigating an archaeological deposit in the tropics is that so many organic materials do not survive. It is difficult, therefore, to establish what vegetable foods were available to the people of ancient Ife and even what domestic animals they had, since bone decays with very great rapidity.[90] Nowadays most of the staple foods cultivated in West Africa are of either American or Asiatic origin, but a number of minor crops which are still used are indigenous to Africa and many of them were probably much more important in times gone by. From an archaeological point of view, however, maize is of particular interest, for this is quite certainly a crop of American origin, and its existence can be inferred from the fact that the cob was commonly used, after the seeds had been eaten, to decorate pottery by rolling it over the wet clay as a roulette giving a simple roughened surface. It has been argued that maize could not have been grown in West Africa earlier than about 1500 if it were brought back from America across the Atlantic by Columbus,[91] but it has been suggested that it could have crossed the Pacific from America at some earlier date and have entered Africa from the east coast, so that the date of origins of maize growing in Africa is not yet certainly established.[92] It is, however, to be remarked that a few of the potsherds incorporated in some of the pavements have impressions of maize cobs. This may give a lead in dating these pavements and may indeed help us to establish the date of introduction of maize if we can date the pavements independently.[93] Although we may not know precisely what foods were cooked, we have discovered signs of clay hearths not unlike those still in use in which the clay is piled up to form a semicircular bank to support the cooking-pot.

MUSIC

Music and dancing play an important role in African life. Indeed it has often been suggested that these are the principal African art forms, although, of course, they are very difficult to discuss because there is no easy way of recording them in print. However, there is some evidence in the archaeological material for musical instruments. Drums are represented on the elaborate ritual pots, whilst metal bars have been excavated which resemble the *ewo* which are struck in rhythm during modern festivals. Iron gongs have been found, but only in recent deposits.[94]

VIII

Ancestors in Terracotta

THE NOK CULTURE

IN CONSIDERING where the art of Ife can have originated we do not need to look far afield, for there is in Northern Nigeria a culture of great antiquity which has produced very rich remains in terracotta sculpture. It has been named by Bernard Fagg the Nok culture, from the name of the mining village of Nok where the first specimens were found. Most of the examples we have of the culture have been found in alluvial deposits which are being mined for their tin content. At Nok itself there are large quantities of carbonized wood in the deposits, and samples have been subjected to radiocarbon testing; one from a layer of grey-black clay which contained figurine material gave a date of AD 207 ± 50, whilst another of abraded logs in the basal gravels and sands below gave a date of 918 BC ± 70.[95] These dates were interpreted by Bernard Fagg as indicating that the culture probably began some time in the middle of the first millennium BC and continued at least until the second century AD and probably later.[96] The idea that this was the time range had already been reached tentatively on purely geological grounds some years earlier.[97] In September 1960 two terracotta figures of women sitting on round stools or perhaps upturned mortars were discovered at Taruga, south-east of Abuja. The heads of these figures were both missing, but the small excavation conducted on the site in December 1960 by Bernard Fagg discovered the head of one of them *in situ*. The site also produced evidence of iron-working and abundant charcoal, a sample of which was dated by radiocarbon to 280 BC ± 120.[98] This date falls conveniently in the middle of the range of dates already established and adds further weight to them, particularly as this site is not an alluvial river deposit but is evidently an occupation site, where these people worked even if they did not actually live. It is hoped that further excavations on this site will extend very greatly our knowledge of the Nok culture and the way of life of the people.

THE ART OF NOK

Fig. 1

Plates 80–85, X–XIII; *Figs. 18–20*

Plate X

The sites which have produced Nok terracotta sculptures are spread across Northern Nigeria in a wide band running diagonally across the country, as seen on the map. There are many sites in this area: at least twenty are already known, apart from a large number grouped together close to Nok. They have produced sculptures showing considerable variation in style and treatment yet all quite clearly in an African mode, as can be seen from the illustrations. It is impossible to doubt that all these pieces are distinctly African for they all show a very free use of the imagination in representing humanity, although the animals are not so impressionistic. Indeed, although the eyes of animals (like the elephant) are represented in much the same way as the eyes on the human heads, the animal sculptures achieve a much greater sense of realism than do the human figures. The reasons for this are difficult to establish. If one were able to ask a Nok sculptor why he represented human beings in one way and animals in another he would no doubt give the same kind of answer as a modern African carver does: 'This is the way in which we do it.' All art is symbolic to a greater or lesser extent, and very probably the difference in representation here in the Nok culture is entirely subconscious. In modern Nigerian societies like the Bini and the Yoruba we find the concept that every human being has a spiritual counterpart which needs to be nourished to ensure the person's well-being.[99] Witchcraft operates in many cases by attacking the spiritual counterpart. Whilst we have no direct evidence about the Nok sculptors' ideas, it would seem not unlikely that they were inhibited to some extent from making naturalistic representations, because they felt that it might give them power over the individual recognizably represented. On the other hand, it was perhaps desirable to exercise power over the animals around them. It would be unwise to attempt to press this explanation very far, but it is interesting to note that in the Upper Palaeolithic cave paintings of Europe the animal figures, although treated in a stylized manner, are very lively representations which are easily recognizable, yet the human figures are extremely rare (at least in the Franco-Cantabrian group of caves) and extremely schematic when they do occur. It may well be that some fundamental spiritual reasons account for this fact both in Nok and in the earlier Stone Age paintings of Europe.

FROM WOOD TO TERRACOTTA

The principal medium of sculptural expression in the whole of Africa is wood and the forms of the sculptures at Nok are in many

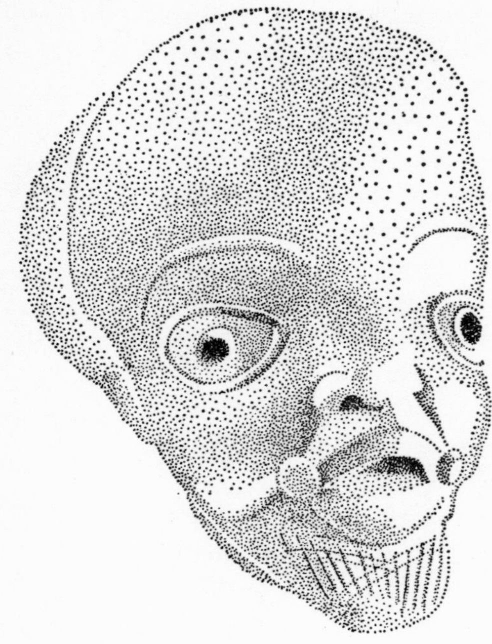

18 Terracotta head from Wamba, the most naturalistic of the human heads in the Nok style

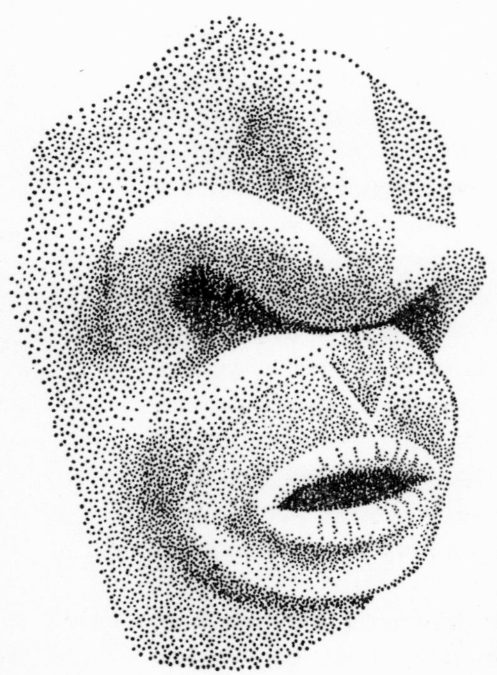

19 Terracotta fragment from a stream bed at Tonga Nok, in which the mouth has been blocked out as if it were a wood carving. The head appears to have been cylindrical in shape

20 Partially reconstructed terracotta figure from Katsina Ala

cases reminiscent of wood-carving. One fragment of a face shows the blocking-out of the lips in a manner which would be much more appropriate to wood-carving than it is to the plastic medium of moist clay. Similarly, many of the sculptural forms seem to derive from the fundamental cylindrical form of a log of wood. In wood-carving the limits of the trunk of the tree set a boundary to the outside shape of the sculpture, unless resort is had to carpentry, which is uncommon in African sculpture and usually late. The effect of transferring from wood sculpture, in which a tradition had evidently been well evolved, into the more pliable medium of terracotta, was one of liberation for the artist. He was able to conceive his forms in plastic terms instead of in such rigid forms as wood had made him use. As a result, beautifully rounded and soft forms became possible for him in a way which would have been hardly practicable in wood. The head from Katsina Ala, in contrast, is much more cylindrical in form. There are several heads of this general type, either a cylinder or a cone set at an angle on another cylinder which is the neck. This is one of the characteristic forms of Nok sculpture. It is a basic structural form which is found in the later sculptures of

Fig. 19

Plate XII

Plate XI

Figs. 21, 22

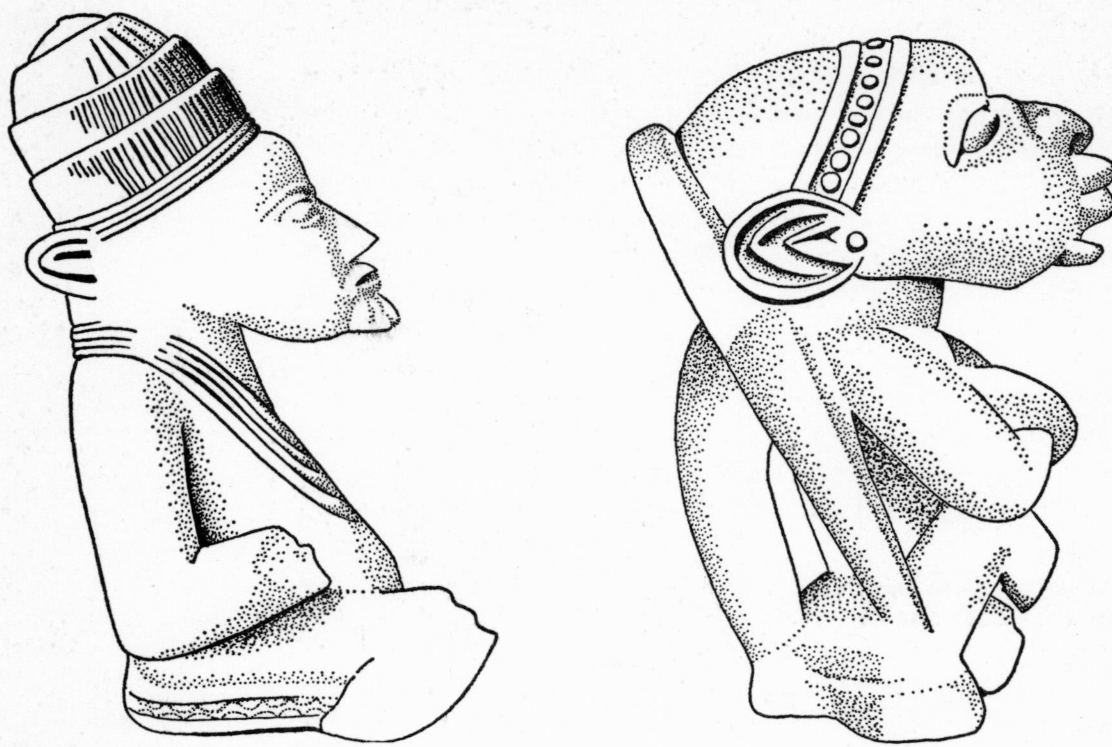

21, 22 A characteristic form found in Nok sculpture is a cylindrical or cone-shaped head set at an angle on another cylinder forming the neck. This is found in later sculptures as the stone figure from Esie, left, *and the soft stone carving of a* nomoli *figure, from Sierra Leone*

Esie and in the *nomoli* figures of Sierra Leone. The small head from
Plate 81 Jemaa is again an intensely plastic form. More restrained is the larger
Plate 83 head from Jemaa which was one of the first examples of Nok sculpture to be published.

It will be noticed in comparing the various heads illustrated here that in all cases the eyes are pierced, as are the ears, and usually the mouth as well. The eyes normally take the form of an inverted triangle or a semicircle with eyebrows above, often arched in counter-
Plates 80, 82, 83 poise to the sweep of the lower edge of the eye. This form of eye is not only very characteristic of Nok sculpture but is also very closely
Fig. 3 similar to the eyes of modern Yoruba *gelede* masks. Indeed Bernard Fagg[100] has pointed out a great many parallels between the art of Nok and the arts of the present day in Southern Nigeria. One head
Fig. 18 from Wamba, although clearly in the same style as these others, is rather more naturalistic in its form. It is quite sensitively modelled and appears to be somewhat infantile, although the chin has a beard

and there are what appear to be keeloid scarifications at the corners of the mouth. Other fragments of sculpture from deposits of the Nok culture also show fairly naturalistic treatments of some details. Perhaps the most interesting characteristic of all in the Nok sculpture is typified by the fragmentary figure of a man from Katsina Ala.[101] *Fig. 20* About two feet six inches in height, he is seated on a stool or upturned mortar. The size of this sculpture is quite striking: originally it must have been even taller. Yet there are other fragments of sculptures which suggest that the originals were far bigger than this —they were indeed quite close to life-size if not larger. The head illustrated in Plate 82, for example, is 14 inches in height. All the heads from Nok appear to come from whole figures, so that a head of this size implies a figure which was itself approaching life-size. To end up approaching life-size allowing for shrinkage in drying and in firing, the sculpture must originally have been life-size or larger. At the other extreme, however, there are a number of quite small sculptures of very great delicacy, like the figurine from near Abuja. Plate 85 The very great proliferation of beads on the arms, legs, and body is charactersitic. Many of the figures have very heavy collars of beads round the neck; this figurine and the life-size head are examples. Plate 82

The purpose which these terracotta sculptures served is of course completely unknown to us. Until we are able to excavate them *in situ* we can only guess or go by analogy. There are in Northern Nigeria close to and even within the area of the Nok culture, people who still make terracotta sculptures, such as the Dakakari and the Tiv. The Dakakari terracottas are placed on graves as commemorative sculptures with a symbolic meaning, whilst one of the Tiv sculptures was recorded by the collector to be intended for use as a dwelling for a spirit. The Jaba who occupy the area around Nok itself still make pottery decorated with human figures like round globular pots with an open base, which are intended as finials to sit on the apex of the thatched roof. Plate 80 *Fig. 23* These three different functions, namely that of grave furniture, of shrine furniture, or for domestic use could, any or all of them, have been the purpose for which these Nok terracotta sculptures were made.

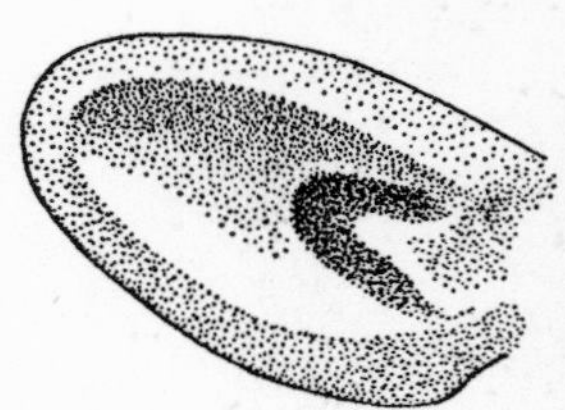

23 Ear of the Nok terracotta shown in Plate 80

Although the Nok style has been referred to as if it were unitary, there are a number of sub-styles which can be distinguished. The most striking is that of the Gold Coffer Mine, the characteristic feature of this is the very large ear. It is likely that as evidence Plate 86 Plate 87 continues to be found from the different sites of the Nok culture we shall be able to distinguish developments in time and in space; in fact, the culture will probably resolve into a group of different art sub-styles which may reflect differences in time. For our present purpose it is sufficient to draw attention to the richness and variety of the artistic concepts which are already known from these ancient terracottas, which are the oldest sculptures known from negro Africa. Many of the characteristics of this style occur in later art forms, particularly at Ife.

THEIR WAY OF LIFE

The Nok people lived in a period which saw the introduction of iron-working into West Africa. The deposits have produced large quantities of stone axes and evidence also of iron-working in the form of slag and nozzles for bellows, as well as a small number of iron artifacts, including two iron axes which closely resemble stone axes in their form. Three of the sculptures, indeed, show figures carrying axes over their shoulder, but it is impossible to be sure whether these are of stone or of iron. Many of the stone axes from the deposits are extremely small, and it is likely that these were intended for use as wood-carving tools whilst at the other end of the size range, some very large ones may have been used as hoes for cultivating the swampy river banks on which they lived. They evidently used vegetable food, for the seeds of the *atili*, an oil-bearing plant, have been identified as well as the shells of the oil palm, together with small stones with pits in them which are thought to have been used in cracking open the nuts to extract the kernel, and stone querns for grinding these and probably other seeds. Since the oil palm cannot grow in the savannah because of the bush fires which destroy it in its early stages,[102] it appears that at this time Nok itself was in a forested area. Stone arrowheads are also found, and these suggest that they also hunted as well as collected. The extent to which they can be considered farmers is difficult to determine: whether they were deliberately cultivating crops or merely encouraging wild plants by weeding is quite obscure. One of the terracotta figurines carries on its head what appears to be a bowl of eggs, whilst another has been thought to represent a domestic cow, but no bones of any kind have been found in the deposits to support the idea that they were in any way a pastoral people.

The sculptures are richly bedecked with beads, and many stone beads have been found in the archaeological deposits, together with quartz cylinders which are thought to be ear, nose and lip plugs. A grinding-stone, too, has been found which appears to have been used for making these ornaments. There is no sign at all of cloth on most of these figurines. Those from Taruga, for example, wear beaded waistbands from which hang a small apron, but this is not clearly of cloth and is more likely to be of beadwork, though it may possibly be of bark cloth or leather. One incomplete but originally large figure from Kuchamfa, however, wears a wrapper which hides the feet and carries a groove parallel to the edge apparently representing a hem. The treatment of this detail is almost identical with a fragmentary terracotta from Ife and is very similar to the hems represented on the bronze figures from Ita Yemoo. The other figurines wear ornaments on the pubis which are evidently composed of basket-work, whilst one has beadwork and a bell which appears to be of iron. Plates 84, XII

A great deal of domestic pottery has been found with the figurines, most of it rather heavy and coarse though well fired. They seem to have been more or less globular vessels with slightly out-turned rims.

Some evidence of buildings survives, for pieces of burnt clay bearing the impression of wattle-work have been found quite frequently, together with more strongly fired clay from furnaces.

Many of the details of dress and of hair-dressing can be paralleled among pagan tribes still living in the area covered by the Nok culture. This suggests that the Nok terracottas may have been made by their ancestors, and it is not improbable that their way of life was quite similar to that of these small tribes of the Plateau who eke out a rather precarious existence nowadays in refuge areas on the hill-slopes and between the rocky outcrops where they have been forced by the later incoming groups of Muslim Northerners, the Hausa and the Fulani. Yet so many features of the Nok culture, particularly of its art, are found in later cultures elsewhere in West Africa, that it is difficult not to believe that the Nok culture as we know it represents the ancestral stock from which much of the sculptural tradition of West Africa derives. Whilst it is conceivable that there were other cultures, not yet discovered, in different areas, producing work similar in style to that of the Nok culture, it is more convenient at present to regard the Nok culture as the ancestral stock, not simply a collateral representative of it, from which these other art forms sprang, and it is in this sense that we shall discuss the Plates 82, 84 influence of the Nok culture. When we do this it must be borne in mind that the amount of archaeological work that has been done in West Africa so far is remarkably small, and it is quite likely that entirely unknown cultures will be found in the future. These might show that Nok is not really the ancestor, but merely the only manifestation known to us at present to indicate what the true ancestral art forms were like.

IX

The Origins of the Yoruba and of the Art of Ife

NOK AND IFE ART

MANY OF THE ELEMENTS we have described from Nok are also found at Ife. These two cultures are the only ones we know from the whole of Africa which have attempted anything near life-size sculpture in terracotta. The human figures in both wear profusions of beads, anklets and bracelets, but particularly heavy beaded collars. In both cultures we see reflected an interest in disease and deformity.[103] Body and limb fragments are often very similar: they are normally rather stylized and simplified at Ife, despite the intense naturalism of the faces; indeed, William Fagg has gone so far as to suggest that if fragments of the limbs and bodies from Ife and Nok should become confused, whether in an archaeological deposit or in a museum, it would be very difficult on grounds of style alone to distinguish them.[104] The close similarity in the representation of hems in terracotta sculptures has been alluded to. Two feet show

Figs. 24, 25

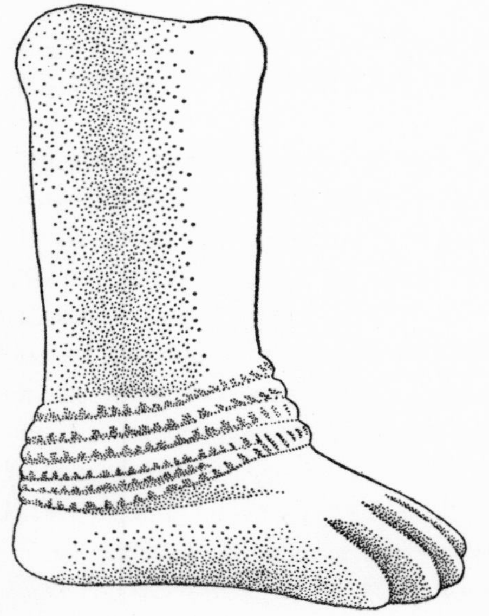

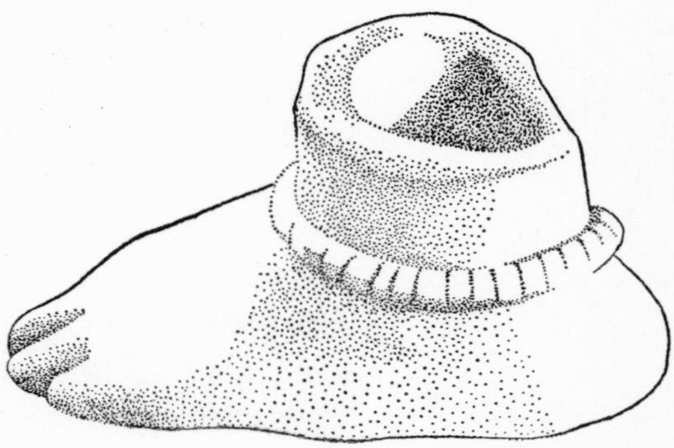

24, 25 Fragments of the limbs of terracotta figures from Nok and Ife are at times very similar, as may be seen in the comparison between the leg, left, *from Nok, and the foot and ankle,* right, *from Ife*

Plate 53

Plates 83, VII, IX

Plate XII
Plates 13, 14

Fig. 27

Plates 80, 83

just how similar these two art-forms can be in some cases. Usually the feet of Nok sculptures are remarkably square cut, and this type of foot is found in stone-carvings in Ife, as in the small figure in the Ore Grove.[105] At Nok, we find naturalism chiefly among the animal figures, whilst at Ife it has become the predominant characteristic of the style. There are many details in both arts which are unlikely to be similar by chance, for example rings are worn on the foreheads; and the figures are sometimes set on upturned pots like the female loins,[106] which should be compared with the terracotta heads from Obaluru. The noses at Nok vary in form, but one particularly characteristic form consists of a vertical ridge with very marked wings projecting strongly at the sides: this is illustrated well in Plate 82 and Fig. 19, which should be compared with Plate 23 and Fig. 26 from Ife. It should be noticed, too, that although the noses of these latter two are similar, the lips of the piece shown in Plate 23 are quite naturalistic, but those of Fig. 26 are very highly stylized. The fragment from Ire, thirty-five miles north of Ife, has been considered to be a link between the two art styles. The lips are not pierced as one would expect them to be if it were a work of Nok sculpture, and it is moderately naturalistic—more so than is usual at Nok. Yet the nose could be from Nok—the groove round the wings is quite characteristic of the principal style of Nok nose. The writer is inclined to regard this piece as being rather closer to the Ife tradition of sculpture than it is to Nok. It is indeed, in its geographical location, just on the edge of the known area of the Ife culture and is some distance away from the southern limits of the Nok sculptures that have so far been found.

Such remarkably close similarities in so many different characteristics do suggest strongly that there is a connection between these two art-forms. We have already suggested that the stylization of the human figure in Nok may be due to some sort of spiritual inhibition. The greater sophistication of the art of Ife suggests that whatever inhibitions there may have been at Nok had been thrown off by the time of the Ife culture. William Fagg has drawn attention to the remarkable similarities between the myths of the gods of the Yoruba and the adventures of the gods in ancient Greece, and has suggested that perhaps there was a similarity in the intellectual and philosophical conditions of life in pre-Classical Greece and in ancient Ife.[107] Certainly there was a similarity of political organization, as both

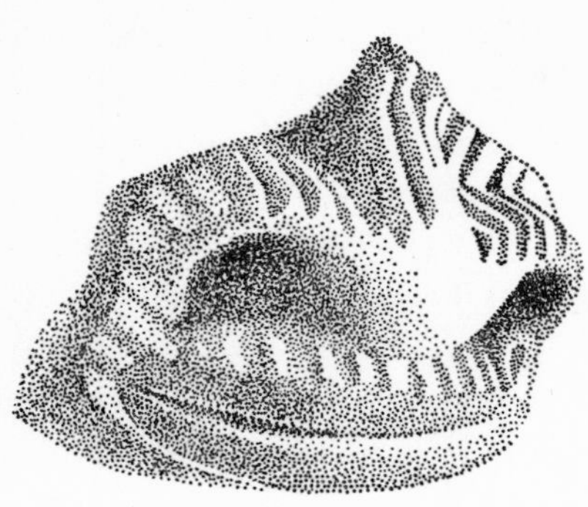

26 Terracotta fragment from Modakeke, Ife. Compare with Plate 23

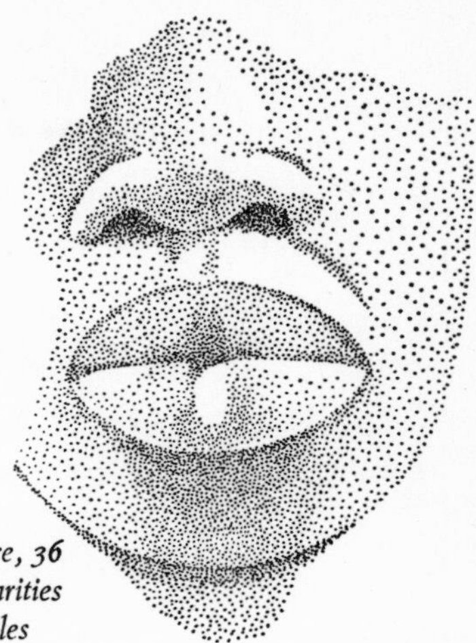

27 Terracotta fragment from Ire, 36 miles north of Ife. It shows similarities to both the Ife and the Nok styles

the Yoruba and the ancient Greeks organized their society in city-states. Although we are only able to guess how the changes between Nok and Ife occurred, the similarities are sufficient for us to be quite certain that there is some kind of a link. Before examining its nature, we need to consider the Ife traditions which throw light on their own origin.

THE LEGEND OF CREATION

The usual myth of origin tells how the high god Olodumare sent sixteen lesser gods to found the world and start life upon its way. He gave to Orishanla,[108] who is also known as Obatala, the necessary materials to make the world itself, a calabash of sand and a five-toed chicken. On the way down from heaven he drank palm wine, which caused him to fall into a deep sleep. This gave Oduduwa the opportunity to seize the calabash and the chicken and to descend first on to the primordial ocean. He emptied the calabash on the water and set the chicken upon it, whereupon it scratched at the sand and scattered it across the face of the deep, making the land appear. The other gods descended after him by a chain, which could be seen in Ife in the Grove of Olose until this grove was destroyed some years ago.

Although Orishanla lost his chance to make the world he was still allowed the privilege of making mankind. Yet once again he became intoxicated with palm wine, and in this condition he made dwarfs, hunchbacks, cripples and albinos who in consequence are considered to be especially protected by him. In the old days there were said to have been no beggars in Yorubaland, apparently because the handicapped were looked after by the devotees of Orishanla. Because of the misfortune which resulted from his liking for palm wine, this drink is forbidden to his devotees.

Oduduwa, however, after a war in which the other gods took sides, became the first ruler of Ife. He gave crowns to his children and sent them out to found kingdoms of their own. This stage is recorded in many different versions in which not only the total number of crowns varies, but also the names of the recipients, for each *oba* wishes to establish his claim to wear a beaded crown, a privilege which is reserved only for descendants of those *obas* who received their crown directly from Oduduwa.[109]

AN INDIGENOUS POPULATION

Alongside this creation legend there are myths and ceremonies which refer to an indigenous population whom the Yoruba met when they arrived.[110] For example, the King of Ibokun claims that his ancestors subdued the aborigines of the country because they had the advantage of iron weapons. The Iron Age in Nigeria cannot have begun before about 500 BC at the earliest, by which time the Yoruba appear to have been already there.[111] Therefore this reference to people coming in from outside can hardly refer to a whole population but rather to a small group. The indigenous population would have been speaking Yoruba, but they probably had a less evolved culture than they were to develop later, when these incoming groups had been largely absorbed. Luckily for the modern historian this fusion is not everywhere total. At least on ceremonial occasions an indigenous group is recognized. In the case of Ife they are known as the Igbo, and come into their own at the Edi Festival.[112]

THE IGBO

Many stories are told in Ife today which refer to the wars with the Igbo. The best known tell how these people used to attack the Ifes and were extremely successful against them, for the Ifes could not understand what nature of being the Igbo were. They had a very forbidding appearance and did not seem to be human. In order to find out what their secret was, a woman called Moremi offered to make any sacrifice demanded by the spirit of the stream, Esinmirin, if he would help her to find out the secret that would lead to the defeat of these creatures. She was told to allow herself to be captured by them on their next raid. This she did and, being a very beautiful woman, she was taken to the Igbo king and became his consort. In due course she saw suits made of raffia fibre lying out in the sun to dry, and she was told by the king that it was very important to make sure that no flame came near them for they would burn very easily. She realized then that the Igbo were ordinary human beings who had worn these raffia costumes in their attacks on the Ifes, and that if she could get back to her own people she knew how they could be defeated. She therefore escaped, came back to Ife and told her people that they should take fire brands with them the next time the Igbo attacked. This they did and the Igbo were duly defeated. Moremi was asked then to pay to Esinmirin the sacrifice that she had offered; her only son Oluorogbo was chosen.[113] Now in the Edi Festival each year in Ife this legend is re-enacted and the representatives of the Igbo, dressed in raffia fibre costumes, are driven out of the town with flaming brands. The part of the Igbo is played by the family of Obawinrin, who is the priest in charge of the Groves of Iwinrin and Osongongon Obamakin. That the head of the family who represents the Igbo should be in charge of two of the groves which have produced such a large proportion of the Ife art in terracotta is striking, suggesting as it does that the art may really be that of the original indigenous population who were employed in the service of the new ruling class.[114]

THE LEGEND OF ORE

The Ore Grove commemorates Ore, a hunter who was living in the world before Oduduwa arrived. He had no wife or children, but Oduduwa had many children who passed Ore's house every day so that he became jealous and began to shoot at them. One day he shot Oduduwa's son. Oduduwa made inquiries and gave Ore a chance to explain his grievance, whereupon he provided him with a wife. Now this legend clearly supports the idea that there was a population here when Oduduwa arrived to make the world (if one queries the logic of this situation, one is told that Ore must have lived in a boat on the primordial ocean), and it is interesting that he should be remembered as a hunter, for this may mean that this legend harks back to days before agriculture was introduced. The priests in charge of the Ore Grove, however, do not claim any connection with the Igbo or with the family of Obawinrin, so we seem here to be dealing with two independent traditions which help to corroborate each other.

The arrival of this incoming group occurred a long time ago, but we can get some understanding of what probably happened from more recent events of a similar character in other parts of Africa, where a separation of political and ritual functions can be clearly seen. Among the Anuak,[115] for example, the political power in many villages has been seized by an immigrant lineage which has become more powerful than the line of headmen descended from the original occupiers of the village site; this old line of headmen, however, still retains ritual association with the earth which could not be broken. Similar retention of ritual functions by an original group, despite the seizure of political power by immigrants, is found also among the Acholi, the Bari and the Lotuko.[116]

It is easy to understand that an incoming group, in order to avoid offending the indigenous gods, who are often associated with specific natural features, should permit the indigenous priests to continue to practise their cults on behalf of the insurgents. That something like this may have happened at Ife is suggested by legends recounted in other parts of Yorubaland about the origins of the Oniship of Ife.

THE LEGEND OF ADIMU

The Oyo, for example, tell this story: Oronmiyon, the son or grandson of Oduduwa,[117] left Ife to go on a military expedition which ended in his founding Oyo (on the site known as Old Oyo). So that the shrines should not be neglected he left behind a servant called Adimu to take charge of the ceremonies, to whom he sent from time to time for objects from the royal treasury. Adimu consolidated his position as chief priest of the national deities and dispenser of the royal treasures, yet he was of humble origins, being the child of a woman condemned to die as a sacrifice to Orishanla, but who, being pregnant with him, was granted a stay of execution until her child was born. He was therefore himself dedicated to the god Orishanla. When people asked who he was that he should be placed in charge of the shrines and treasures, it was said '*Omo oluwo ni*': He is the son of a sacrificial victim, which was later said to have been contracted to *Owoni*, or *Oni*.[118] When the seat of government was later moved to Oyo, the national shrines remained in Ife, and Adimu and his successors became the principal priests of Yorubaland. Adimu seems to be unknown in Ife, and, indeed, it is commonly asserted that Oronmiyon never reigned on the Ife throne, although he is still regarded with respect and his stone shield and stool are still preserved, as well as his staff, in Ife.

Plate 73

Whatever truth there may be in Johnson's story, it seems clear that the Oyos regarded the line of Onis who reigned in Ife after the foundation of Oyo, as being descended from a servant, though it seems highly unlikely that in this distant mythical past that the individual names like Oronmiyon really represent a single person: they are better understood as symbolizing a group of people. The significance of Johnson's story appears to be that after a ruling group had spent some time establishing themselves in Ife, they spread out to found new kingdoms elsewhere, whilst the indigenous population who had continued to provide the priests for the shrines were able to consolidate their position in the ritual life of the people and to seize some temporal power too, if only on a relatively local scale. The majority of Yoruba kings nowadays are proud to claim descent from the rulers of Ife, and, indeed, a number of cases are known where rulers having denied any connection with Ife now claim one.[119]

If the rulers of Ife after the foundation of Oyo were members of the indigenous population, it could explain why Obawinrin, the head of the family still recognized as Igbo, should have charge of two of the richest groves of sculpture in Ife. It could also help to explain why the traditions associated with all the antiquities of Ife show signs of confusion and contradiction, for if the priest in charge of them wished to consolidate his position among his own people, it would be aided by neglecting the shrines of the royal ancestors of the recently established rulers in favour of his own claims, and encouraging the cult of local gods instead. Indeed many of the Ife cults today are unknown outside Ife; for example, Oramfe, Eleshije, Oluorogbo, Teko, and Ijugbe. Such an attitude could have contributed to the decline in the naturalistic art. Unfortunately we have no means of dating the period of Oduduwa and Oronmiyon, the days when the gods were men.

CONNECTIONS BETWEEN NOK AND IFE

It is difficult at present to tie in these ideas in any precise way with the Nok culture. The Ife culture of the classical period evidently draws much of its artistic tradition from that of Nok, or from an undiscovered common ancestor. It is conceivable that the early Yoruba-speakers of the forest were carving in wood when the Nok culture was flourishing farther north, and only at a later stage did they begin to sculpt in terracotta, and even later in bronze. That some elements of Ife culture were brought in from outside is strongly suggested by Ife myths. Probably only a small group of people was involved since they became completely absorbed linguistically. They seem to have come from the savannahs to the north, and to have fused into a new people and a new culture along the edge of the forest. It is possible even that the Nok culture itself spread as far as the forest's edge—perhaps some of the Nok people followed the edge of the forest as it retreated with increasing desiccation, bringing their sculpture with them, for the clearly separated areas of the two cultures which can be seen on the map probably represent the distribution of influence of the archaeological museums at Jos and Ife, rather than any true limits of the cultures. Certainly there is no compelling reason to consider it necessary to have successive 'waves' of invaders coming in large numbers and with new ideas every few centuries.[120] There seems to be only one element of the Ife culture which must have been introduced from outside, namely the knowledge of bronze-casting, which could have been introduced by a single craftsman travelling one of the trade-routes along the Sudan to the south of the Sahara, or across the Sahara from the Mediterranean. He would certainly have needed to keep in touch through these trade-routes with the original sources of his metals until such time as he was able to find local ores that he could exploit. The impluvial form of architecture occurs all round the Mediterranean and has been considered to be an example of Mediterranean influence in West Africa, but so slender is the evidence about this that the impluvium could well have been invented in West Africa and spread from there to the Mediterranean where it was first known to the European travellers, who were later to see it in West Africa. African archaeology is at present severely handicapped by a lack of real data about such questions, but it does not help the subject to assert that because traits of culture have been found outside negro Africa that they must therefore have been invented outside Africa. A couple of decades ago it was thought that mankind had originated in Asia; now the weight of evidence points to Africa. It is surely wiser to keep an open mind and to be critical of explanations which rely largely on a lack of information about the early history of Africa.

Fig. 1

A number of Northern Nigerian tribes have been reported to have traditions of an Eastern origin, usually associated with the name of Kisra.[121] It seems most likely that these traditions refer only to a relatively small ruling group, not to the whole population. Some of these peoples, however, also have traditions of bronze-casting, so that it is possible that this craft was introduced via the Sudan and the Benue Valley. The interpretation of these traditions, however, is made difficult by the fact that most of the peoples to whom they refer have been converted to Islam, whilst the Europeans who have written about them seem to have been influenced by the Egyptian discoveries of Flinders Petrie and others, and to have been inclined to assume an Egyptian origin for anything that could be paralleled there simply because they knew about it.

NATURALISM IN OTHER ART TRADITIONS

Similarly, it has been fashionable to look for the origins of the naturalistic art of Ife in other forms of naturalistic art with little regard for chronology. It has been suggested, for example, that a bronze mask from Nubia in the British Museum[122] affords an example of a style of bronze-casting from which the art of Ife could have been derived, but this mask is very much smaller than the bronze-castings of Ife and is in a style far removed from that of Ife, being much more highly stylized. In discussing analogues of Ife art, most writers seem to have ignored the very obvious fact that once one has decided to represent human beings in a naturalistic manner, since human beings resemble each other all over the world, the resulting copies, if they are at all close to nature, will themselves resemble each other in a general way. It is only the degree of idealization of a representation and the stylized techniques, the schemata as Gombrich calls them, which will serve to distinguish one style of art from another. If one looks closely at Egyptian art, at Renaissance sculpture, even at the Gandhara sculpture which was made in India under Greek influence, one can see quite clearly stylizations which are individual to each of them and not shared by the art of Ife. The same objection applies to Jones's suggestion that Ife art is analogous to Khmer sculpture, even though some details of the crowns are similar.[123] There remains the possibility of an influence from the European Renaissance. European sculpture of this period is distinguished particularly for the attention it pays to the anatomical substructure of the human body, based on the knowledge which was being discovered at the time by dissection. The only evidence one can see in Ife art of the substructure of the human body is in the bony eyebrow-ridges, occasionally, but very rarely, in the form of the eye, and once in the cheek-bones. In all these cases it could be as much observation of the surface as any understanding of the hidden anatomy, so that here again the feeling of the art is not the same as that of Renaissance sculpture. Plate VI

NATURALISM IN TRIBAL ART

To discuss naturalism at Ife in these terms, however, is to ignore the striking fact that naturalism not infrequently occurs in the arts of tribal societies alongside more common stylized forms. Boas drew attention to this in 1897 when writing of the naturalistic masks of the North Pacific coast of America, where sculptural forms are normally so unnaturalistic as to have become decorative symbols.[124] Similarly in New Guinea and the New Hebrides, naturalistic portraits in clay are regularly modelled on the skulls of ancestors, despite the extreme formalism of most of the art in these areas.[125] Even the aboriginal Australians, occasionally, come close to naturalistic sculpture.[126] It is evident then that naturalism lies neither beyond the conception nor beyond the skill of tribal artists. It needs only to be called to the fore by social conditions. In Ife the need to commemorate and to glorify the divine kings and their courtiers was sufficient to swing the emphasis from the restricted naturalism of the Nok sculptures to the paramount portraiture of Ife.

X

The Date of the Art of Ife

THE INTRODUCTION OF BRONZE-CASTING

SUCH EVIDENCE as we have about the date of the art of Ife relates to the bronzes rather than to the terracotta sculptures. Stylistically, however, the bulk of the terracotta can be associated with the bronzes in the Classical Period, so that the dating of one will date the other medium. Unfortunately there is in Ife itself no evidence which can throw light directly on the date of the art. There is, for example, a tradition that bronze-casting was introduced by Obalufon II, the third Oni after the creation of the world. This might mean that it was introduced by, or soon after the arrival of, the Oduduwa Dynasty, but this is an event which we cannot date.

One of the complications in tracing the history of bronze-casting is that any style which becomes old-fashioned can be completely replaced by a newer style, by melting down the old objects and recasting them to suit the new taste. Luckily terracotta sculpture once made cannot be unmade, so that we can trace the history of sculpture through the evidence of terracotta whereas bronzes are liable to appear fully fledged. It seems indeed that the art of Ife evolved in terracotta, and that it was translated bodily as an evolved naturalistic art-form into bronze when the technique of bronze-casting became known to the people of Ife. The technique could have been introduced by a single itinerant bronzesmith, or perhaps a small group, casting utilitarian objects such as bells or knife-handles. Such a smith would have had to keep in touch with supplies of metal, at least until he had found ores locally. The techniques of bronze-casting in West Africa suggest that there were at least two separate introductions on to the Guinea Coast from the hinterland. William Fagg[127] has pointed out that the Dan-Ngere to the west and the peoples of the Cameroons Grasslands to the east use decorative motifs made of threads of wax about a sixteenth of an inch in diameter; among the Baule and Ashanti less far to the west and among the Tiv and Jukun and at Igbo Ukwu less far to the east, a finer thread is used, whilst

Plates 103, 104

in the central area, which includes Ife and Benin, such motifs are absent, except on the eastern edge of the area, *e.g.*, at Obo Ayegunle. We cannot be sure whether the technique of the central area was introduced into a previously continuous area of bronze-casting, or whether an incoming group was unable to affect the established technique of the centre and so spread round it. Archaeological evidence may one day provide an answer. Whichever way it happened, the people of Ife appear already to have been skilled sculptors in terracotta and to have had considerable skill in firing them. They would not have found it very difficult to translate their sophisticated art into the new and more permanent medium. They may not even have found it necessary to recast any of the bronzes to keep abreast of changes in style, for some basic characteristics of the Nok sculpture have persisted through a period of two thousand years to survive in modern West African sculpture.[128] It seems therefore that there is a very strongly conservative element in African artistic traditions which makes it possible for the fundamentals of an art-form to persist for so long, and we might therefore expect even the more superficial characters to persist for perhaps two or three centuries, but it would seem very unlikely that the bronze-castings of Ife could have been made over a longer period than that without showing noticeable change.

THE DURATION OF BRONZE-CASTING IN IFE

If the bronze heads were made for funeral effigies, then this may provide an indication of the length of time during which they were made. They are evidently commemorative, yet if they were all of different reigns this would represent a period of three to four hundred years if we allow twenty years for a reign. If, however, the king was put to death after seven years, as is supposed to happen to divine kings (and Ulli Beier tells me that he was told in Ijebu that this used to be the practice in Ife), then the period covered would be about a hundred and five to a hundred and twenty-six years, depending on whether or not the three smaller heads are included. On the other hand, we do know that it was a common practice to sacrifice other human beings with the king when he died. The royal grave excavated by the writer at Ilesha, twenty miles from Ife, showed that the practice continued there into the nineteenth century.[129] It is not inconceivable, therefore, that these heads may have been cast in groups commemorating not only the deceased Oni but also the members of his court who chose or were compelled to die with him, in which case there must have been an equally elaborate second burial in which effigies of the accompanying victims were also buried. This would presuppose that in this case the attendants wore chiefly emblems; the chiefs of modern Ife wear distinctive hats, one type of which is shown in Plate 69. If this was the custom, the bronzes which have survived might not cover a very long period of time at all, perhaps only a couple of generations, just as the naturalistic art of the *ako* figures of Owo appears to have flourished for only half a century.

It was suggested (p. 26) that the bronze heads might originally have been buried in the Olokun Grove. Until recently the Onis were buried at Igbo Odi, outside the town wall to the south-east. Here there are about thirty or forty mounds each reputed to be the burial place of an Oni. This might indicate that the practice of royal burial which we have inferred at the Olokun Grove was abandoned a long time ago, but it is more likely that the second burial effigies were not buried in the same place as the bodies. The name Igbo Odi means 'secret grove', and it is a place which is still held in some awe. In Ilesha, until the middle of the nineteenth century, the king's body was dismembered and scattered so that no one would know where it was buried; similarly, in Ife the place where the Oni was buried seems to have been kept secret. The number of graves at Igbo Odi cannot therefore be used as an indication of the date of abandonment of the Olokun Grove, and by implication, of bronze-casting. On the other hand, the purchase of a glass object by the Landers at Old Oyo in 1830 (p. 108) suggests that the use of the Olokun Grove for burial must have ceased a long time earlier, since by that time the trade in mined glass seems to have been well established.

IFE BRONZES SENT TO BENIN

At the time the first Europeans visited Benin about 1485 they recorded that it was the custom when the King of Benin acceded to the throne for him to send ambassadors with rich gifts to a ruler called the Ogane, who appears to be the Oni of Ife (who is known among the Bini today as the Ogene). Moreover, the Ogane was described as being a spiritual overlord, who was to them what the Pope was to the Europeans of the time. This further suggests that it is the Oni of Ife to whom these gifts were sent. In return he sent a staff, a hat and a cross all made of brass, which were regarded as the symbols of authority for the King of Benin and confirmed him in his office.[130] Clearly, then, bronze-casting was going on in Ife at the time the Europeans arrived in Benin.

According to traditions in both Benin and Ife, Oronmiyon was sent from Ife to Benin to control the town when it fell into a state of anarchy. He did not himself reign as king there but, having pacified the town, he took as wife a daughter of one of the native chiefs and by her begat a son whom he left behind to reign as the Oba Eweka I of Benin. From him all succeeding Obas of Benin have been descended. Their dynasty is therefore a Yoruba one, and the Obas of Benin have for a long time regarded the Oni of Ife as their elder brother. Moreover, it became the custom when an Oba of Benin died to send his head to Ife for burial on the site there known as Orun Oba Ado, which is the place from which Oronmiyon is alleged to have set out for Benin. Excavations on this site have revealed a number of pits which might well have been graves, although no skulls were found. It seems very likely that it was not the real head that was sent but some token of the body, such as the fingernails or hair; these pieces of the body, which show apparent signs of growth after death, are regarded as symbols of continuing life and are commonly used, both in Benin and among the Yoruba, when a man dies and is buried away from the home, as a token body to be interred by his family at home. Bradbury has recorded the details of the last occasion on which the 'head' of a king of Benin was taken to Ife for burial, and has interviewed one of the people who was in the party which visited Ife in 1888. The Benin historian, Jacob Egharevba,[131] tells the story of the Oba Oguola before whose time, when the head of an Oba was sent to Ife for burial, it had been the custom for a bronze head to be sent back from Ife to Benin. Oguola suggested that it would be much simpler if the Oni of Ife were to allow one of his bronzesmiths to visit Benin to teach the Bini how to make such heads for themselves. The Oni agreed to this[132] and sent Igueghae to Benin, where he is still worshipped to this day as the patron of the bronze-casters, and indeed on his shrine there used to be terracotta heads comparable to the bronze heads which were used on the royal ancestor shrines in Benin. Now the Oba Oguola was reigning apparently at the end of the fourteenth century.[133] We may therefore infer from the Benin evidence that bronze heads were being cast in Ife before the end of the fourteenth century, and the European visitors confirmed that bronze-casting was continuing there about a century later although they do not refer to bronze heads.

Plates 94, 95; *Figs. 28–30*

55, 56 Post-Classical sculptures in terracotta found in 1955 at a site on the Ondo Road fourteen miles from Ife. The head shows the bulging eyes and flat protrusive lips characteristic of the later Ife sculptures, whilst the stylized ear bears some resemblance to those of the Esie stone sculptures (*Fig. 21*). The male figure, *right*, is clearly a crude version of the Classical figures

57, 58 Some of the fragments of five figures found at Lagere, Ife, in 1958. The foot is from a life-size figure of which eight pieces survive including crotals and tassels. The two arms show the only representation of this type of bracelet at Ife. All the pieces from this site show characteristics which are not found in other sub-styles of Ife art

59 Terracotta head of a man found in 1959 by gold-miners panning the gravels of the Mokuro stream about three miles from Ife. This piece appears in style and technique to belong to a more recent date than the Classical Period of the naturalistic bronzes and terracottas. The ear of this head is shown in *Fig. 10* and two pieces of the body in *Fig. 11*. Red paint still covers the face

60 Terracotta head collected by Frobenius in Ife in 1910. It has been broken from a figure which had a flat collar on the neck, which is much shorter than usual and slopes back from the head instead of being vertically beneath it. The bulging eyes remind one of the smaller gagged heads (Plate 62), whilst the ear is unusually highly stylized for Ife (*Fig. 12*). It seems very probable that this is a late work. The faint engraved circles on the forehead correspond to the raised rings on heads of the Classical Period (Plates VII, IX), but the relief modelling of the eyebrows is so far unique in Ife sculpture

61, 62 Ife heads are not invariably naturalistic. The highly stylized pieces *above* symbolize rather than portray human heads. The first, *left*, was found in 1961 by students clearing the precincts of the Oronmiyon Memorial College. The second, from the grove of Osongongon Obamakin, shows a blend of naturalistic features on a highly stylized conical head form. The third was found in Ife in 1963. The fourth head, *extreme right*, was found at Abiri in 1947. It contrasts with the ram's head and human head from the same site (Plate 24). The three stylized heads with rope gags, *below*, apparently represent victims for human sacrifice. The first, *left*, was found opposite Ita Yemoo in 1957; the second was excavated in the grove of Osongongon Obamakin in 1953 by Bernard Fagg; the third is of uncertain provenance, but may also be from Osongongon Obamakin since the roughish micaceous clay is very similar to terracotta sculptures known to be from the grove. All three heads have flat, protruding lips, but the ears and eyes of the last two are moderately naturalistic. The Ilesha Road head is much closer in style to modern Yoruba sculpture (Plates 106, 109, 110, *Fig. 3*)

63 One of the three legs of a quartz vessel, two inches in diameter around the legs, though it may well have expanded above into a shallow bowl of the type used nowadays for the cult of Ifa. (Several are illustrated in *Bibl. 55 a, I p. 259, 261, 263* and *265*.) The piece was found by one of Frobenius's labourers 'on the hill of the old Ifa temple' (*Bibl. 55 a, I, p. 332*). The contorted posture of the figure with his arms passed behind his flexed kness should be compared with that of the bronze figures supporting a bowl in the British Museum, attributed to the Lower Niger Bronze Industry (illustrated in *Bibl. 50 j, pl. 63 a*). It appears to represent an acrobat

64 Sherd of a ritual pot found with the head illustrated in Plate 62 *left*. It shows a decapitated male body lying naked, with the hands tied behind the back; the head lies beside it, with a rope gag between its teeth. When in Ife today animals are sacrificed as substitutes for human beings they are gagged and their forelegs are tied behind the back as a man would have been treated. The gag was to stop the victim from cursing his executioner as he expired. This sherd confirms that the gagged heads in bronze and terracotta represent sacrificial victims (Plates 62, V, VI)

65, 66 *Above*, terracotta fragments being excavated at Ita Yemoo, Ife, during 1963. Nearest the camera is a left heel and ankle on a broken plinth, with another ankle and piece of plinth to its left. Beyond is a crowned head with fragments of the torso and sashes in the corner. The scales show feet and inches. *Below*, detail of the pavement excavated at the Catholic Mission, Ife, during 1958, composed of double lines of potsherds forming hollow rectangles, filled in with quartz pebbles. A plan and a detail of it appear as *Figs. 16, 17*

67 A very unusual terracotta head, excavated in 1964 at Igbo Obameri, Ife, by Oliver Myers, representing a man wearing a mask. The lips and chin can be seen to the left of the photograph, visible through a gap in the patterned material which hangs from the round flat hat and hides the rest of the face. On the opposite side are two eyes resembling those frequently found on the 'pot' (*ikoko*) which encloses the head on modern *epa* and *are* masks in Ekiti. (*Fig. 5* shows this more clearly.) The clear portrayal of the person wearing the mask, who would in reality be hidden, is perhaps intended to make it clear that the sculpture is of a man wearing a mask, not of some strange spirit in the form of the mask, though nowadays it is considered dangerous to see the man inside (*Bibl. 16 h, p. 27; 30 b*)

68 Terracotta head found beside the road from Ife to Ifewara about a mile beyond the Ore Grove by boys hunting for rodents in 1959. This sculpture was made as a head; it is not broken from a larger sculpture representing a full length figure, as many of the terracotta heads are. The hair is dressed up to a disc on the crown

69, 70 Priests of the god Orishanla during the Itapa festival wear their chiefly caps and badges of office; their faces and torsos are decorated with white paint and they strike iron bar gongs (*ewo*) as they kneel in worship before a small shelter in which is kept this small striated terracotta head which is not normally seen, but is kept covered by a large piece of broken pot

71, 72 The Oni of Ife, Sir Adesoji Aderemi, wearing a traditional beaded crown with a crest over the forehead and a long fringe of beads hiding his face. He is taking part in the Olojo festival in honour of Ogun, the god of iron and patron of hunters, one of the two occasions each year when, in the old days, the Oni used to appear in public. He carries a ceremonial sword with which he 'fights' the chief, Oshogun, who is in charge of the cult of Ogun. *Below*, a granite mudfish in the Ogun Ladin shrine in the Palace at Ife. The shrine is associated both with Ogun, the god of iron, and with the welfare of the royal family

73 The Opa Oronmiyon, or staff of Oronyon, now turned to stone. Oronmiyon was a great warrior of the mythical phase of Yoruba history. Ogun, the god of iron, was the war captain of his father Oduduwa, who created the world and ruled as the first Oni of Ife. During one successful campaign Ogun captured a beautiful woman, Lakange, with whom he had sexual relations on the way back to Ife. On his return Ogun handed over the rest of his prisoners, not mentioning Lakange. His father found out about her, and took her as one of his own wives. He asked Ogun if he had made love to her, but did not believe his son's denial. Now Oduduwa was a white man and Ogun was black. When in due time Lakange bore a child, he was half black and half white, divided vertically down the middle. Thus Oduduwa was able to say when he saw the baby '*Oro mi yon*' (my word has come to pass). At the Olojo festival (Plate 71) some of the court messengers (*emese*) paint themselves half red and half white in memory of Oronmiyon, and run up and down the hill on which the principal shrine for Ogun is situated. Oronmiyon established dynasties in Benin and Oyo and promised always to return to help the people of Ife when they were hard pressed in war. On one occasion when they called for him he appeared suddenly among them, swinging his staff in a blind fury. When the Ifes cried out to him that he was killing his own people, he set down his staff in disgust and went away and died. It carried originally 140 spiral-headed iron nails, closely similar to those decorating the statue of Orodi at Eshure (Plate 75). They are likely to have been no more than decoration

74 Stone figure of a man from the Ore Grove, Ife, sometimes known as Idena (the gate keeper). He wears a heavy collar of beads, not closely paralleled in the bronze and terracotta sculptures; similarly his hip knot is only paralleled in a general way, although the posture is known in terracotta. The hair is represented by wrought iron nails inserted into holes already drilled, and hammered to fit by expansion. The form of the face is much less naturalistic than the bronze and terracotta sculptures, possibly because the granite was a less tractable medium, or perhaps because stone working was carried out by a different group of craftsmen. The lips and nose do indeed resemble in a general way the Nok sculpture shown in *Fig. 19*

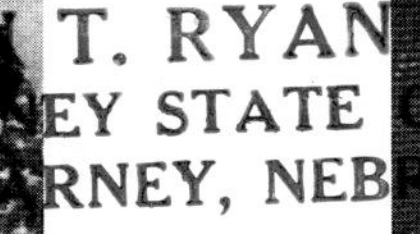

75 One of a group of stone carvings clearly related to those of Ife, but found at Eshure in Ekiti. It comes from the Grove of Orodi, and is decorated with iron nails on the head and body similar to those on the Opa Oronmiyon (Plate 73) and on the head of Idena. These nails prompted the local belief that Orodi was a man who was shot in war and turned to stone. The face has been left without features, but his left hand holds a ceremonial sword (*ada*), and his right a fly whisk. (*See also Bibl. 119 p*)

76–79 Four examples of stools from Ife. The terracotta sculpture, *above*, from the Iwinrin Grove represents a round stool with a looped handle supported on a rectangular stool with four legs. A figure was seated on the round stool with his legs astride the loop, and his feet resting on the rectangular stool. The larger pieces used in the restoration have been in the Iwinrin Grove since time immemorial (see the photograph taken by H. L. Ward Price in 1931, in *Bibl. 50 n, p. 60*), but the smaller pieces were recovered by excavation in 1953 by Bernard Fagg and in 1959 by the writer. The figure is about three-quarters life-size, so that originally the sculpture must have been about four feet high. It is the largest known Ife sculpture. *Opposite* are three stone stools, the upper of quartz, one of three presented by the Oni of Ife, Adelekan Olubushe, in 1896 to Captain Bower (*see Bibl. 49 j, p*). All three came originally from the shrine of Oluorogbo, a 'white god' who carried messages between heaven and earth. *Centre*, an unusually simple stool of granite-gneiss, one of a pair from the Apere Oro (stool for the bull-roarer) Grove. *Below*, a broken stool of white quartz from the Epinbodo shrine where it lay upside-down and had recently had a white chicken sacrificed over it when it was brought into the museum in 1958

80 Terracotta head found at the Gold Coff
Mine at Jemaa in 1958. The ears of this hea
are unusual in the Nok sculptures, both
their form and in being naturalistically place
Similar ear forms occur at Ife (Plate 43) ar
in modern Yoruba sculpture (*Fig. 37*). Th
eyes are completely typical of the Nok styl
with the semi-circular (or triangular) eye ba
completely pierced by the pupil, and the we
arched eyebrows counter-balancing them.
this example the hairs of the eyebrows and
the upper lid are indicated by cross-hatchin
The raised area beside the mouth original
represented a keeloid tribal mark. The ve
fresh condition of this and of many oth
heads, shows that they could not have bee
washed far from their original position befo
being incorporated in the river gravels

81 An unusual terracotta head from Jema
The inflated cheeks were perhaps inspired
a musician blowing a reeded flute or chant
an instrument which is now widespread in t
savannas of West Africa, but there is no indic
tion that there was a flute between the lip
This too is broken from a figure

82 Terracotta head of about life size found at a depth of about twelve feet during tin mining at Nok in 1954. The eyes are typical of Nok art, as is the low position of the ear (just visible on the left of the photograph). The lower lip has been broken, so that the mouth now looks more open than the sculptor intended. There was a rope of thin strings of beads round the neck, which was modelled hollow to keep the clay even in thickness for better firing. Bernard Fagg has pointed out that the five buns into which the hair is dressed resemble the present-day hair style of the Kachichiri and Numana tribes who live about thirty miles east of Nok. Holes in these buns, he suggests, may have been used to carry real feathers (*Bibl. 49 h*). The head is broken from a figure which, if standing upright, could hardly have been less than four feet tall

83 Terracotta head found during mining
Tsauni camp, Jemaa, in 1943. The clerk
charge of the mine was sufficiently interes
in this head to take it home with him. So
time later, deciding that it would serve w
as a scarecrow, he set it up on a stick in
farm, where it was exposed to sun and r
for a year. The slightness of the erosion wh
this produced gives testimony to the f
quality of the pottery. The impressed corn
of the eyes are unusual and give it life. T
setting of the ears, at the angle of the jaw,
feature regularly found in Nok sculpture. T
raised ring on the forehead should be co
pared with the Ife heads on Plates VII and
Like them, this was originally part of a fig

84 Human loins from Nok wearing elaborate beadwork ornaments, which include a kind of sporran facing the right and a small bell hanging on the right hip. Married women of the Aten tribe used until recently to wear similar bells with a long clapper during the *nep* rites

85 This kneeling man found at Bwari, twe
miles from Abuja, the smallest Nok sculp
so far found, yet shows great delicacy
modelling. The rope of beads round his n
is identical with that shown on the lar
(Plate 82). His right arm is raised as if
straighten his cap

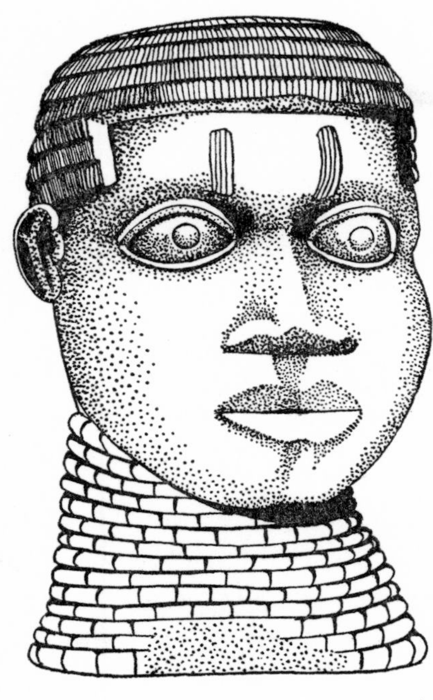

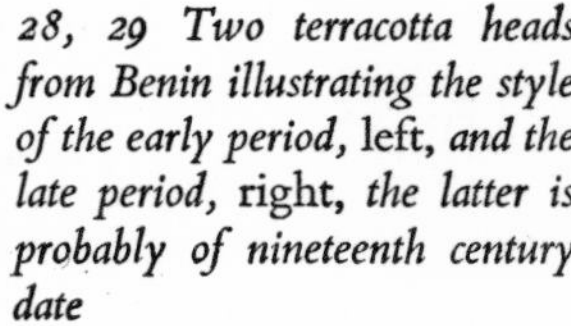

28, 29 Two terracotta heads from Benin illustrating the style of the early period, left, *and the late period,* right, *the latter is probably of nineteenth century date*

The last reference we have to emblems of royal authority being sent from the Ogane to the Oba of Benin is in 1540.[134] Later visitors to Benin such as Nyendael[135] described the bronze heads on the ancestor shrines but do not refer to Ife. Evidently once Oguola had got bronze-casting established in Benin his successors had the heads made there and did not need to import them from Ife. Gradually, although they continued right up to the end of the nineteenth century to send the Oba's 'head' to Ife for burial, they did not bother to collect the insignia from there. This Benin evidence suggests that bronze-casting was being carried out on a substantial scale in Ife in the fourteenth century, and that it may have been only on a reducing scale in the fifteenth and sixteenth centuries. We have already suggested that the close similarity of style in the thirty or so bronzes we have from Ife suggests that they were made over a relatively limited range of time. It is therefore likely that they should be dated to the thirteenth or fourteenth century, but the strong indications of a connection with the Nok culture make it difficult to accept a date as late as this for the peak of the art. The terracotta sculptures are a good deal more varied than the bronzes, and it seems very likely that they flourished for a considerably longer time. It may be, but we cannot yet prove it, that some of the art in terracotta is of much greater antiquity than the bronzes, but the puzzling gap of a thousand years between the latest date we have of the Nok culture and the earliest date we can suggest for the bronzes of Ife is a major difficulty which should not be minimized. No doubt we shall eventually find some evidence to fill in this missing millennium, perhaps by showing that the Nok culture persisted much later or that the Ife culture began much earlier than we can assume on the evidence we have at present obtained. The technique of thermo-luminescence in particular is likely to help us soon to assign dates to the terracotta sculptures of both cultures.

THE END OF BRONZE-CASTING IN IFE

The naturalistic bronze-casting of Ife appears to have died out very quickly, even if bronze-casting continued on a small scale for the objects which were sent to Benin. The story of Lajuwa (p. 57) may well afford us evidence of why the bronze-casting ceased, and Idowu tells what may well be a different version of the same legend. According to this, when a certain well-loved Oni died his courtiers decided not to announce the fact, but instructed the bronze-casters to make an effigy of him to which the other members of the court came to pay their homage. In due course the deception was discovered, and the Oni who succeeded was so angry at having been kept from the throne that he ordered the execution of those who had been responsible for making the effigy. As a result the bronze-casters and terracotta sculptors were all killed; consequently both these arts died out at once in Ife.[136] Some possible corroboration of this story is perhaps afforded by the mask known by the name of Obalufon. This was evidently intended to be worn over the face and could well have been used, hidden by the beaded fringe of the crown, by someone who wished to masquerade as the Oni. Of course, this is merely an interpretation which we put on the story. It is quite possible that the story collected by Idowu was an invention intended to explain why it was that bronze-casting ceased in Ife so suddenly. We have already pointed out that terracotta and stone sculpture continued much later than bronze-casting: it is possible that the reason for the decline in Ife bronze-casting was of an economic nature. The earliest European contacts with Southern Nigeria were with Benin, and Ife is only referred to as being somewhere in

Plate I

the interior. The Europeans did not have any contact with Ife at all before the nineteenth century. Benin remained in more-or-less continuous contact with the Europeans and, once bronze-casting was established there, had no difficulty in obtaining the required metals from the coastal trade with Europe. Ife, on the other hand, with no contact with this European trade, probably depended on supplies from farther north; from the trade-routes across the Sahara or down the Benue Valley, which might well have been interrupted with the spread of Islam in the fifteenth and sixteenth centuries.

William Fagg has suggested that metallurgical analysis of the Ife metal-castings adds some support to the idea that the Ife bronzes were cast earlier than those of Benin. Relatively few Benin castings have been analysed in relation to the large numbers which survive, but according to Fagg the analyses that have been done suggest that the earliest Benin pieces (we shall discuss in a moment which pieces are to be considered early) are of brass, whereas the later ones are of true bronze.[137] All the Ife pieces have been demonstrated to be of brass. It seems therefore that the same sources of material used in Ife were available when bronze-casting began in Benin in the time of Oguola, but that later the necessary supplies were obtained through the European trade, and that these supplies were not of brass any more but of bronze. Unfortunately, however, the early analyses of Benin bronzes on which this interpretation is based[138] do not sufficiently identify the individual pieces which were analysed. A recent unpublished series of tests showed a great many late Benin pieces to be of brass,[139] so a systematic programme of analyses is now being undertaken to test this hypothesis. However, the Ife brasses and some of those from Benin show a different composition from European brass, so there can be little doubt that there were independent African sources.

Oronmiyon is credited with having established the city of Oyo and placed his son Ajaka on the throne there, and also with having founded the Yoruba dynasty in Benin, where he fathered Eweka I. If Oronmiyon were a real person this would suggest that these two events were very close together in time, but he is so evidently a mythical creature, an archetypal hero-figure, that there is no good reason for assuming that these events were contemporaneous. It is possible, indeed, that the Yoruba dynasty in Benin was founded much earlier than the city of Oyo. It is also quite possible that the

Classical Period of Ife art preceded the founding of Oyo, in which case if the political capital had moved away from Ife to Oyo and a member of the indigenous group had been left behind in charge of the shrines (see p. 124) it is easy to understand how these crafts could have died out, associated as they evidently were with the royal cults. So far, however, nothing has been discovered at Old Oyo which would support this hypothesis in any satisfactory way. One small terracotta head was found there in the 1956–7 excavations, but this was of a crude style and was quite impossible to date but it certainly bore little or no resemblance to any of the work of Ife.[140] It is reported, however, that when Oyo was overrun by the Ilorins there were many hundreds of brass house-posts which were seized and taken away to be melted down to make cannons. This would suggest at any rate that bronze-casting had continued in Oyo, but this is such a long time after the founding of the city that in itself it does not give any indication of whether the craft centre from Ife was moved to Oyo with the capital, for we find that bronze-casting was being conducted throughout Ijebu, Egba and elsewhere in Yorubaland during the last two or three centuries, if not earlier.

Plate 101

XI

Descendants in Bronze

THE ART OF BENIN

HOW MUCH FAITH can we put in the Igueghae story of the Ife origin of Benin bronze-casting? Igueghae is said to have taken examples of Ife work in bronze and terracotta to Benin. The small figure found in the centre of Benin appears to be an Ife work, and was claimed by Egharevba to be the work of Igueghae himself. A bronze pendant, obviously made in Benin, was found in Ife. The face of a terracotta figure, although found in Ife and without parallel in the same medium, is clearly in Benin style and is closely paralleled by a late bronze face mask from Benin. That there was artistic contact between Ife and Benin is beyond doubt, and here is evidence that there was traffic in both directions.

Plate 89

Plate 90

Plate 92

Plate 91

BRONZE HEADS

The typology of Benin bronze-casting has been closely studied by William Fagg, who has much improved the groupings postulated earlier by Von Luschan and Struck by eliminating from the sequence a number of pieces which are quite certainly in a series of different styles, separate from the tradition of the Benin court. Philip Dark is working out a more refined chronology of the true Benin pieces. The heads which remain in the Benin sequence fall into a series beginning with thin castings in a naturalistic style. In this group, assigned to the Early Period, the beaded collar is close to the neck and the features of the head, although stylized to a considerable degree compared with the Ife bronzes, are yet much less so than the great bulk of Benin art. The well-known Queen Mother heads in the British Museum and in Lagos[141] are of this general type, but these cannot be dated before the early sixteenth century when the Oba Esigie introduced the title of Queen Mother. Some of the Queen Mother heads have flanges at the bottom and are to be assigned to a still later date. To the Middle Period are to be assigned the heads with a deep high collar and no flange, which are probably of the seventeenth century, whilst similar heads with a flange seem to belong to the time of Eresoyen (mid-eighteenth century). The Oba

Plate 94

Plate 95

Fig. 30

Osemwede (1816–48) introduced a more elaborate crown with upswept projections which are characteristic of the Late Period.[142] The development of the heads in this sequence is also supported by their increasing thickness, as metal became more freely available through trade with Europe, until some of them weigh about a hundredweight.

THE PLAQUES

Besides the commemorative bronze heads there is a large series of plaques which seem to commemorate historical and ceremonial events. Many of them show Portuguese in mid-sixteenth-century dress, and Dark places these at the beginning of the sequence.[143] The latest ones show figures of the Benin court with high collars like those on the heads. These plaques were described in 1668 by Dapper: 'wooden pillars, from top to bottom covered with cast copper, on which are engraved the pictures of their war exploits and battles, and are kept very clean'.[144] But by 1702, when Nyendael described the palace in considerable detail, he made no reference to them.[145] They had evidently been taken down in the interval and put into store, where they seem to have remained until the Royal Navy carried them away in 1897. Evidently no more were cast after about 1700, but their manufacture might have ceased even before Dapper's time. Bradbury was told by an old chief, who had been a young court attendant before the punitive expedition, that the plaques had been stacked away rather like a card index and whenever there was a dispute about traditional dress or some other aspect of courtly etiquette, a chief was sent to check up on this great catalogue of precedents.

TERRACOTTA HEADS

The bronze-casters of Benin are organized, like all the Benin craftsmen, into a guild and still have their own quarter in the town. There they have an altar for Igueghae, who is their patron, on which used to stand a group of terracotta heads which he was said to have brought with him from Ife, although they were clearly in a Benin style. They used also to make terracotta heads themselves in his honour and these reflect the styles of the bronzes. One of those illustrated resembles the early bronzes and may itself be of comparable date, whilst another example is clearly fairly recent work.

Fig. 28
Fig. 29

ORIGIN AND DEVELOPMENT OF THE BENIN STYLE

The art objects of Benin are all, even the least stylized, quite distinct from those of Ife from which they are derived. William Fagg[146] has suggested that there is a gap of perhaps a century between the Igueghae Period and that of the earliest surviving Benin bronzes,

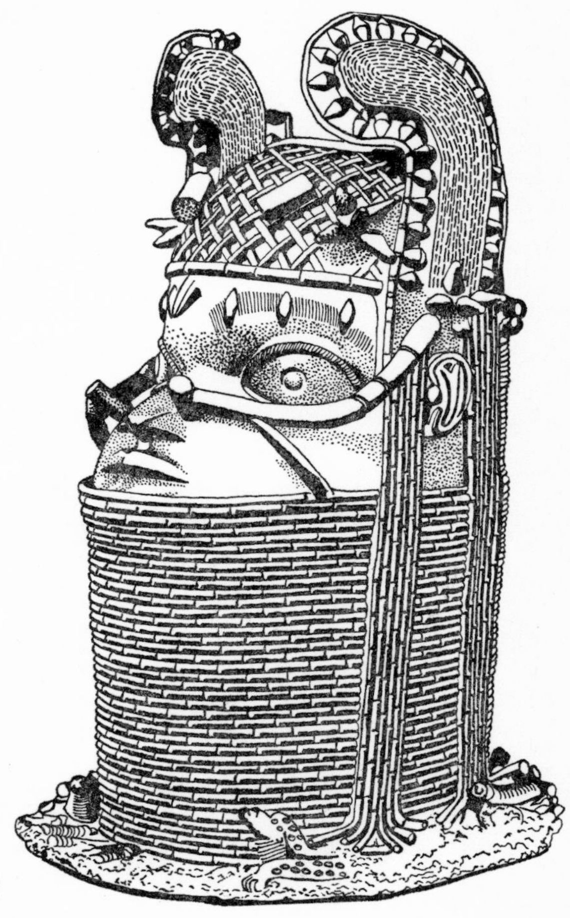

30 Benin bronze head of the Late Period

to account for this change in style, but it is not necessary to assume such a gap. The Benin craftsmen taught by Igueghae (whether he was a single person or indeed a real person at all could be disputed, but it is more convenient to write as if he were) were quite probably experienced wood- or ivory-carvers, who would bring to the art of bronze-casting their established schemata or concepts of representation which they would employ in making the initial wax models. We should note that wooden commemorative heads are said to have been introduced by Oba Ere, an Ogiso king who reigned before Oronmiyon's time.[147] Even if they were totally inexperienced in artistic work, say blacksmiths, as they might have been, they could not be expected to produce identical copies of the sophisticated

VII Terracotta head excavated at Ita Yemoo in 1958. The upper part of this head was impacted into the potsherd pavement which formed the floor of the shrine, and had to be separated out by Chief Akeredolu in the workshop of the Ife Museum. At the time of discovery this was the only example known of this type of crown, with a square top separating into four panels below, overlying a beaded crown, but a similar head (Plate 65) was excavated in a different part of the site during 1963, and Oliver Myers excavated another rather abraded head of the same type and two fragments of a similar crown at Igbo Obameri in 1964. More red paint than usual survives on this head, which has lost its crest, but retains the forehead ring seen in Plate IX, and in the Jemaa head (Plate 83). The treatment of the hair below the crown resembles the technique shown on the queen of the bronze pair in Plates 10 and III. The lower lip is striated, although the face is smooth. A fragment of this head too, like that in Plate 12, was recovered from the bricks

VIII Terracotta head from a figure, possibly representing an attendant since it is shown without a crown, excavated at Ita Yemoo in 1958. Traces of red paint still adhere to it. The modelling of the eyes on this head is particularly striking, for the sculptor shows an awareness, uncommon at Ife, that the eye is really a globular object in the socket. When excavated, this piece lay face downwards, with its nose about a sixteenth of an inch above the potsherd pavement which formed the floor of the shrine

IX The most elaborate terracotta head so far found in Ife. This lay face upwards beside the one shown in Plate VIII. It wears a very complex beaded crown with five concentric tiers, which are believed to indicate a queen. There is a curtain hanging down the back of the neck, whilst the front edge is engraved to represent feathers. Traces of red and white paint survive on the crown, and there is red paint on the necklaces, lips, ears and forehead. A crest has broken from the crown, leaving traces of a ring of beads on the forehead. This feature should be compared with Plate VII and with the Nok head from Jemaa in Plate 83. (A rear view of the head appears in *Bibl. 50 n, p. 61*, and a profile in *Bibl. 119 d, pl. VII b*)

VII

VIII

IX

X

XI

XII

XIII

CALVIN T. RYAN LIBRARY
KEARNEY STATE COLLEGE
KEARNEY, NEBRASKA

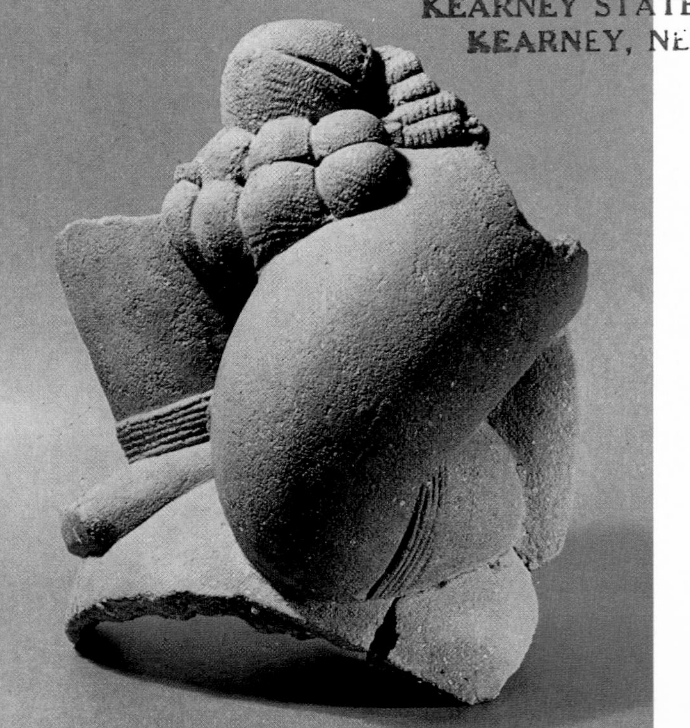

X Terracotta head of an elephant from Agwazo Mine, Odegi, in Nassarawa Division. Despite the fact that the eyes are in typical Nok style, this head is quite naturalistic, yet it appears to have been fixed vertically on a neck so that the rest of the figure could not have resembled an elephant very closely, unless it were represented as sitting on its haunches

XI Terracotta head found in 1951, when a shea-nut tree was uprooted in preparing a hockey pitch for the Benue Middle School at Katsina Ala. This is a fine example of the conception of the form of the human head as a cylinder (or, in other cases, as a cone) which is typical of Nok sculpture. The curious ears, partly hidden by a ridge of hair, are also typical, as are the flaring wings of the nose and the pierced nostrils and eyes. The body illustrated in *Fig. 20* was found at the same time, and other pieces were found three years later, one of which is illustrated in *Bibl. 50 n, p. 9 left*

XII The loins and kneeling legs of a terracotta figure of a woman, found at a depth of about forty feet during tin mining in the Big Paddock at Nok. She wears an elaborate decoration, perhaps of basketwork or of bundles of fibre, hung from beads which apparently passed round her waist. Her voluptuously rounded limbs are in an asymmetrical posture, which is relatively rare in African sculpture, though it is found again in the huntsman figure in the British Museum in which, just as here, the lower leg resting on the ground presented a problem to the sculptor. In this example he joined the ankle to the front of the foot; the sculptor of the huntsman simply omitted the lower leg entirely (*see Bibl. 45, Fig. 173*). The base of the figure should be compared with the Ife heads from Obaluru (Plates 13, 14) and the horse from Zuru (Plate 86)

XIII Terracotta sculpture of a monkey sitting on a base which is shaped like an upturned pot (*cf.* the preceding piece and the chameleon from Ife, Plate 51). Headless when found in 1944 at Nok, a piece of the head turned up eighteen months later. The proportions and pose, with the left hand holding the tail, are very naturalistic naturalism of Ife, which must have been alien to their traditions. They would have copied as best they could, evolving their own schemata, if they had none to begin with.[148] It is possible then that the relatively naturalistic heads, few as they are, need to be spread out over a longer period, beginning in the late fourteenth century.

Fig. 31

Some idea of the stylization of the Benin heads is conveyed by the ears illustrated here. The first of these shows the naturalism of Ife at its most idealized, while Fig. 31b shows a more marked division or *fossa* in the upper part of the inner ridge or *anti-helix*. This feature was chosen for emphasis by some of the Benin sculptors, like the one who made the ear of the Middle Period head illustrated in Fig. 31e. The ear from a head cast in a distinctive style to which William Fagg has given the name Udo, after a group of bronzes in the same style known to have been kept, but not necessarily made, in the village of that name, is shown in Fig. 31h.[149] Although the general form of the human ear is retained, it has developed into a y-shaped ridge, the stem of which sweeps round to form the edge of the ear. This head is probably to be assigned to the Early Middle Period.

Fig. 31 g

The ear of the mask used in the Oduduwa masquerade which was introduced to Benin by Eresoyen in the middle of the eighteenth century (though this mask is probably not so old), has this y-shaped ridge reduced to its simplest form, whilst the edge of the ear is simply a raised kidney-shaped line.[150]

Yet it would be wrong to imagine that the development of Benin art is simply one of gradual development away from a relative naturalism. Figs. 31c and 31d showing ears from an unusual but early head in the Fuller Collection[151] and of an Early Middle Period head in Cambridge, are both further away from anatomical accuracy than the Middle Period ear, Fig. 31e. The ear of the Queen Mother head in the British Museum, Fig. 31f, is perhaps the most stylized of all the Benin ears here illustrated, although it is to be assigned to the sixteenth century.[152]

A COURT ART

Plates 90, 93–95

The examples of Benin art illustrated in this book show unmistakably that it is a court art. The people represented are either the king himself, his attendants, or his servants. Indeed, bronze-castings could only be made with the Oba's express permission, so it is little wonder that the vast bulk of them seem to have come from the Palace itself, which used to cover about half the area of the town, so important was the Oba in the traditional life of Benin.[153] Besides

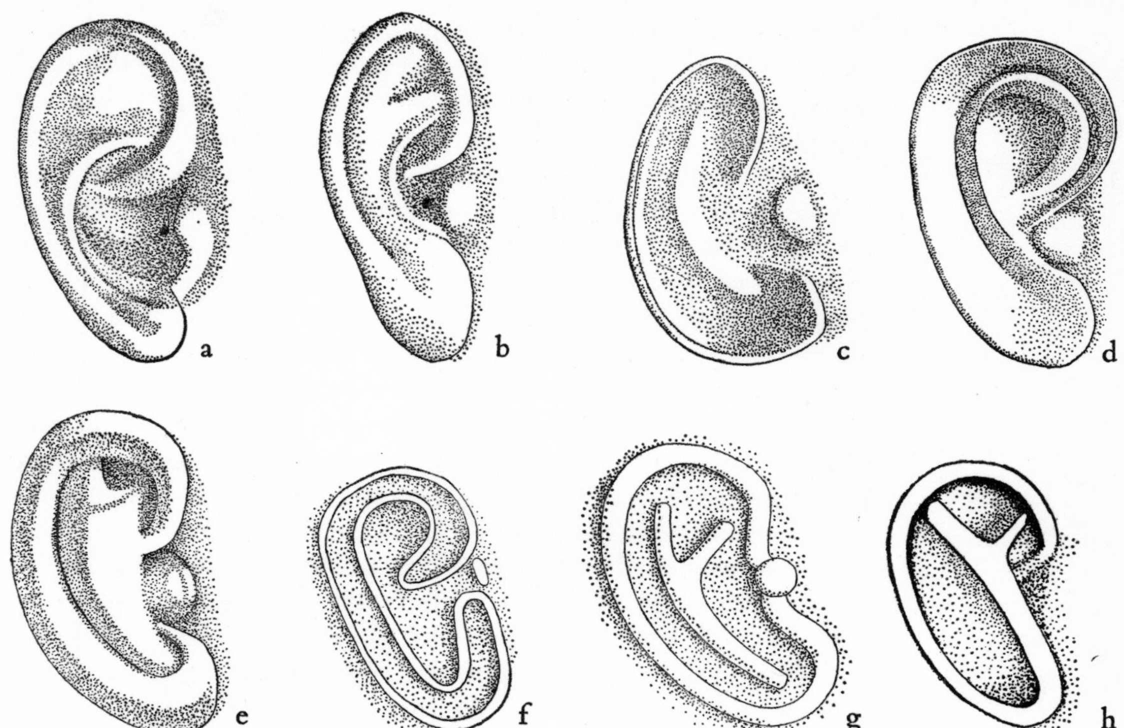

31 Details of ears of various styles: a *from the Ife bronze head shown in Plate II;* b *from Ife bronze head no. 10;* c *from a Benin bronze head in unusual but early style;* d *from a Benin bronze head of the Early Middle Period;* e *from a Benin bronze head of the Middle Period;* f *from the sixteenth century Benin bronze head of a Queen Mother;* g *from a Benin bronze mask for the Oduduwa masquerade;* h *from a bronze head, in the 'Udo' style, probably of the Early Middle Period*

the heads, which symbolized the deceased Oba, without in any way being considered to portray him, a number of other large bronzes were cast such as the cocks which used to stand on the altars commemorating the Queen Mothers. Cocks used, indeed, to be sacrificed on these altars, so evidently these are permanent memorials of such sacrifices like the terracotta ram-heads in Ife. Altar groups of royal figures and attendants were also made, standing on hollow rectangular bases in which the offering was placed. It seems, however, to have been easy to obtain royal permission to have brass masks cast for wear on the hip, whilst wooden heads covered with sheet brass are still to be found in ancestor altars in private houses. Another of the royal pre-emptive rights was over ivory. Many uncarved tusks brought back from Benin bear the Oba's mark of possession, and

Plate 91

there was a group of palace servants whose duty it was to look after the royal ivories, which included not only carved tusks which stood on the sturdier of the bronze commemorative heads[154] but also double gongs,[155] large figures,[156] bracelets,[157] boxes,[158] and some beautiful masks of the early period.[159] These early pieces have probably only survived because of the special care which was taken of them in the Palace. The ivories were carved by the same craftsmen who carved wood into a great variety of boxes[160] as well as into wooden commemorative heads,[161] a type of head said to have been in use before Oronmiyon established the Yoruba dynasty there. They also carved ram-heads for paternal ancestral shrines.[162]

THE RELIABILITY OF BENIN TRADITIONS

Various dates in Benin history have been mentioned in this very sketchy outline of the development of Benin art. These are based primarily on the oral traditions brought together by Chief J. U. Egharevba whose *Short History of Benin* was first published in 1934. More recently Bradbury[163] has attempted to assess the reliability of Egharevba's dates, in so far as he could obtain other sources or external confirmation. He concludes that over the last two hundred and fifty years Egharevba's dates are approximately correct; indeed it is astonishing to find that the date of Akenzua I's death and of Eresoyen's accession, given as 1735 by Egharevba, has received independent confirmation from the recent discovery by Ryder in papers of the Dutch West India Company of the record of the death of an Oba of Benin in 1734 or 1735. A greater margin of error is to be expected as one gets further back, but the persistent tradition that Ozolua was the reigning Oba when the first Portuguese arrived would fix his reign in the last quarter of the fifteenth century. As he is the fifteenth Oba, the dynasty is likely to have begun not later than 1300,[164] but as the principle of succession by primogeniture did not apply in early Benin and may only have become the regular practice in the late seventeenth century under Ewuakpe,[165] the dates of this early period are not reliable at all. The earlier Ogiso dynasty is shadowy in the extreme. Nevetheless, the fundamental sequence seems to be sound enough and it furnishes an adequate basis for a cultural history of Benin, since the names of particular Obas are associated with particular cultural innovations. For example, Akenzua I is remembered as having inaugurated a period of great prosperity which continued during his son Eresoyen's reign, which is remembered also for a resurgence of bronze-casting. It is said that more brass was available at this time (the middle of the eighteenth century) than ever before. Dutch trading records confirm that there was a renewal of intensive trade with Benin at this time, in which objects made of brass are conspicuous. This period corresponds to the Later Middle Period of the bronzes when they became bigger and heavier, leading to the extravagant castings of the Late Period. We are fortunate to have such a consistent history of one forest kingdom of Southern Nigeria, for it does help to throw light on the history of neighbouring areas.

XII

Relatives in Bronze of Ife and Benin

THREE PLAQUES IN BENIN

THERE ARE SEVERAL groups of bronzes whose associations with Ife and Benin are still obscure. Many of them were found in Benin, but they do not form part of the regular Benin sequence and tend in general to be more flamboyant and unrestrained. One small group of pieces may, however, be crucial in tracing the relationships between Ife and Benin and between these and the variety of styles which William Fagg has grouped together temporarily as the Lower Niger Bronze Industry; they also have links with the Tsoede bronzes in three Nupe villages farther north. The group in question consists of a large semicircular pendant plaque resembling Plate 90 in general form, but much larger; some fragments of a second object of similar type; and the central figure from a third.

Plates 97–99

Plate 98

The central figure of the first piece has Ife-type striations on his face, which is more stylized than that of any Ife bronze so far known. Round his neck is a choker similar to those of the Early Period Benin heads, below which is a beaded collar, comparable in a general way to those worn by the Ife figures, whilst a loop of beads which hangs from it is tied in a knot where the Ife figures have their badges. His head-dress is a simplified form of that worn by the small Ife figure found in Benin, whilst the wrappers worn by this figure and by the two figures on the pendant are decorated with the incised diaper of lozenges with dots which also occurs on some of the Lagere terracotta sculptures (see page 66). The hip knots which secure the wrappers of both figures are very simplified and stylized, although a naturalistic ram-head mask hangs at the hip of the central figure. Below his feet are a pair of mudfish, whose stylized treatment is similar to that of a terracotta sculpture from Ife.

Plate 89

Plate 96

Plate 99

The second piece, in a more bizarre style, has kept only one supporting figure with a fantastic head; part of the outer margin with figures perhaps of monkeys eating fruit; and parts of the central figure and the second supporter. Below the feet of the central figure are a pair

32 Detail of an ivory armlet of Yoruba workmanship

of mudfish which are even closer in style to the Ife terracotta than those in the piece just described. The two mudfish here seem to emerge from the feet of the figure, and there can be little doubt that this is the prototype of the figure whose legs are entirely fish who occurs frequently in Benin art of the Middle Period,[166] in other Lower Niger bronzes,[167] and in later bronzes and ivory and wood sculpture from Yorubaland. Later, the fishes may become snakes. It is quite clear that, fragmentary though it is, this piece was originally similar to the one just described. What little remains of the clothing of the central figure is covered with the same diaper pattern and also includes sashes, which are especially common at Ife.

Plate 96

Figs. 32–34

The third piece is the central figure from another similar plaque. In general, it resembles the main figure on the first piece quite closely; but the choker is wider and shallower, and the collar below it has become a single row of large beads. The central loop of beads with the knot has disappeared. The ram-head mask is more stylized, as are the feet. There are no signs of pendants from the head-dress. The head itself is now missing, but Mrs Meyerowitz's photograph[168]

Plate 97

33 Detail of an openwork bronze armlet, formerly part of the regalia of the King of Wukari, but probably of Yoruba manufacture

shows a large part of the face from which one can see that it was not striated nor did it resemble at all closely either the Ife or the Benin style. Indeed, its closest affinities seem to be with some of the Tsoede figures to be described next, such as the small figure with a similar staff at Tada whose mouth, navel and nipples are similar, whilst his eyes are more rounded. The head of the female figure from Jebba is also similar. These three pieces seem, therefore, to hark back to Ife and at the same time to look forward to the established Benin style, whilst also sharing characteristics of the Tsoede figures and of the Lower Niger bronze industries. Egharevba's suggestion, when he was curator of the Benin Museum, that these were pieces brought from Ife by Igueghae as exemplars, may not be far wrong.[169]

Plate 100

THE TSOEDE BRONZES: TADA

It is interesting that they should look also towards the Tsoede bronzes, of which there are ten known, all kept in Nupe villages on the Niger, whither they are said to have been brought from Idah, the Igala capital, by the founder-hero Tsoede in the sixteenth century.[170] He is said also to have brought brass-smiths with him to teach the craft of *cire perdue* casting which the Nupe still practise on a small scale, though their beaten and chased brasswares are better known. A series of independent genealogies collected by Nadel all agreed in fixing Tsoede's birth in the early fifteenth century, and the links between the bronze figures associated with his name and the three plaques described and of these with Ife suggest that they do, indeed, belong to the period just after Oguola sent to Ife for a bronze-caster to teach his people. Moreover, the Igala are a Yoruba-speaking

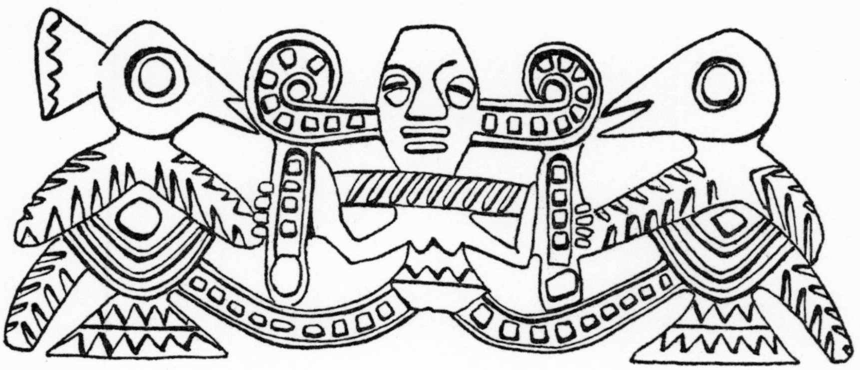

34 Detail of an ivory armlet excavated by Frobenius in Modakeke

people who have also had contact, often of a warlike nature, with Benin, so these bronzes could have been made at Idah, where the seated bronze figure in Ife style might conceivably have served as a model. Three of these Tsoede figures stand on square bases like many of the Ife terracotta figures, whilst the feet of one are similar to those of the dwarfs from Benin,[171] and another holds a disc-topped staff like the figures in the pendant plaques.

Plate 8

Plates 97, 98

Seven of the figures are kept at Tada, two at Jebba, and the tenth has lately come to light at Giragi, an island forty miles downstream from Tada. The Ife bronze from Tada has already been described (p. 51); of the remainder, the largest, 3 feet 9 inches in height, is a male figure called Gara, a very elaborate casting indeed.[172] It stands on a square base (now damaged) and wears a double cloth; the outer one being a sleeved tunic richly embroidered with knotted ribbons and birds. Over this is thrown a garment covered with cowrie shells; the anklets also are of cowries. His arms are very thin and short and resemble those of the Jebba woman. On his chest hangs a pectoral, with its straight edge at the bottom.[173]. It carries a ram's head and three birds, which can all be paralleled in a general way from Benin and in Yoruba pieces. Most interesting, however, is the pair of discs worn on the front and back of the head. These have relief castings of a horned human face with snakes or fishes issuing from the nostrils. This motif we have seen in a fragmentary terracotta at Ife, which may also have been horned. The Tada face, however, has Bini tribal marks over the eyes.

Plate 8

Plate 100

Fig. 36

Fig. 35

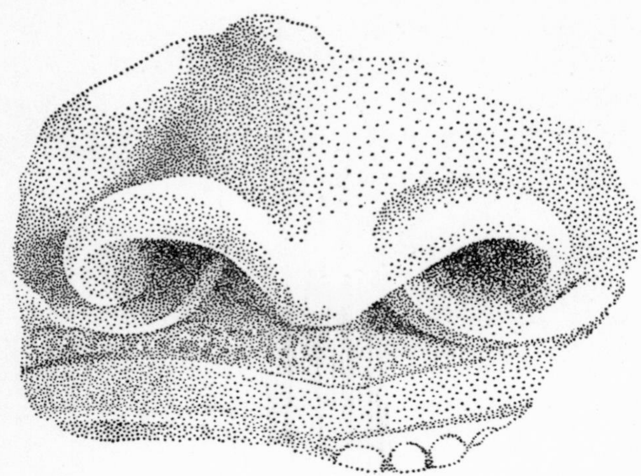

35 Terracotta fragment of a large grotesque head from the shrine of Kubolaje, Ife, with snakes (or fishes) issuing from the nostrils

The smallest figure at Tada, called Sarauniya,[174] is only 16 inches high. Like the previous piece, it stands on a rectangular base and is in the same style, to judge from the eyes and mouth, but is different in every other particular, for he wears only a simple hat with decoration, partly cast and partly incised, spiralling round it in a way
Plate 25 reminiscent of an Ife head in terracotta; a single string of beads round his neck, and a plain wrapper round his loins. In his right
Plates 97–99 hand he holds a disc-headed staff like the figures on the pendant plaques from Benin.

The fourth figure is 22 inches high and is rather different in style from the rest of the group, for it has large feet and very bulging
Cf. Plate 101 eyes and its hands are held above each other in an Ogboni gesture.
Plate 100 Its ears, however, resemble the last piece, the Jebba woman, and the Giragi figure, whilst its wrapper, although tied with tapes apparently sewn on the corners of the cloth, has a raised lozenge diaper reminis-
Plate 8 cent of the Ife piece in the same shrine. Most of the Tsoede bronzes show burnt-in repairs, but an unusually large proportion of this figure has had to be made good in this way. The writer was told that this figure, like the seated one, was called Tsoede.[175] The three remaining pieces at Tada are quite unparalleled. Two are ostriches, 4 feet 4 inches and 3 feet 4 inches in height. Both have lost their feet, but must have had flat bases originally to make them stand. The remaining piece represents an elephant and is 2 feet in height.

Its feet, too, are damaged, but one has retained part of a square base. The tip of the trunk is deeply split and is clearly prehensile.

JEBBA
Plate 100

Of the two pieces kept at Jebba, one is illustrated. It is 3 feet 9½ inches high and is in the same style as the tallest and the smallest of the Tada figures. Her pendulous breasts are rendered with unusual naturalism for an African sculpture, for these organs are normally treated in a stylized, if not in an idealized and symbolic, way. The male figure was attacked about 1940 by a religious fanatic, who wanted to have it melted down to make pennies to pay for the faithful to make the pilgrimage to Mecca. It has recently been restored at the British Museum.[176] It is just over three feet high and, like its partner, stands on a rectangular base, but has the left foot forward and the right one turned outward in an unusually informal pose. He wears anklets made of cowrie shells and has a heavy ring collar of them as well, whilst his outer garment consists entirely of pendant sashes. His arms, now incomplete, were like the female's, short and thin, though partly hidden by the sleeves of his tunic. His face is in the same style as hers, though it is very deeply striated in an unusual pattern: lines radiate from the corners of the mouth and are cut across by parallel diagonal lines crossing the cheeks from the bridge of the nose, whilst the forehead is striated vertically.[177] He has a quiver on his back and wears an elaborate helmet covered with wire attachments (which are probably modern replacements of decorations which may originally have been quite different). Like that of the standing figure at Tada, the helmet has a disc on the front, on which the motif is a curious bird with its wings forming loops; a motif repeated many times on the tunic of the Tada figure, and found once at Benin on an ivory gong, thought to be of the sixteenth century.[178]

GIRAGI

The remaining piece, from Giragi, was found on the eve of Nigeria's independence in 1960, and was thus able to be shown to the world as part of the Independence Exhibition. It is 18½ inches high and represents a man with a flat-topped hat, beating a small cylindrical drum hung round his neck. He wears a featureless wrapper and has feet similar to the one figure from Tada which has no base; and his face looks like an unworn version of that on this same figure. The ears are of the usual type in this group, and the arms are short and thin. Nevertheless, this piece seems to be inferior to the rest of the examples known.[179]

36, 37 The same motif shown in Fig. 35 in terracotta at Ife is found again in bronze in the detail of the head-dress of a standing figure from Tada, left, *and the mask in Benin,* right.

These Tsoede figures include the largest bronzes ever found anywhere in Africa: no less than five of them are over three feet in height. The technical difficulties in making such large castings by traditional African techniques are enormous, so it is not surprising to find that their ambition outstripped their skill, with the result that some of them needed extensive burnt-in repairs. Even the seated Plate 8 figure which is, of course, an Ife piece, had to be made good in this way, though the process was better handled in this example.

These large bronze-castings, so many of them on bases, resemble in general form the terracotta sculptures from Ife and serve to give us a general impression of what these must have looked like when they were complete.

In describing these pieces, a number of parallels have been pointed out from both Ife and Benin, but this does not exhaust the possible ramifications, for the motif with fishes or snakes emerging from the *Fig. 37* nostrils is found again in various places. One of the two small masks in the Benin Museum, which seem to be copies one of the other, has Benin marks on the forehead (*cf.* Fig. 36), whilst the eyes are shaped like those of the majority of the Tsoede bronzes. The teeth and beard resemble the Tada motif very much, yet the animals being swallowed by the snakes resemble figures on a different group of bronzes, best exemplified in a bell from the shrine of Enowe in Benin,[180] which has a face closely similar to Fig. 37, but with a frog in the mouth and horns on the head. On top of the head is, surprisingly, a human foot, which explains the indeterminate projection on Fig. 37. The animals in the snakes' mouths resemble the apes on the margin of the fragmentary pendant plaque, but they are closer to those on the bowl brought back from Benin in 1897 and now in the British Museum, which Fagg has assigned to his 'Huntsman Style'.[181] These figures, in turn, are in a posture similar to that of a quartz-carving from Ife.

Plate 99

Plate 63

The interconnections then are numberless. There are not simply one or two threads running through the history of bronze-casting in the Niger Valley which need only to be unravelled. We have rather a piece of woven cloth with many threads in both the warp and the weft which will take a long time to sort out.[182]

XIII

Neighbours in Bronze and Stone

IGBO UKWU

In many parts of Nigeria the supply of water in the dry season is a matter of great concern. In the Eastern Region it is a common practice to excavate cisterns in which water can be collected during the rains for use during the dry season. In 1939, Isaiah Anozie was digging such a cistern in his compound at Igbo Ukwu near Awka when he struck a number of bronze objects of remarkable beauty and interest.[183] It was not possible to undertake excavations on this site until the end of 1959, when Thurstan Shaw undertook the first of two digging seasons there. He recovered the remainder of the group of bronze objects which were still undisturbed, and he was able to demonstrate that they had originally lain in a storehouse. Near by, he undertook a further excavation where other bronzes had been found later but had been left in the ground. Here he uncovered the grave of a ritual chief of considerable importance, richly accompanied with elaborate bronze ceremonial objects.[184]

All the bronzes from Igbo Ukwu are in a very distinctive style of casting. They represent a tradition distinct from that of Ife and Benin, yet they include hip ornaments which are hung with crotals and correspond, functionally at least, to those of Benin, whilst the human faces have raised lines upon them in patterns which closely resemble those of the stone-carvings of Esie and are occasionally paralleled, rather less precisely, at Ife. Most of the objects are of unique form in Nigerian sculpture. Many of them are bowls in the form of a calabash, whilst a number of handles were found still attached to fragments of real calabashes. Particularly striking is a vase mounted on a pierced stand and surrounded by an open knotwork design of ropes, whilst there are also a number of vessels in the shape of snail-shells and several elaborate objects which appear to be the heads and lower ends of staffs. There are also sword-hilts and scabbards. The ornamentation on these objects is often applied in very fine threads of material in the modelling stage, in a way which

Plates 102, 103, 105

Plate 105

is found nowadays in the Obo style of bronze-casting of Northern Ekiti, which in the preliminary stages of modelling uses not wax but a latex specially prepared from a cactus. It is possible that a similar material was used in preparing these bronzes at Igbo Ukwu.[185]

These bronzes appear to be associated with a treasure house and a grave, both of an Eze Nri, a divine king. Kingly offices are rarely found among the Ibo, indeed they are only found among them where there has been cultural influence from another people, *e.g.*, at Onitsha where much of the chieftaincy structure derives from Benin; and here at Nri, of which Igbo Ukwu was formerly a part, where the kingship seems to be derived from Idah. This is the same place from which Tsoede set out with his bronzes when he was founding the Nupe kingdom farther up the Niger. Such similarities as the Tsoede figures have to Ife and Benin have been discussed above, yet they seem to have even less in common with the Igbo Ukwu bronzes despite this tradition that the Nri kingship, with which the bronzes seem to be associated, derives from Idah. The facial striations of the Jebba bowman[186] seem to be the only point of similarity, and these Plate 103
are no closer to each other than either is to the usual Ife pattern, although one Ife terracotta affords a general parallel to both. How- Plate 102
ever, radiocarbon dates from both of Shaw's excavations have just been announced. They are AD 840±145 (I–1784) and AD 850±120 (I—2008): much earlier that anyone had dared to surmise. It appears therefore that there was a flourishing of culture already in the ninth century in Ibo-land which probably had nothing whatever to do with Idah. Although stylistically distinct from Ife, this early date for the casting of copper and bronze (*cf. Bibl.* 101 e) helps to make more plausible the suggestion that the Classical Period of Ife art may have been earlier than the thirteenth to fourteenth centuries to which it has usually been assigned (p. 149).

IDAH

Nevertheless, Idah does seem to have played a very important role in the history of the Lower Niger, despite the obscurity of its influence on the art, for it had connections with Benin as well as with Nupe, with the Northern Ibo and the Jukun.[187] It may be that Idah diffused works of art made in other centres, for no evidence of ancient or recent bronze-working has been adduced from the Igala area.[188] Indeed, the principal emblem of the royal regalia is a well-polished brass mask made in Benin probably in the early sixteenth century, which the Atta wears hanging round his neck. It is known as *Ejube 'auilo* (the eye which brings fear to other eyes) and was intended to be worn over the face, for slits are provided below the eyes.[189] Shaw records that there is a similar Benin bronze mask in the regalia of the present Eze Nri at Oreri.[190] Two others are in the possession of the Olugbo of Ugbo.[191] These are all of the early period and may reflect the former extent of Benin conquest.

THE JUKUN

Similarly, the Jukun were an influential people in Nigerian history, but whether their importance has been exaggerated simply by the fact that Meek's study of them was one of the first major accounts of a Nigerian people to appear (in 1931) is not clear. This book seems to have influenced many other writers who have been inclined to follow his example (and that of Palmer) in bringing in customs, institutions and techniques on a wholesale scale down the Benue Valley as a route of migration of Hamitic peoples from Upper Egypt. The uncritical acceptance of this thesis has marred a lot of later work. It is time for another study of the Jukun, for Meek's data, invaluable though it is, was collected with a marked bias towards the Egyptian concept of the divine king. It would be interesting to know more of their brass-casting traditions about which very little is known. They are said to employ the pagan Hausa Aba Kwariga, who live south of Wukari, to do their brass-casting, but very few of their bronze objects have reached museums. An openwork bracelet from the royal insignia is now in the Lagos Museum, but this seems most likely to be a Yoruba piece, probably obtained by trade.

Fig. 33

THE TIV

The near-by Tiv, however, still have a lively bronze-casting tradition of their own, which has nothing at all to do with divine kingship or royal patronage, for their social system acknowledges no supreme ruler at all.[192] Tiv bronzes are only a few inches high, but very skilfully produced, using a latex preparation, not wax, which thus permits rather different initial constructions, for the latex can be formed into loops which do not collapse during the investment with clay, whereas similar forms in wax need to be supported in some way. Their finest castings are snuff-takers: finger-rings with a slightly concave disc to hold the snuff to the nostril, the support between the two parts often taking the form of elaborate human or animal groups;[193] and voice disguisers (*mboivungu*), which are used by members of secret societies when imitating the voices of spirits.[194]

In addition to casting bronze, the Tiv also still sculpt in pottery to produce terracotta heads which are the homes of spirits. They might be a vestige of the continuing Nok tradition of sculpture in terracotta. Unlike the Yoruba, Bini, Igala and Ibo, who all speak Kwa languages, but like the Jukun, the Tiv speak a Bantu language; and Greenberg considers that it was in the Benue Valley that the Bantu languages arose, within part of the area of the Nok culture, and probably whilst that culture was flourishing.[195] The material evidence that might support (or refute) this hypothesis has not yet been examined from this point of view. Plate 87

Although this book is principally concerned with one central sculptural tradition deriving from that of the Nok culture, reaching a seminal peak in the Classical Period of Ife, then proliferating in a variety of sculptural traditions in bronze, terracotta and wood, it is important to realize that there are these other traditions which appear to be quite separate from it. Nevertheless, it is surprising how frequently concepts found in the sculpture of Nok seem to appear again much later. An outstanding example of this is the very large group of stone sculptures at Esie, on the northern edge of Yorubaland.

ESIE

Practically nothing is known about their origin. Mr Ramshaw, a schools inspector, was, in 1933, one of the first Europeans to hear about this large group of stone figures in a grove of *peregun* trees[196] in a patch of woodland still surviving in the savannah. Yet Frobenius had obtained the heads of three of these figures in 1912, which he published as having been excavated at Offa.[197] Ceremonies are conducted annually in the grove at Esie,[198] yet the local people, who are Yoruba, seem to have no idea when or by whom these figures were made. They declare that the face-marks shown on many of them are Nupe, but unfortunately we know nothing of Nupe art before their conversion to Islam. Certainly these hundreds of stone sculptures, and there are some fragments of terracotta too, show echoes of Nok and of Ife. Very clearly many different sculptors are represented with varying styles.

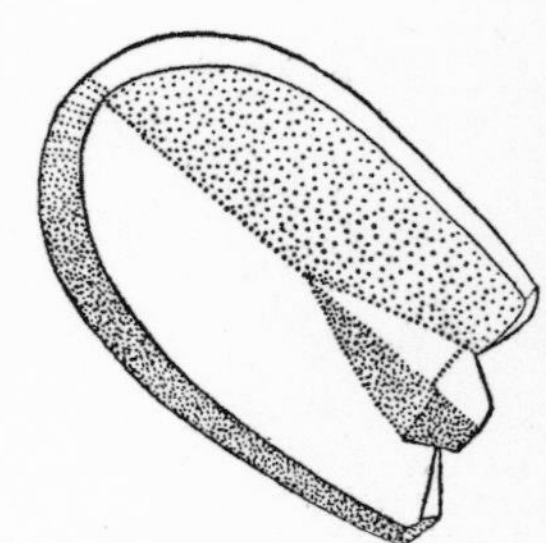

38 Ear of a wooden figure carved by Lamidi Fakeye. Note the similarity to that of the figure in Plate 109

One group of figures has a structure of the head and neck which is very similar to that of many of the Nok sculptures, whilst the form of the ear echoes some of the Nok and modern Yoruba pieces. Some of the figures sit on round stools which resemble those of Ife, but lack the characteristic loop. The facial marks of some heads

Fig. 21

Figs. 23, 38
Fig. 39
Plates 103, 105

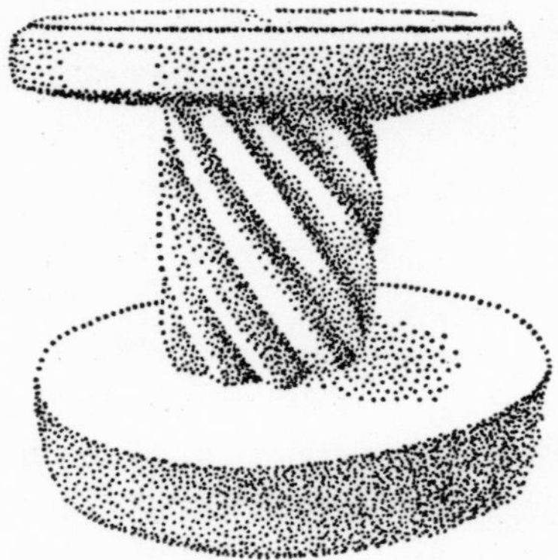

39 Detail of a stone figure at Esie, representing a common type of wooden stool

resemble those of Igbo bronzes, whilst others have only three horizontal strokes between the ear and the eye.[199] There is an interest shown in bead decorations, but these are very simple compared with the elaboration of the hair-styles, which are one of the most fascinating aspects of these figures; the soft stone has allowed the sculptor complete freedom to represent their complications to a degree unmatched elsewhere. Another remarkable feature is the way in which sculpture in the round is combined with incision, not merely of surface decoration, but of such essentials as the feet of seated figures, which are often incised on the base of the stool. As at Nok, the feet, whether incised or sculpted, are square cut. Two of the carvings represent calabashes of palm wine, a motif already noted at Ife. One head indeed has been considered by William Fagg to show some
Plate 74 affinity with that of the Idena figure at Ife.[200]

There are so many sculptures at Esie (estimates range between 800 and 2,000) that an analysis by statistical techniques might usefully be attempted. Such a study would help to isolate the work of individual carvers, and might provide a better basis for understanding the relative significance of the various influences they reflect.

It has been suggested that these figures were brought to Esie from elsewhere (principally because their arrangement in the grove seemed to be completely unsystematic) by refugees, perhaps from Old Oyo. Whatever their origin, they do seem to have been traded fairly widely, for a number of small groups of figures in the same style have been found at Ofaro, Effon Alaye and Ijara, and recently in Ife itself.[201]

XIV

Recent Yoruba Sculpture

ILESHA

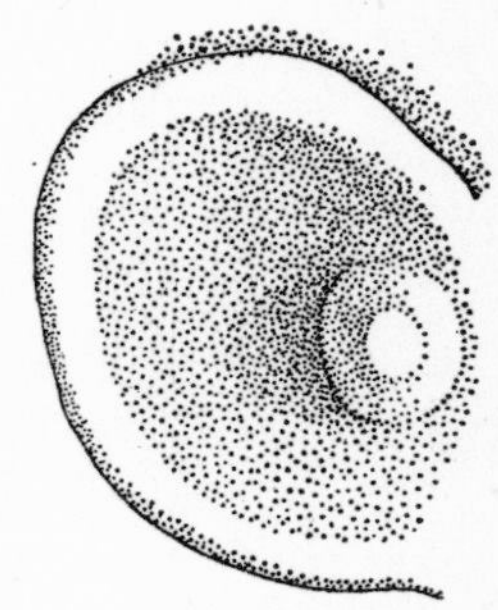

40 Typical ear from the series of baked mud sculptures of nineteenth century date excavated at Ilesha

ONE OF THE LINKS between ancient Ife and modern Yoruba sculpture has been found. Within the area of the palace at Ilesha, twenty miles to the north-east of Ife, a group of sculptures came to light in 1959 when workmen were levelling ground to build a telephone exchange. An excavation revealed that they had lain in a shallow pit close to deeper pits which might have been associated with their manufacture. These deep pits had in turn been cut through by the grave of a king of Ilesha, who must have been either Atakunmosa or his son Gbegbaje, the only two kings who were buried inside the palace. Their reigns covered the second half of the nineteenth century, so the sculptures must have been earlier than this, but probably not much earlier, for pottery found with them appears to be of the middle of the nineteenth century, or possibly even a little earlier.

These sculptures were modelled from solid blocks of clay, very lightly fired, and consequently extremely fragile. Most of them had been very badly damaged, but several were luckily almost intact. Only a few are complete figures; most represent only heads, usually on basin-shaped bases, whilst there were many bases which were evidently complete in themselves. The most striking features of the style are the protruding globular eye, divided above the centre by an eyelid, with a strip of clay round the lower circumference to represent the lower lid, the flat ear with a knob for the *tragus*, and the protruding flat parallel lips, whilst complete figures are always shown kneeling with the hands on the knees. Recent ivory-carvings from Ilesha portray eyes in the same way, while the lips can be paralleled all over Yorubaland. A similar posture is found in representations in mud of Eshu, the Yoruba trickster-god, such as those set like sentries beside doorways in the palace at Owo, eighty miles to the south-east of Ilesha. It may be that these Ilesha pieces had a similar protective purpose, for they all contain magical substances,

Plate 107

Fig. 40

Plates 106, 109, 110; *Fig. 3*

e.g., an animal tooth, bone or vegetable matter, and all have a groove on some part which appears to serve no functional end.

Plate 108

There are in the shrine for Oduduwa at Ife two mud sculptures in a rather similar style. They may be of similar age or perhaps more recent, but they seem to be different in function, since they represent either Oduduwa and his wife Ogido or else servants of these gods.

MODERN YORUBA SCULPTURE

Plate 101

Plates 55, 60, 62

The style of these nineteenth-century sculptures, like that of the earlier bronze figure from Apomu, shows clear affinities with modern Yoruba sculpture. Some of these characteristics have already been observed among those Ife terracotta sculptures which we have considered to be post-Classical. Yoruba sculpture can indeed be characterized as showing a gradually devolving naturalism, as if the social pressures which produced the naturalism of Classical Ife have gradually weakened. Yet the Yoruba area of ancient linguistic and allegedly political unity has retained a hold on its ancient central tradition. Their social system has no doubt contributed to this. The Yoruba live in very large family compounds, grouped together in towns ruled by kings who still, in most parts, claim to get their authority from Ife. In contrast to this, the Ibo live in very small family groups in hamlets scattered fairly evenly across the countryside.[202] The village used to be the limit of their social unit. In consequence, Ibo sculpture shows far greater variation in its concepts, to such an extent that unless one has seen an example of a particular style of sculpture before, one might well find it difficult to identify as Ibo at all.[203] Such a difficulty is almost inconceivable in the case of Yoruba sculpture, which is only rarely abstract and usually quite clearly recognizable as Yoruba, from whatever part of Yorubaland

Plates 106, 109, 110

it may come. The styles of the two female figures, one from Ilesha, the other from Ilaro, separated by about a hundred and twenty miles in space and perhaps a century in time, are clearly similar.

Fig. 3

Even in objects serving quite different purposes, like the *gelede* society mask from Otta, the mouth, nose and eyes are similar.[204]

EXTERNAL INFLUENCES

This does not mean, of course, that Yoruba art in the years since the Classical Period of Ife sculpture has not been subject to influences from outside. Most conspicuously there has been mutual contact between Benin and Owo, which contributed to the importance of Owo as a centre of bronze-casting and of ivory- and wood-carving. Indeed, Owo sculptures were found in Benin, whilst at one time both towns used very similar carved wooden ram-heads on their ancestor shrines, a practice which has died out in Benin, but which continues in Owo, where there are also similar heads with human faces.[205] In consequence, Owo has developed a style of sculpture, particularly in ivory, which is intermediate between the Yoruba and the Benin styles.[206]

In northern Yorubaland the influence of Islam has discouraged humanistic sculpture, so that the Yoruba of Ilorin city carve only geometric designs like those on the drum-posts outside the Emir's Palace,[207] although in the adjacent part of Ilorin province, which is northern Ekiti, the humanistic tradition of Yoruba sculpture is still strong, the carver taking great delight in representing scenes of everyday life.[208]

There are many important centres of Yoruba sculpture in bronze and in wood, each with its own characteristic local style. It would, however, be a mistake to imagine that working within an established traditional style inhibits invention or masks individuality. Whilst it is true that the many thousands of Yoruba sculptures in museums throughout the world can in many cases be attributed only to the town or district in which they originated, we can often identify the style of individual carvers, many of whose names we know. The importance of the artist as an individual was first recognized by Kenneth Murray, whilst Father Carroll has worked closely with northern Ekiti carvers and has described their methods and their individual characteristics.[209] There are standardized ways of representing the component parts of a figure or design, which the carver repeats in an increasingly personal way as time goes by, whilst he is always free to employ them in any combination he may choose. This does not preclude the observation of nature, nor the introduction of new subjects: *gelede* masks in south-western Yorubaland nowadays often represent sewing-machines and aeroplanes, whilst bicycles have become a regular feature of northern Ekiti door panels.

Yet the amount of external influence has varied in different parts. Northern Ekiti is still an area of villages and small towns with few Europeans. Here life still goes on in many ways much as it must have done before the Fulani wars of the nineteenth century. Traditional forms of sculpture still continue, though, as the traditional religion wanes and as modern building methods spread, the demand for masks, drums, doors and house-posts declines. Carvers are forced, therefore, to look increasingly to the European market, for which they are producing a greater variety of carvings than any master-carver would have been expected to produce only two generations ago. Fourteen house-posts carved by Areogun of Osi show only three different subjects, though his doors show more variety. The limitation of the repertoire brought increasing skill in treating the same subject repeatedly, whereas carvers nowadays are being pressed to change their subjects frequently as the customer demands increasing novelty. Yoruba sculptors are thus adapting themselves to the modern world before their traditional methods have been adequately studied. There is an urgent need for field-workers to study the relatively few carvers still practising their art in the traditional way, not only in the area of Africa we have been discussing, but all over the world. There is a great deal of inadequately documented art in museums which needs to be studied alongside intensive field-work. If this can be done urgently we may be able to name the carvers of masterpieces which are at present anonymous, for the study of the art of tribally organized societies is not different in kind from the study of the art of other societies. The same principles of connoisseurship apply, and the same understanding is required of both the society and the period which produced each successive art-form.

XV

Elements of Continuity in West African Sculpture

IN THE COURSE of this book, references have been made to the repeated occurrence of similar structural forms, subjects or details of treatment at different times in the history of West African sculpture. Many of them already occur in the Nok culture, which demonstrates that the essential canons of African sculpture were already established more than two thousand years ago. Indeed an examination of predynastic Egyptian sculptures suggests that they were already established five thousand years ago. We may some day find sculptures to fill in the details of this remote past, but for the present we must be grateful to have such a wide range of terracotta sculptures from the Nok culture which show that many features of more recent art have a long history behind them.

The typical Nok eyes are very similar to those of Yoruba wood sculpture and to many of the Benin bronzes; the most vigorously treated type of nose at Nok, with widely flaring wings appears again in some Ife heads, and at Tada, as the basic form of nose at Benin and in Yoruba sculpture. Some of the Nok heads have forehead-rings, a feature repeated at Ife; rarely, the heads in both these cultures have the hair treated as a raised ring with a hole in the centre at Nok,[210] or an iron nail at Ife. The treatment of the lower leg of the kneeling figure from Nok is in the same spirit as the Ilesha pieces in which the leg is attached to the middle of the foot, whilst the left leg of the male of the Ita Yemoo pair shows a comparable approach in making anatomical structure subservient to sculptural form. The globular base which supports the Nok piece is found again at Ife and at Zuru. Nok figures wear heavy rolled, beaded collars similar to those worn by some early Benin heads and the Jebba bowman, whilst the Ife figures wear a great variety of heavy collars.

Plates 80–83
Fig. 19
Plates 22, 23; *Figs. 35, 36*
Plates 83, VII, IX
Plates 30, XII
Plate 107
Plates 10, III
Plates 13, 86, XII
Plates 82, 85
Plates 6, 7, 9, 10

A cylindrical or conical head mounted on a cylindrical neck is very characteristic of the Nok style and reappears at Esie and, farther afield, in the *nomoli* figures found in Sierra Leone and in the

Plate XI; *Figs. 21, 22*

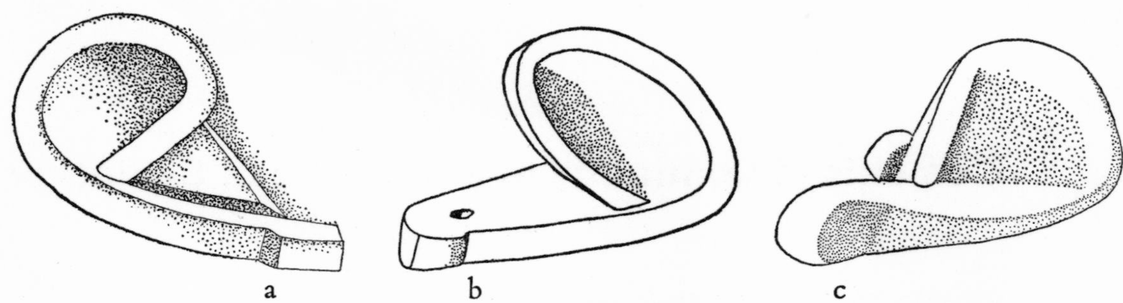

41 Details of ears from gelede *masks:* a *from western Yorubaland;* b *from an unidentified town to the north-west of Otta destroyed by Governor Glover between 1864 and 1870;* c *from the mask in Fig. 3*

Afro-Portuguese ivories, which were the first and best form of 'tourist' art to be produced in Africa.[211] (The last two also show the widely flared nose.) Possible echoes of this structural form can also be found in sculptures of the Baga of Guinée,[212] the Senufo of the Ivory Coast,[213] and even as far away as the Babembe on the Lower Congo,[214] and the Bajokwe of Angola.[215] Unfortunately we cannot be sure that these are not rediscoveries of the same structural principles, but the latter two examples, among Bantu-speaking peoples, should be viewed in the light of Greenberg's suggestion that the Bantu languages originated in the Benue Valley about the time of the Nok culture.

The Ife sculptures share many general characteristics with those of Nok, whilst shifting the major emphasis on to naturalistic representation, probably reflecting a modification of religious ideas. The
Fig. 31 naturalistic ears of Ife provide a basis for the freely stylized inter-
Plates 60, 62; *Fig. 12* pretations of Benin, whilst the stylized ears of post-Classical Ife heads
Fig. 41 afford a start for the development of some modern Yoruba ears. At
Ife we meet ram-heads in terracotta, associated with the sacrifice of this animal; both the sacrifice and its representation in bronze and wood are found elsewhere in Yorubaland, as well as in the Lower
Fig. 35 Niger bronzes. Ife also introduces us to the figure with snakes emerging from his nostrils which occurs often in Benin, sometimes
Fig. 36 on pieces not made there[216] but also on typical Benin pieces.[217] We
Fig. 37 see it also farther up the Niger at Tada. On the stone-carvings of Ife we meet the motif of a snake swallowing a frog or lizard;[218] this, too, is found at Benin, sometimes combined with the preceding figure.[219]

86 Terracotta sculpture from a Dakakari man's grave at Zuru, probably representing a horse, indicating that a chief was buried below. Zuru is close to the known area of the Nok culture (*Fig. 1*) so it is interesting to find terracotta sculpture on the same scale produced there until the present century. (*See also Bibl. 52 a, b; 61; 62 and 107*)

87, 88 Two terracotta heads, *right*, apparently from a figure found near Wukari, and *left*, a Tiv head, *atsuku*, in which a spirit may dwell. The hair is dressed into three ridges

89 Small bronze figure, found in Benin, but probably made in Ife to represent an Oni. This piece was found during alterations to the Palace in Benin, and is claimed by Chief Egharevba, the historian of Benin, to be a sample of the work of Igueghae, the bronze-caster sent from Ife to teach the art in Benin probably in the late fourteenth century. Most of the details of dress and ornament can be paralleled in Ife, though the crossed baldricks of beads which this figure wears are rare in Ife, but common in later Benin works. This may well be a fashion introduced from Ife which developed more feely in Benin. Two diagonal strokes over the nose are recent scratches and appear on many of the most unusual pieces in the collection of the Benin Museum, as if many years ago someone had carefully marked all the pieces which were not of Bini workmanship. The ridge running from nose to ear appears to represent, as Dr Justine Cordwell has suggested, the upper edge of a ceremonial metal filter covering the nostrils, such as she has photographed a Dahomean *oba* wearing. The casting is barely one millimetre thick in places. The proportions of the head are slightly smaller than on the other Ife bronze figures

90 A bronze pendant made in Benin but found in Ife about 1940 or 1941, when digging mud for bricks for the house which is now No. 3, Iyekere Street. It was found at a depth of about four feet in a relatively recent rubbish pit which was excavated in 1961. It shows the Oba of Benin flanked by attendants, who support his arms to ensure that he will not fall, for since he is a divine king his well-being and that of the state are intimately associated. Below his feet is a human head with mudfish springing from the nostrils, a motif seen also in *Figs. 34–36*. Beneath the attendants' feet are frogs; there are mudfish beside them; and another pair of mudfish spring from the Oba's waist. There are loops for suspension behind the attendants' heads. Crotals were originally attached to the loops round the edge

91 Bronze mask from Benin, probably o nineteenth century date

92 Terracotta head found in 1962 eroding from the ground in Ogbon Oya quarter, Ife. The similarity of this piece to the bronze mask illustrated *above*, despite the difference of the medium, is striking. It also resembles the heads of a number of free standing figures of the middle period of Benin art, while the line down the centre of the forehead and nose can be paralleled in the ivory head in the Egerton Collection (*Bibl. 50 j, Fig. 53*), the wooden head in the Field Museum, Chicago (*Bibl. 36, pl. 39*), and the bronze mask in the Fuller Collection (*ibid. pl. 22*). There can be little doubt, therefore, that this piece is of Bini workmanship, and as the texture and colour of the clay do not match any of the very large number of Ife terracottas, it is quite possible that it was actually made in Benin

93 Bronze figure of the middle period of Benin art. João Afonso d'Aveiro, the first Portuguese visitor to Benin around 1485, reported that when the King of Benin succeeded to the throne he sent a messenger, apparently to the Oni of Ife, to ask for confirmation in his office. As signs of his approval the Oni sent a staff, a hat and a pectoral cross all made of brass (*Bibl. 38, I, iii, cap. iv*). This figure appears to be wearing these emblems, so perhaps he is the newly confirmed king. However, the king is nowhere certainly represented as wearing a cross, although crosses are shown sometimes as part of the decoration on his clothing (*e.g. Bibl. 50, i, Fig. 24; Bibl. 113, pl. 81*). D'Aveiro goes on to say that as a reward for the labours of the journey to and from Ife, the messenger receives a small cross similar to that which he carries to the king, and wears this round his neck to indicate that he is in future a privileged person (*Bibl. 38*). Now there are altar groups (*e.g., Bibl. 113, pls. 84, 85*) in which an attendant figure is shown with a short hammer-like staff in his left hand (like this figure), a long staff in his right (apparently lost from this figure), a brimmed hat on his head, a cross round his neck and 'cat's whisker' tribal marks. It would appear then that this figure represents a messenger who has been to Ife, although his tribal mark is a puzzle for it is rarely found in Benin art except on figures of this type. It occurs, of course, on Ife terracottas where it may indicate an ancient Ife marking (Plates 14, 31, 32). Perhaps Ife men were used as messengers between the two cities. The Beni-Nupe, who wear the mark nowadays, took it from the Yoruba (*Bibl. 89, p. 22*), but it occurs also among the Igala, the Jukun, and even the Senufo of the Ivory Coast. Tribal marks then cannot be regarded as reliable evidence

94 Bronze head of the early period of Benin art, probably of the fifteenth century. The break beneath the chin reveals the thinness of the casting, which failed at the back of the head where a burnt-in repair was needed. So thin a head could not have supported the weight of a tusk as the later heads did. The features are only moderately stylized compared with the later heads. The vertical lines above the nose are of iron as are the pupils of the eyes. The diagonal line across the hair above the ear is due to a crack in the mould which probably developed during drying

95 Bronze head of the end of the middle period of Benin art, probably around the middle of the seventeenth century. In comparison with the previous specimen the change in the profile of the face is noticeable in its marked prognathism; the beaded collar has been increased in size and hides the chin, and a beaded crown is now worn. This is a much thicker and heavier casting than the preceding one, and could easily have supported a carved tusk

97–99 Three fragmentary plaques found in Benin, but showing characteristics found at Ife and among the Tsoede bronzes, thus suggesting interconnections of these three styles. (*See* p. 166 ff.) The right forearm and upper part of the staff of the plaque, *below right*, are detached and are not shown >

96 Terracotta found by Frobenius among the ruins of the Palace at Ife, and thought to have been a decorative wall tile. The strange animal appears to be a mudfish with a head at each end. The form of the head, especially the eye, resembles the mudfishes on Plates 98 and 99

oo The upper part of a figure of a woman kept in ıe Nupe village on Jebba Island in the River Niger. 'his is another of the bronzes alleged to have been rought up the Niger from Idah by Tsoede, the ounder-hero of the Nupe in the sixteenth century f. p. 168, note 170 and Plate 8). The trunk of this gure is treated in an unusually naturalistic way, lthough the legs are fat and straight whilst the arms re very short and thin, resembling in proportions nd attitude those of the dwarfs from Benin in the 'ienna Museum (*Bibl. 50 j, pl. 25*). The left hand olds a fan which has been bent over. The stylization f the head is also typical of the three large standing gures in the group and in the smallest figure at 'ada, with the almost round eye with applied strips or the edge of the lids, and the rather kidney-shaped ps with a raised edge. The very simplified ear is ound in the smallest Tada figure and on a bronze gure found at Giragi, farther down the Niger, in 960. The chased design on the hair is unusual, but ıe body striations are found at Ife and Benin, as well s at Tada. On her right hip a patch can be seen, oorly executed by the process of burning-in (p. 54)

oı Female figure in bronze from a meeting house f the Ogboni Society at Apomu. The hands are ıaking an Ogboni greeting. This is a very fine xample of Yoruba casting, probably of the eighteenth entury. An inlay has been lost from the channel own the nose. Her almost complete nudity can be aralleled in the arts of Nok and Benin, but not at fe, although the aperto-labial representation of the enitals seems to be a later development which may e restricted to Ogboni bronzes. A similar figure, erhaps a copy of this one, is still in use in the Ogboni ouse at Ede, whither it was brought by the wife of he king (the Timi Ajeniju) about 1830 from her ome town, Owu (*Bibl. 16 h, pl. 2*). The Nigerian Auseum has recently acquired a similar but even ırger one (42 ins) from Iperu (*reg. no. 65. 4.53*), vhilst a fourth is reported to be in use in an Ogboni ouse in Ibadan. A related but smaller male figure also in the Nigerian Museum (*reg. no. 61.5.10*). Aorton-Williams identifies this figure as representing ıjagbo, a terrible Alafin of Oyo, who was deified as vengeful spirit whose image is used in the detection nd punishment of those who betray Ogboni secrets *Bibl. 86*). Denis Williams however, reports that the gure in Ibadan is said to represent Onile, the earth pirit, to whom Ajagbo is closely related (*Bibl. 20 a*)

102–104 Similar striation patterns occur on the faces of sculptures from Ife, Igbo Ukwu and Esie. The terracotta sculpture, *above left*, was collected by Frobenius in Ife in 1910. It is one of the most extraordinary pieces in the whole corpus of Ife art (*see* p. 60). The striation pattern on the man's face is unusual in Ife but is close to those of Igbo Ukwu, eastern Nigeria, *above right*, where the pattern of striations is raised, not incised, and may be compared with the scarification on the face of the stone figure from Esie, *below right*. The head from Igbo Ukwu is supplied with loops below the chin from ear to ear, from which bronze-wire chains and crotals were originally strung.

105 *Below left*, is a bronze casting representing the shell of a giant land snail (*Achatina achatina* Linn.) found at Igbo Ukwu in 1939 in digging a water storage cistern. These bronzes are characterized by lavish decoration applied to the surface, often including mantids, beetles, and, as here, crickets

Wood carving representing a deceased twin, carved in Ilaro. This was formerly the collection of Georg Emil Schüz, who d in 1877. It was evidently carved before t date

07 Solid sculpture in lightly aked clay excavated at the alace in Ilesha. This appears to ave been made about the middle f the nineteenth century. The implified ear, the flat horizontal ps, and the bulging eyes are haracteristically Yoruba; carved vory representations of Eshu sed in Ifa divination were still arved in this same style in lesha until very recently. The quatting posture is entirely ypical of this group of sculp- ures

08 One of two mud figures in he shrine to Oduduwa at gbodio, Ife. This is nowadays he most important shrine in Ife, nd is still surrounded by a grove f forest trees despite its being n the centre of the town. Kenneth Murray was told in 946 that this represented Odudua himself, but the writer vas told in 1962 that both igures were of his servants. The tyle resembles that of the fired nud figures of Ilesha (Plate 107) nd may well be of a similar ineteenth century date. Feathers nd blood of sacrificed chickens re on the head of the figure, the ower part of which is hidden by piece of decayed cloth. Behind s part of a domestic pot. The mall objects hanging from the aw are pupa cases of a moth probably a species of Tineid) vhose caterpillars had fed on the acrifices. The two white spots on the left hand are egg-cases of piders. In this same grove is kept the drum of Oduduwa, a broken glass-making crucible discussed on p. 24

109, 110 Wood carving of kneeling woman holding a bow probably carved at Ilesha b used in a house in Ife for mar years

Benin art, in its turn, introduces us to the figure whose legs are fishes,[220] and this we find frequently in Yoruba sculpture in wood and ivory, whilst the bronze bracelet from Wukari, which has replaced the fishes with snakes swallowing frogs, is probably another Yoruba variation on the theme.

These examples are but a few of the elements which indicate connections across time and space in the history of West African sculpture. Bernard Fagg has given examples of many more similarities between the Nok culture and more recent ones nearer the coast.[221] Despite the sporadic—and to varying degrees, uncertain—distribution through time of the art-styles illustrated in this book, there is an unavoidable impression of continuity of artistic tradition in West Africa through more than two millennia. The Nok culture has been dated by radiocarbon, which has provided three dates which combine together and with the geological evidence to make reasonable sense. There follows the Ife culture, which, at present, can only be dated by inference from evidence relating primarily to Benin. It may be necessary to revise this dating, pushing the Classical Period of Ife much farther back to bring it closer to the Nok culture. Benin art is clearly seen to be derived from Classical Ife whilst some continuity can be seen between post-Classical Ife and modern Yoruba sculpture. This is the general outline. We can look forward to the discovery of new evidence bearing on the topics discussed in this book, which has tended to emphasize what we know rather than what we do not know. We can expect the discovery of sites to fill in the gaps in our knowledge between the Nok culture and Classical Ife and between post-Classical Ife and modern Yoruba sculpture. The evidence we lack will be found by the farmers and labourers of West Africa, who will always make more initial discoveries than the archaeologists can. It is up to them to report the discovery of the artistic remains which are their own heritage, a heritage which has already won international recognition for Africa in the world of art.

Figs. 32, 34

Notes

Bibliography

List of Illustrations

Index

Notes

Chapter I

1 Terracotta is a term used for sculptures made in pottery. Its colour depends on the conditions in which it is fired.
2 First published in *Bibl.* 97 a. The original is illustrated in *Bibl.* 50 j, Pl. 3.
3 See *Bibl.* 60, pp. 466–7.
4 *Bibl.* 55 a; b.
5 See *Bibl.* 25. Illustrated also in *Bibl.* 45, Fig. 155; 110, Pl. 1.
6 See *Bibl.* 50 o. The traditional method is described in Chapter IV.
7 For references see Chapter VIII.
8 For references see Chapter XI.
9 Other early accounts of Ife are *Bibl.* 39; 44; 46.

Chapter II

10 See *Bibl.* 88 a; f. Other information is in the files of the Department of Antiquities, Nigeria.
11 *Bibl.* 13 a; b.
12 On this topic and on the whole subject of the psychology of looking both at the real world and at its representation in painting *Bibl.* 56 is invaluable.
13 As Mrs Caroline Sassoon has pointed out to me.
14 The ear in Fig. 31a has a very European look, but the population of Yorubaland nowadays is very mixed and variable. I have observed many ears in Ife which could have provided a basis for this particular convention.
15 *Bibl.* 50 d.
16 *Bibl.* 93 b in which he compares them with the terracotta heads from Memphis (*Bibl.* 93 a, Pls 36–41).
17 The terracotta heads, however, are often represented with hair covering the heads in these same shapes.
18 Dr W. G. van der Sleen identified one of the beads from Head 9 as a

'black cylindrical Indian Trade-wind bead' (letter of 12th January 1962). Such beads he reports to have been found at sites in East Africa dated between the third and fourteenth centuries AD (*Bibl.* 111).

19 *Bibl.* 50 p.

20 *Bibl.* 65, p. 51.

21 *Cola nitida*, the fruits of which are always offered to guests and shared with them as a gesture of hospitality. The sculpture in Pls. 109, 110 would probably have been used to offer kola nuts to guests.

22 Nos 1 and 8, illustrated in *Bibl.* 110, Figs 12 and 7.

23 *Bibl.* 50 p.

24 A conclusion which Bernard Fagg also reached in his explorations there in 1953. See *Bibl.* 90, 1952–3, §49.

25 Illustrated in *Bibl.* 49 k, Fig. 5.

26 I am indebted to Fr Kevan Carroll, S.M.A., for this text and its interpretation.

27 These pavements are described on pp. 104–5.

28 Dr R. E. Bradbury informs me that in Benin these figures are made by the brassworking Chief Ihamanigun, a fact which lends support to the suggestion that the Ife bronze heads were used in a similar way.

29 A detailed account of these ceremonies and figures will be found in *Bibl.* 119 n.

30 Examples are shown in *Bibl.* 50 g; 119 e; l.

31 *Bibl.* 68.

32 *Bibl.* 119 n.

33 *Bibl.* 117 a, p. 24, records that an Oni whom he does not name reduced the size of the palace, thus excluding from it a group of people who had been preying on the townsfolk. In gratitude, he was buried inside the palace compound 'and succeeding Onis have been accorded the same privilege'. Three Onis lie buried in the palace: Lajodogun, Adelekan Olubushe (1894–1910) and Ademiluyi (1910–30). The 'Oni' before Olubushe, Derin Ologbenla, was never more than Oni elect and 'reigned' over the exiled Ifes at Oke Igbo. His elder brother Orayigba Ayikiti, known as Ojaja, was forced on the Ifes (*Bibl.* 65, pp. 646–8). He reigned from 1878 to 1881. His predecessor, Degbin Kumbusu, was a tyrant, and ruled over the Ifes during the later part of their exile at Ishoya. He reigned from 1849 to 1878. Adegunle Abeweila was not popular in Ife, since he gave Modakeke to the Oyos (see p. 102). He was poisoned after a few years on the throne. His two predecessors, Wunmonije and Gbegbaje, seem also to have been murdered after short reigns (*Bibl.* 65, p. 230). Before these came Odunle Akinmoyero, who was reigning at the time of the collapse of Old Oyo, about 1837. Lajodogun's name does not appear among

these, nor do any Onis later than Akinmoyero appear to have been held in the respect which Ward Price's story implies. It would appear, then, that we must date the reduction of the size of the palace to the first half of the nineteenth century. I am grateful to Mrs Catherine Fagg for allowing me to use her notes on the king list of Ife.

34 Kindly identified by Mr J. Tankard of the Shirley Institute, Manchester.

35 These two samples were examined by Mr E. B. Jones at the Testing House of the Manchester Chamber of Commerce.

36 One of the *ako* figures surviving in Owo had a strip of black hairy cloth nailed over the forehead to represent hair. The Ife heads could have been furnished with cloth or with animal skins below the crowns to give a similar effect.

37 *Bibl.* 111. See note 18.

38 *Bibl.* 110, p. 27 ff.

39 *Bibl.* 28 c; d; 119 q.

40 The facial features of the Obalufon mask are very similar to those of Head 7 illustrated in *Bibl.* 110, Fig. 8.

41 *E.g., Bibl.* 92, Pls 3, 4, 22, 23 and 27; 96, Pls 22, 23, 27 and 28; and 109, Pls 6 and 31. In many museum specimens the cloths have been removed or the fibre has decayed (*e.g.*, most masks in *Bibl.* 96).

42 *Bibl.* 24 f, pp. 111–12.

43 But compare the alternative explanation on p. 150.

44 *Bibl.* 50 a. Kenneth Murray had earlier pointed out that these proportions in figures on Benin plaques proved that the art could not have been introduced by the Portuguese (*Bibl.* 88 a).

Chapter III

45 *E.g., Bibl.* 119 r, Fig. 67.

46 See *Bibl.* 50 b, Fig. 1.

47 *Bibl.* 95.

48 *Bibl.* 40.

Chapter IV

49 *Euphorbia kamerunica.* This variation was observed at Obo Ayegunle in Ekiti in 1959. The latex is heated over a slow fire till it solidifies. In use it is broken into pieces which are softened in hot water and worked in the hands into threads or sheets. These are applied to a cone and to each other, fusion of the pieces and smoothing of the finished form being achieved with a hot knife. This latex burns to a fine ash when

the mould is heated and is easily shaken out before the metal is poured in.

50 This is illustrated in a Benin example in *Bibl.* 26, p. 251, and facing page.

51 *Bibl.* 120 b describes a variation of the process.

52 *Bibl.* 50 o.

53 *Bibl.* 11; 119 c and m give details.

54 *Bibl.* 81 b.

55 *Bibl.* 11; 88 a.

Chapter V

56 *Bibl.* 3.

57 In modern Ife, the remains of the sacrificed animal (most of which is usually eaten) are normally laid on the ground where termites and ants quickly consume them. In Ondo, Idanre and Benin, the cleaned skulls of the sacrifice are hung over the shrine and are thus kept indefinitely. At one time these skulls sacrificed at annual festivals were used to record the passing of the years.

58 Information from Dr R. E. Bradbury.

59 Illustrated in *Bibl.* 55 a, I, p. 341, Figs 3 a, b; and in *Bibl.* 69, Fig. 3.

60 *Bibl.* 55 a, I, p. 337, shows three views of this piece, Figs 1 a, b, c.

61 They may at some time have stood in a building, for a potsherd pavement was excavated there in 1958.

62 Igbo = grove, a sacred place in the forest. Several of them are now within the built-up part of the town, where the forest trees are still preserved so far as possible, though many no longer in use have been built over.

63 *Bibl.* 13 c, p. 62.

64 *Bibl.* 106, II, pp. 492–3: Kalabari and Lower Ijo; and pp. 501–4: among the Ibo in Degema, Owerri and Aba divisions.

65 There is also an unprovenanced face (reg. no. 43) with a nose eaten away by gangosa or some similar disease.

66 On the important political role of this society in the traditional Yoruba state see *Bibl.* 86.

67 Palm wine is the natural sap of the tree (either *Raphia vinifera*: the wine palm or *Elaeis guineensis*: the oil palm) which is rich in yeast and so ferments naturally. Containers for it are therefore closed with a porous stopper of wood wool.

68 One is illustrated in *Bibl.* 50 b, Pl. F, *f.*

69 Illustrated in *Bibl.* 49 e, Pl. H, *a* and *d.*

70 Illustrated in *Bibl.* 88 f, p. 6.

71 Many of these pieces are illustrated in *Bibl.* 74.
72 See *Bibl.* 89, p. 22.
73 See also the caption to Pl. 93.
74 Quartz and mica serve as a 'backing' to bind the clay together when it is fired. European potters use ground-up fireclay or 'grog' for this purpose. Without it, the clay would disintegrate in firing.
75 *Bibl.* 114, p. 128.
76 The elaborate clay tobacco-pipes of the Cameroons Grasslands are made in this way. See *Bibl.* 64 a.

Chapter VI

77 Illustrated in *Bibl.* 88 g, Fig. 2.
78 Illustrated in *Bibl.* 55 a, I, p. 325, Fig. 1.
79 *Bibl.* 88 g gives a full account of this grove.
80 Described and illustrated in *Bibl.* 119 p.
81 Illustrated in *Bibl.* 88 g, Pl. L and Fig. 4.
82 *Bibl.* 49 p and 119 i.
83 Related forms from the Igala are illustrated in *Bibl.* 49 p, Fig. 3; and *Bibl.* 102 b, Figs 2 to 4.
84 See *Bibl.* 24 b, p. 203.
85 Illustrated in *Bibl.* 49 p, Pl. K, *g* and *h*.
86 *Bibl.* 110, p. 5.
87 Most of the stools not illustrated here can be seen in *Bibl.* 49 p.

Chapter VII

88 The earliest use of brick was at Little Wenham Hall in the thirteenth century and at this time bricks were still extremely scarce in England. Until the late fifteenth century most of them were imported from the Low Countries, whilst it was as late as the eighteenth century before small houses for the well-to-do came to be built of brick. Wattle-and-daub still prevailed for the cottages of ordinary people, because there was a tax on bricks, which was not repealed until 1850. One of the grounds Lord Halifax mentioned for its repeal was that this would increase the comforts of the lower class by improving their dwellings. See C. F. Innocent, *The Development of English Building Construction*, Cambridge, 1916, and Stephen Dowel, *A History of Taxation and Taxes in England*, London, 1888, IV, 376–84.
89 *Bibl.* 71, I, 180.
90 Some domestic animals, of course, are represented in terracotta.
91 *Bibl.* 119 j.
92 *Bibl.* 29 a, b, c.

93 Experiments are at present in progress on sample sherds from pavements to establish their age by thermo-luminescence. *Bibl.* 104 discusses the possibility of relative dating by statistical analysis of maize impressions on pottery.

94 Life in ancient Ife has been more fully discussed in *Bibl.* 50 p.

Chapter VIII

95 *Bibl.* 10. These dates are numbers Y-474 and Y-142–4 respectively. Other samples from the sands gave much earlier dates (Y-475: 2103 ± 140 BC; Y-142–3: 3533 ± 85 BC; Y-142–3′: 3703 ± 90 BC) and are thought to have been derived from older deposits.

96 *Bibl.* 49 k, p. 292.

97 *Bibl.* 20; 49 g.

98 Sample number I-1457. *Bibl.* 49 m; o.

99 The Bini concept of *ehi* is discussed in *Bibl.* 24 d. The Yoruba concept of *orun* seems to have similar implications.

100 *Bibl.* 49 n.

101 The head in Pl. XI quite possibly belongs to this figure.

102 *Bibl.* 4 a.

Chapter IX

103 See p. 61 and *Bibl.* 49 k, Fig. 11.

104 *Bibl.* 45, p. 59.

105 Illustrated in *Bibl.* 88 g. Fig, 1.

106 There is a similar sculpture of squatting male loins on an upturned pot from Ankiring, though the forms of this sculpture are much less rounded.

107 *Bibl.* 45, p. 60.

108 Whose very name means 'Great God'.

109 There are many variations on this creation legend, *e.g.*, *Bibl.* 46, pp. 89–92; 55 c, pp. 161–3; 63, pp. 19 ff; 121 a; b.

110 See *Bibl.* 16 b, where many examples of these legends and ceremonies are gathered together.

111 See Bradbury's comments on the length of time the Yoruba, the Edo and the Ibo must have been settled in their present area. *Bibl.* 24 e, p. 150.

112 Described in detail in *Bibl.* 116.

113 Johnson gives a very similar version of this legend. *Bibl.* 65, p. 147.

114 The Ibo of Eastern Nigeria, who are generally considered to represent an early West African stock, relatively uninfluenced from outside

before the advent of European missionaries, are still known to themselves and to the Yoruba as the Igbo. Perhaps they do indeed retain the name of the original population of Southern Nigeria.

115 *Bibl.* 48, pp. 48–9.
116 *Bibl.* 100, pp. 115–16, 249–50 and 310.
117 See the caption to Pl. 73.
118 Many of the Ife legends include etymologies of a highly dubious kind, like the name of Oronmiyon himself (p. 142).
119 See *Bibl.* 16 b, pp. 30–1.
120 *E.g.*, *Bibl.* 18 b, pp. 21–3.
121 *Bibl.* 91 a, II, pp. 61 ff.; c, pp. 131–2, 165.
122 Illustrated in the *British Museum Quarterly*, VII, 1932, Pl. 29 *a*.
123 *Bibl.* 66.
124 *Bulletin of the American Museum of Natural History*, IX, 1897, pp. 123–76.
125 *Bibl.* 14. Pl. 25; 37, Pls. 20, 21; 75, pp. 23, 41; 77, pp. 115, 157.
126 *Bibl.* 27 p. 224.

Chapter X

127 *Bibl.* 45, pp. 60–1.
128 *Bibl.* 49 k; n.
129 *Bibl.* 119 g. There were nine people buried with the king.
130 *Bibl.* 38, decada I, libro III, cap. iv, fol. 28. This is discussed further in the caption to Pl. 93.
131 *Bibl.* 43, p. 12.
132 Bradbury reports that it is generally said in Benin 'that they came against the Oni's wishes'. *Bibl.* 24 c, p. 286.
133 Egharevba made the mistake of regarding as successive generations a sequence of kings who were two groups of brothers, thus producing an error of about a century in his dates.
134 *Bibl.* 38. The passage referred to in note 130 recounts that an ambassador from Benin to the Portuguese court in 1540 was wearing one of the crosses which was his reward for making the journey between Ife and Benin. The translated text of the whole passage will be found in *Bibl.* 99, pp. 26–7, 33 and 36.
135 *Bibl.* 21.
136 *Bibl.* 63, p. 208.
137 *Bibl.* 50 j, p. 35.
138 *Bibl.* 97 b, pp. 16–17; 113, I, p. 508.
139 *Bibl.* 101 e, footnote 14.
140 *Bibl.* 119 b.

Chapter XI

141 *Bibl.* 50 j, Pl. 13, illustrates the less well-known one in the Liverpool City Museum.
142 Though Fagg, *Bibl.* 50 j, p. 37, believes that heads with this feature were being made in the late eighteenth century.
143 *Bibl.* 53, pp. 21–2.
144 *Bibl.* 35, quoted from *Bibl.* 98, p. 160.
145 *Bibl.* 21.
146 *Bibl.* 50 j, p. 32.
147 *Bibl.* 53, p. 22.
148 A modern painter, copying a work of an older master produces something entirely different in style. Compare Van Gogh's copy with the original of Millet's painting 'The Cornfield', *Bibl.* 56, pp. 308–9.
149 They are distinguished not only by stylistic characteristics, but also by the possession of rectangular slots in the back of both heads and figures. Examples of this sub-style are in *Bibl.* 53, Figs 75, 76; 50 j, Fig. 56; n, p. 142.
150 This head is illustrated in *Bibl.* 53, Figs 77, 78 and 50 j, Fig. 17.
151 Illustrated in *Bibl.* 36, Pl. 6; and 45, Fig. 165.
152 Illustrated in *Bibl.* 53, Figs 65–7.
153 *Bibl.* 24 b gives an interesting account of the ceremonies associated with the king.
154 They are shown in position in *Bibl.* 53, Figs 71, 72; 26, Pls 1 and 2 between pp. 250 and 251.
155 *Bibl.* 50 j, Figs 38 a, 39.
156 *Bibl.* 50 j, Fig. 48.
157 *Bibl.* 53, Figs 53, 54; 50 j, Fig. 32.
158 *Bibl.* 98, Fig. 220.
159 *Bibl.* 50 j, Fig. 61; 50 n, p. 66.
160 *Bibl.* 98, Fig. 243; 53, Fig. 13.
161 *Bibl.* 53, Fig. 74.
162 *Bibl.* 50 j, Fig. 103. Two old antelope heads of similar type from a village outside Benin are illustrated in *Bibl.* 50 n, p. 156.
163 *Bibl.* 24 c; e.
164 This is the date suggested also by Talbot, *Bibl.* 106, I, p. 153.
165 *Bibl.* 24 e, pp. 155–6.

Chapter XII

166 *E.g.*, *Bibl.* 50 j, Fig. 16; n, p. 104; and 53, Figs 32–4.
167 *E.g.*, *Bibl.* 50 n, p. 105.

168 *Bibl.* 83 d, Pl. 1 d. The right forearm and staff are missing from her photograph.

169 Although we should not ignore the possibility that they might have been made at a later date under influences from Ife and Benin, perhaps at Owo.

170 See Nadel (*Bibl.* 89, pp. 72–6) for his story, although Nadel's informant, the Emir of Pategi, denied that these figures were brought by Tsoede, though agreeing that he came in a bronze canoe with bronze trumpets and iron chains, one of which is kept with the figures on Jebba Island. The canoe is said to be sunk in the river at Egan where sacrifices are still made to it annually. On page 406, Nadel gives '1463?' as the date of the birth of Tsoede, 1493 as the date when he was taken as slave to Idah, 1523 his flight from Idah, 1531 his establishment as king of Nupe, and 1591 as the date of his death. However many 'written records of Nupe history which were compiled by Mohammedan scholars and court historians' (pp. 72–3) may agree in this, a life of 128 years is hard to accept as literally true. The period is evidently mythical, and it may be that he belongs only to the end of it or perhaps to the early part of it and has been extended to cover the gap to the first historical king. The stylistic data cannot be employed to produce a closer limit of time than this, but the sculptures do not suggest a date outside the period from the early fifteenth century through to the end of the sixteenth century.

171 Illustrated in *Bibl.* 50 k, Fig. 28.

172 Illustrated in *Bibl.* 50 h, Figs 4, 5.

173 Unlike the Benin objects of this type but like one in the British Museum illustrated in *Bibl.* 50 n, p. 105.

174 According to Abraham's *Dictionary of the Hausa Language*, London, 1962 (under *Sarki* p. 785), this means a chieftainess. The writer has found that male figures with bare chests and a wrapper are frequently considered to be female in Yorubaland just as here.

175 These four pieces were first illustrated in *Bibl.* 72, opp. p. 196. The photographs are said to have been 'obtained with great difficulty, and at some personal risk, by the late D. Crocombe', who was the agent for the Niger Company at Jebba, and died in May 1917.

176 The restoration is described and illustrated in *Bibl.* 50 m.

177 Illustrated in *Bibl.* 50 j, Fig. 57; k, Fig. 32.

178 *Bibl.* 50 j, Fig. 38 a.

179 *Bibl.* 90, 1958–62, pp. 39, 43.

180 Illustrated in *Bibl.* 50 n, p. 123.

181 Illustrated in *Bibl.* 50 j, Fig. 63 a.

182 Most of the work in this field, like that of Benin, has been done by

William Fagg, whose published accounts of it appear in *Bibl.* 45; 50 j; n; and in various exhibition catalogues, notably *Bibl.* 50 i.

Chapter XIII

183 The original accounts of these discoveries are *Bibl.* 67; 51.

184 See *Bibl.* 101 a; b; c. The second season's excavation in 1964 is described in *Bibl.* 101 f.

185 *Bibl.* 108, Pl. 31, shows a calabash bowl in bronze identical in form and decoration with those from Igbo Ukwu. It was bought in the Tikar area but was said to have come originally from Bamum, both in Cameroun.

186 *Bibl.* 50 j, Fig. 57.

187 *Bibl.* 22.

188 Mr Philip Allison informs me that he was told in Idah that they learnt brass-casting from Koton Karifi, but this could be a recent reflex movement after the original craft had died out.

189 Illustrated in *Bibl.* 88 c, p. 91; 50 n, p. 67.

190 *Bibl.* 101 b.

191 Illustrated in *Nigeria Magazine*, 26, 1947, p. 359.

192 *Bibl.* 19.

193 See *Bibl.* 50 j, Pl. 30 a; n, p. 131; 103, Pl. 12.

194 See *Bibl.* 9, especially Figs 20, 21, and Pl. I *c* and *d*.

195 See *Bibl.* 59, and 58, pp. 184–7.

196 *Dracaena fragrans* Gawl, used to mark boundaries and sacred places.

197 *Bibl.* 55 a, I, opp. p. 400.

198 Described in *Bibl.* 88 d, and more recently by P. Stevens, 'The Festival of the Images at Esie,' *Nigeria Magazine*, LXXXVII, 1965.

199 See *Bibl.* 50 j, Fig. 75.

200 *Bibl.* 50 f; j, Fig. 76.

201 *Bibl.* 4 b; 34 b; 54. On the original site see *Bibl.* 5, 34 a; 83 c; 85; 88 d, and Stevens's article referred to in note 198.

Chapter XIV

202 The exceptional cases where they live in towns established before European administration are all on the northern and western edges of the area, where influence from neighbouring groups like the Bini and the Igala made themselves felt.

203 Compare the essential unity of style of the Yoruba sculptures in *Bibl.* 50 j, Figs 77 to 101, with variety of the Ibo examples, Figs 112 to 122 and *Bibl.* 109, Pls 5 to 9. See also *Bibl.* 16 d.

204 See also *Bibl.* 16 g.
205 See *Bibl.* 50 n, p. 149; 119 q.
206 See *Bibl.* 50 e; j, Figs 99–105.
207 *Bibl.* 55 a, I, Pl. facing p. 168
208 See *Bibl.* 28 a; b.
209 *Bibl.* 28 c; d.

Chapter XV

210 *E.g.*, the head from Nok itself illustrated in *Bibl.* 90, 1958–62, p. 58.
211 See *Bibl.* 50 l.
212 *E.g.*, *Bibl.* 45, Figs 68, 69.
213 *E.g.*, *Bibl.* 45, Fig. 103; 50 k, Fig. 18.
214 *E.g.*, *Bibl.* 45, Fig. 234.
215 *E.g.*, *Bibl.* 50 k, Fig. 76.
216 See also the piece illustrated in *Bibl.* 98, Fig. 268.
217 *E.g.*, *Bibl.* 98, Fig. 30; 50 n, p. 106.
218 See *Bibl.* 88 g, Pl. L and Fig. 1.
219 *Bibl.* 50 n, p. 106; j, fig. 19; 53, Figs 79–82.
220 See *Bibl.* 50 n, p. 104; 53, Pls 32–4.
221 *Bibl.* 49 n.

Bibliography

Abbreviations

Burl. M	*Burlington Magazine.*
ILN	*Illustrated London News.*
JAH	*Journal of African History.*
JHSN	*Journal of the Historical Society of Nigeria.*
JRAI	*Journal of the Royal Anthropological Institute.*
Odu	*Odu, a Journal of Yoruba, [Edo] and Related Studies.*

References in the text and notes preceded by *Bibl.* are to numbers in the following list.

1 ABRAHAM, R. C. *Dictionary of Modern Yoruba,* London, 1958.

2 ADEMAKINWA, J. A. *Ife, Cradle of the Yoruba,* 2 parts, Lagos, 1958.

3 ADEREMI, H. H. SIR ADESOJI, the Oni of Ife. Notes on the city of Ife, *Nigeria,* XII, 1937, pp. 3–6.

4 a ALLISON, P. A. Historical inferences to be drawn from the effect of human settlement on the vegetation of Africa, *JAH,* III, 1962, pp. 241–9.

b —— Newly discovered stone figures from the Yoruba village of Ijara, Northern Nigeria, *Man,* LXIII, 1963, 115.

c —— A terracotta head in the Ife style from Ikirun, Western Nigeria, *Man,* LXIII, 1963, 194.

d —— A carved stone figure of Eshu from Igbajo, Western Nigeria, *Man,* LXIV, 1964, 131.

5 ANONYMOUS. A Nigerian forest mystery, massed statues of unknown origin used in ancestor worship and fertility rites, *ILN,* 20th August 1938, pp. 334–5.

6 ANONYMOUS. Mud shrines of Olokun, *Nigeria,* L, 1956, pp. 280–95.

7 ARMSTRONG, R. G. The use of linguistic and ethnographic data in the study of Idoma and Yoruba history, in *Bibl.* 112, pp. 127–44.

8 ARRIENS, C. Die heilige Steinfiguren von Ife, *Der Erdball,* IV, 1930, pp. 333–41.

9 BALFOUR, HENRY. Ritual and secular uses of vibrating membranes as voice-disguisers, *JRAI,* LXXVIII, 1951, pp. 45–69.

10 BARENDSEN, G. W., DEEVEY, E. S. and GRALENSKI, L. J. Yale Natural Radio Carbon Measurements, III, *Science*, CXXVI, 1957, pp. 916–17.

11 BARKER, H. Examination of the Ife bronze heads, *Man*, LXV, 1965, 10.

12 BARTH, H. *Travels and Discoveries in North and Central Africa 1849–55*, 5 vols, London, 1858.

13 a BASCOM, W. R. Brass portrait heads from Ile-Ife, Nigeria, *Man* XXXVIII, 1938, 201.

b —— The legacy of an unknown Nigerian 'Donatello', *ILN*, 8th April 1939, pp. 592–4.

c —— The sociological role of the Yoruba cult-group, *American Anthropologist*, XLVI, 1944 (No. 63 in the *Memoir Series of the American Anthropological Association*).

14 BATESON, G. *Naven*, Cambridge, 1936.

15 BATTUTA, IBN. *Travels in Asia and Africa*, ed. by H. A. R. Gibb, London, 1929.

16 a BEIER, H. U. The historical and psychological significance of Yoruba myths, *Odu* I, n.d., pp. 17–25.

b —— Before Oduduwa, *Odu*, III, n.d., pp. 25–32.

c —— *The Story of Sacred Wood Carvings from one small Yoruba Town*, Lagos, n.d.

d —— Ibo and Yoruba art, a comparison, *Black Orpheus*, VIII, n.d., pp. 46–50.

e —— The *egungun* cult, *Nigeria*, LI, 1956, pp. 380–92.

f —— Obatala festival, *Nigeria*, LII, 1956, pp. 10–28.

g —— *Gelede* masks, *Odu*, VI, 1958, pp. 5–23.

h —— *A Year of Sacred Festivals in one Yoruba Town*, Lagos, 1959.

i —— *Art in Nigeria 1960*, Cambridge, 1960.

j —— *African Mud Sculpture*, Cambridge, 1963.

17 BERTHO, J. and MAUNY, R. Archéologie du pays Yorouba et du Bas-niger, *Notes Africaines*, LVI, 1952, pp. 97–114.

18 a BIOBAKU, S. O. Myths and oral history, *Odu*, I, n.d., pp. 12–17.

b —— *The Origin of the Yoruba, The Lugard Lectures*, Lagos, 1955.

19 BOHANNAN, L. and P. *The Tiv of Central Nigeria*, London, 1953.

20 BOND, G. A preliminary account of the Pleistocene geology of the Plateau tin-fields region of Northern Nigeria, *Proceedings of the Third International West African Congress, Ibadan, 1949*, Lagos, 1956.

21 BOSMAN, W. *Nauwkeurige Beschrijvinge van der Guinese*, Utrecht, 1704.

22 BOSTON, J. S. Notes on contact between the Igala and the Ibo, *JHSN*, II, 1960, pp. 52–8.

23 BOVILL, E. W. *The Golden Trade of the Moors*, London, 1958.

24 a BRADBURY, R. E. *The Benin Kingdom and the Edo-Speaking Peoples of South-Western Nigeria*, London, 1957.

b —— Divine kingship in Benin, *Nigeria*, LXII, 1959, pp. 186–207.

c —— Chronological problems in the study of Benin history, *JHSN*, I, 1959, pp. 263–87.

d —— *Ehi*: three stories from Benin, *Odu*, VIII, 1960, pp. 40–8.

e —— The historical uses of comparative ethnography with special reference to Benin and the Yoruba, in *Bibl.* 112, pp. 145–64.

f —— Father and son in Edo mortuary ritual, in *African Systems o, Thought*, ed. M. Fortes and G. Dieterlen, London, 1965, pp. 96–121.

25 BRAUNHOLTZ, H. J. A bronze head from Ife, Nigeria, *British Museum Quarterly*, XIV, 1940, pp. 75–7.

26 BRINKWORTH, I. Benin: 'City of Blood' – and Bronze. *The Geographical Magazine*, XXVII, No. 5, September 1954, pp. 248–57.

27 BÜHLER, A., BARROW, TERRY and MOUNTFORD, CHARLES P. *Oceania and Australia, The Art of the South Seas*, London, 1962.

28 a CARROLL, K. Yoruba masks, *Odu*, III, n.d., pp. 3–15.

b —— Ekiti Yoruba wood-carving, *Odu*, IV, n.d., pp. 3–10.

c —— Three generations of Yoruba carvers, *Ibadan*, XII, 1961, pp. 21–4.

d —— *Yoruba Religious Carving, Pagan and Christian Sculpture in Nigeria and Dahomey*, London, 1967.

29 a CARTER, G. F. Movement of people and ideas across the Pacific, in J. Barreau, *Plants and the Migrations of Pacific Peoples*, Tenth Pacific Science Congress, Honolulu, Hawaii, 1961 (pub. 1963), pp. 7–22.

b —— Maize to Africa, *Anthropological Journal of Canada*, I, pt 2, 1963, pp. 3–8.

c —— Archaeological maize in West Africa: a discussion of Stanton and Willett, *Man*, LXIV, 1964, 95.

30 a CLARKE, J. D. The stone figures of Esie, *Nigeria*, XIV, 1938, pp. 106–8.

b Three Yoruba fertility ceremonies, *JRAI*, LXXIV, 1944, pp. 91–6.

31 CONNAH, G. Archaeological research in Benin city, 1961–64, *JHSN*, II, 1964, pp. 465–77.

32 a CORDWELL, JUSTINE M. The problem of process and form in West African art, *Proceedings of the Third International West African Conference, 1949*, Lagos, 1956, pp. 53–60.

b —— Naturalism and stylization in Yoruba art, *Magazine of Art*, 46, 1953, pp. 220–6.

33 CROOK, J. Ife portraits and Roman portraits, *Ibadan*, XVII, 1963, pp. 9–10.

34 a DANIEL, F. DE F. The stone figures of Esie, Ilorin Province, Nigeria, *JRAI*, LXVII, 1937, pp. 43–50.

b —— Stone sculpture in Nigeria. Stone figures at Ofaro. *Nigeria*, XVIII, 1939, pp. 107–8.

c —— Figures at Jebba and Tada, *Nigeria*, XX, 1940, pp. 282–4.

35 DAPPER, O. *Nauwkeurige Beschrijvinge der Afrikaansche Gewesten*, Amsterdam, 1668.

36 DARK, P. J. C. *The Art of Benin, A Catalogue of an Exhibition of the A. W. F. Fuller and Chicago Natural History Museum Collections of Antiquities from Benin, Nigeria*, Chicago, 1962.

37 DEACON, A. B. *Malekula: A Vanishing People in the New Hebrides*, London, 1934.

38 DE BARROS, J. *Da Asia*, Lisbon, 1552.

39 DENNETT, R. E. *Nigerian Studies*, London, 1910.

40 DITTMAR, K. Zur Herkunft und Bedeutung der altyorubischen Kronen und des äthiopischen Kalatscha, *Festschift für Ad. E. Jensen*. München, 1964, pp. 63–90.

41 DUCKWORTH, E. H. Recent archaeological discoveries in the ancient city of Ife, *Nigeria*, XIV, 1938, pp. 101–5.

42 ECCLES, POLLY. Nupe bronzes, *Nigeria Magazine*, LXXIII, 1962, pp. 13–25.

43 EGHAREVBA, J. U. *A Short History of Benin* (3rd ed.) Ibadan, 1960.

44 ELGEE, C. H. Ife stone-carvings, *Journal of the African Society*, VII, 1908, pp. 338–45.

45 ELISOFON, E. and FAGG, W. B. *The Sculpture of Africa*, London, 1958.

46 ELLIS, A. B. *The Yoruba-Speaking Peoples of the Slave Coast of West Africa*, London, 1894.

47 ESAN, O. Before Oduduwa, *Odu*, VIII, 1960, pp. 75–6.

48 EVANS-PRITCHARD, E. E. *The Political System of the Anuak*, London, 1940.

49 a FAGG, BERNARD E. B. A preliminary note on a new series of pottery figures from Northern Nigeria, *Africa*, XV, 1945, pp. 21–2.

b —— Archaeological notes from Northern Nigeria, *Man*, XLVI, 1946, 48.

c —— Primitive art of problematic age, *ILN*, 26th April 1947, pp. 442–3.

d —— Masterpieces of early Nigerian art, *ILN*, 20th November 1948, 586–7.

e —— New discoveries from Ife on exhibition at the Royal Anthropological Institute, *Man*, XLIX, 1949, 79.

f —— Some archaeological problems at Ife, *Conférence Internationale*

des Africanistes de l'Ouest, Ve Réunion, Abidjan, Compte rendu, 1953, pp. 125–6.
g —— An outline of the Stone Age of the Plateau minesfield, *Proceedings of the Third International West African Conference, Ibadan, 1949*, Lagos, 1956, pp. 203–22.
h —— A life-size terracotta head from Nok, *Man*, LVI, 1956, 95.
i —— The Nok Culture, *West African Review*, 156, pp. 1083–7.
j —— Caribbean treasure hunt, *West Africa*, 6th October 1956.
k —— The Nok culture in prehistory, *JHSN*, I, 1959, pp. 288–93.
l —— Mining for history, *Nigeria Magazine*, LXXI, pp. 34–41.
m —— An ancient site in Niger Province, *Bulletin of News*, Historical Society of Nigeria, V, pt 4, 1961, p. 3.
n —— The Nok terracottas in West African art history, *Actes du IVe Congrès Panafricain de Préhistoire*, Tervuren, Section III, 1962, pp. 445–50.
o —— Radiocarbon dating of the Nok culture, Northern Nigeria, *Nature*, 9th January 1965, pp. 205, 212.
p Fagg, Bernard and Fagg, William. The ritual stools of Ancient Ife, *Man*, LX, 1960, 155.
50 a Fagg, William B. The antiquities of Ife, *Image*, II, 1949. (Reprinted in *Magazine of Art*, XLIII, Washington, 1950, pp. 129–33.)
b —— A bronze figure in Ife style at Benin, *Man*, L, 1950, 98.
c —— L'art nigérien avant Jésus-Christ, *L'Art Nègre*, Présence Africaine, 10–11, Paris, 1951, pp. 91–5.
d —— De l'art des Yoruba, *L'Art Nègre*, Présence Africaine, 10–11, Paris, 1951, pp. 103–35.
e —— Tribal sculpture and the Festival of Britain, *Man*, LI, 1951, 124.
f —— On a stone head of variant style at Esie, Nigeria, *Man*, LIX, 1959, 60.
g —— Another Yoruba hunter's shrine, *Man*, LIX, 1959, p. 335.
h —— The mysterious bronzes of Jebba and Tada, Northern Nigeria, *ILN*, 236, no, 6290, 20th February 1960, pp. 297–9.
i —— *Nigerian Tribal Art*, Arts Council (London), 1960.
j —— *Nigerian Images*, London, 1963.
k —— *Africa, 100 Tribes—100 Masterpieces*; *Afrika, 100 Stämme—100 Meisterwerke*, Berlin, 1964.
l —— *Afro-Portuguese Ivories*, London, n.d.
m Fagg, William B., Nimmo, B. A. and Smith, P. J. The restoration of a bronze bowman from Jebba, Nigeria, *British Museum Quarterly*, XXVIII, 1964, pp. 51–6.
n Fagg, William B. and Plass, Margaret. *African Sculpture, an anthology*, London and New York, 1964.

o FAGG, WILLIAM B. and UNDERWOOD, LEON. An examination of the so-called Olokun head of Ife, Nigeria, *Man*, XLIX, 1949, 1.

p FAGG, WILLIAM B. and WILLETT, FRANK. Ancient Ife, an ethnographical summary, *Odu*, VIII, 1960, pp. 21–35. (Reprinted in *Actes du IVe Congrès Panafricain de Préhistoire*, Tervuren, 1962, Section III, pp. 357–73.)

51 FIELD, J. O. Bronze-castings found at Igbo, Southern Nigeria, *Man*, XL, 1940, 1.

52 a FITZGERALD, R. T. D. Dakakari grave pottery, *JRAI*, LXXIV, 1944, pp. 43–57.

b —— Dakakari grave pottery, *Nigerian Field*, XXIII, 1958, pp. 76–84.

53 FORMAN, W. and B. and DARK, PHILIP. *Benin Art*, London, 1960.

54 FRIEND, D. Carved stones at Effon, *Nigeria*, XVIII, 1939, p. 108.

55 a FROBENIUS, LEO. *Und Afrika Sprach*, 3 vols, Berlin, 1912–13.

b —— *The Voice of Africa*, 2 vols, London, 1913.

c —— *Mythologie de l'Atlantide*, Paris, 1949.

56 GOMBRICH, E. H. *Art and Illusion*, London, 1960.

57 a GOODWIN, A. J. H. Archaeology and Benin architecture, *JHSN*, I, 1957, pp. 65–85.

b —— Walls, paving, water-paths and landmarks, *Odu*, VI, 1958, pp. 45–53.

c —— A bronze snake head and other recent finds in the old palace at Benin, *Man*, LXIII, 1963, 174.

58 GRAY, R. A report on the (third) conference (on African History and Archaeology), *JAH*, III, 1962, pp. 174–91.

59 GREENBERG, J. H. *The Languages of Africa*, Bloomington (Indiana) and the Hague, 1963.

60 HAMBLY, W. D. *Culture Areas of Africa*, Field Museum, Publication 346, Anthropological series, Chicago, XXXI, 1935.

61 HARRIS, P. G. Notes on the Dakakari peoples of Sokoto Province, *JRAI*, LXVIII, 1938, pp. 113–52.

62 HOLLIS, ROSEMARY. Dakakari grave pottery. *Nigerian Field*, 23, 1958, pp. 23–6.

63 IDOWU, E. B. *Olodumare, God in Yoruba Belief*, London, 1962.

64 a JEFFREYS, M. D. W. Carved clay tobacco-pipes from Bamenda, British Cameroons, *Man*, L, 1950, 29.

b —— How ancient is West African maize? *Africa*, XXXIII, 1963, pp. 115–31.

65 JOHNSON, S. *The History of the Yorubas*, London, 1921.

66 JONES, A. M. Indonesia and Africa: The xylophone as a culture-indicator, *JRAI*, LXXXIX, 1959, pp. 155–68.

67 JONES, G. I. Ibo bronzes from the Awka Division, *Nigerian Field*, VIII, 4, 1939, pp. 164–7.

68 KANTOROWITZ, E. H. *The King's Two Bodies, a Study in Medieval Political Theology*. Princeton, 1957.

69 KRIEGER, K. Terrakotten und Steinplastiken aus Ife, Nigeria, *Berichte aus den ehemaligen Preussischen Kunstkammer*, Neue Folge, Berliner Museen, Berlin, 1955, pp. 32–9.

70 LAIRD, MACGREGOR and OLDFIELD, R. A. K. *An Expedition into the Interior of Africa by the River Niger, 1832, 1833 and 1834*, 2 vols, London, 1837.

71 LANDER, RICHARD and JOHN. *Journal of an Expedition to Explore the Course and Termination of the Niger*, London, 1832.

72 'LANGA LANGA' (HERMON-HODGE, H. B.) *Up against it in Nigeria*, New York, 1922.

73 a LAOYE I, H. H. the Timi of Ede. Yoruba Drums, *Nigeria*, XLV, 1954, pp. 4–13.

b —— Yoruba Drums, *Odu*, VII, 1959, pp. 5–14.

74 LEBEUF, J.-P. L'art ancien du Tchad, *Cahiers d'Art*, 26e année, Paris, 1951, pp. 7–28.

75 LEENHARDT, M. *Arts de L'Océanie*, Paris, 1947.

76 LEUZINGER, E. *Africa, the Art of the Negro Peoples*, London, 1960.

77 LINTON, RALPH and WINGERT, PAUL S. *Arts of the South Seas*, New York, 1946.

78 LLOYD, P. C. Yoruba myths: A sociologist's interpretation, *Odu*, II, n.d., pp. 20–8.

79 LOMBARD, J. A propos des pierres sculptées d'Ife, *Notes Africaines*, LXVIII, 1955, p. 1.

80 LUCAS, J. O. *The Religion of the Yorubas*, Lagos, 1948.

81 a MAUNY, RAYMOND. *Tableau Géographique de l'Ouest Africain au Moyen Age*, Dakar, 1961.

b —— A possible source of copper for the oldest brass heads at Ife. *JHSN*, II, 1962, pp. 393–5.

82 MEEK, C. K. *A Sudanese Kingdom*, London, 1931.

83 a MEYEROWITZ, E. L. R. Four pre-Portuguese bronze-castings from Benin, *Man*, XL, 1940, 155.

b —— Ancient Nigerian bronzes, *Burl. M.*, LXXIX, 1941, pp. 89–92; 121–8.

c —— The stone figures of Esie in Nigeria, *Burl. M.*, LXXXII, 1943, pp. 31–6.

d —— Ancient bronzes in the royal palace at Benin, *Burl. M.*, LXXXIII, 1943, pp. 248–53.

84 MEYEROWITZ, H. and V. Bronzes and terracottas from Ile-Ife, *Burl. M.*, LXXV, 1939, pp. 150–5.

85 MILBURN, S. Stone sculptures at Esie (Ilorin Province), *The Nigerian Teacher*, VIII, 1936, pp. 2–7.

86 MORTON-WILLIAMS, P. The Yoruba Ogboni cult in Oyo, *Africa*, XXX, 1960, pp. 362–74.

87 MOSS, A. A. Further light on the Olokun head of Ife, *Man*, XLIX, 1949, 159.

88 a MURRAY, K. C. Nigerian bronzes: works from Ife, *Antiquity*, XV, 1941, pp. 71–80.

b —— Frobenius and Ile-Ife, *The Nigerian Field*, XI, 1943, pp. 200–3.

c —— Idah masks, *The Nigerian Field*, XIV, 1949, pp. 85–92.

d —— The stone images of Esie and their yearly festival, *Nigeria*, XXXVII, 1951, pp. 45–64.

e —— The artist in Nigerian tribal society, a comment, in *Bibl.* 103.

f [MURRAY, K. C., and FAGG, B. E. B.] *An Introduction to the Art of Ife*, Lagos, 1955.

g MURRAY, K. C. and WILLETT, F. The Ore Grove at Ife, Western Nigeria, *Man*, LVIII, 1958, 187.

89 NADEL, S. F. *A Black Byzantium*, London, 1942.

90 NIGERIA. *Annual Report on Antiquities for the Year 1949*, etc., Lagos.

91 a PALMER, SIR H. RICHMOND. *Sudanese Memoirs*, 3 vols. Lagos, 1928–.

b —— Gabi figures, *Man*, XXXI, 1931, 261.

c —— *The Bornu Sahara and Sudan*, London, 1936.

d —— Ancient Nigerian bronzes, *Burl. M.*, LXXXI, 1942, pp. 252–6.

92 PAULME, DENISE. *African Sculpture*, London, 1962. (Original edition: *Les Sculptures de l'Afrique Noire*, Paris, 1956.)

93 a PETRIE, SIR W. M. FLINDERS. *Memphis I* (British School of Archaeology in Egypt), London, 1909.

b —— ed. *Ancient Egypt*, 1914, pt 2, p. 84 (Review of *Bibl.* 55b) and pt 4, p. 169 (article 'Egypt in Africa').

94 PITT-RIVERS, A. H. LANE-FOX. *Antique Works of Art from Benin*, London, 1900.

95 PRINCE, RAYMOND. Curse, invocation and mental health among the Yoruba, *Canadian Psychiatric Association Journal*, V, 1960, pp. 65–79.

96 RADIN, PAUL and SWEENEY, JAMES J. *African Folktales and Sculpture*, 2nd ed., London, 1965 (New York, 1964).

97 a READ, C. H. Plato's 'Atlantis' rediscovered, *Burl. M.*, XVIII, 1911, pp. 330–5.

b READ, C. H. and DALTON, O. M. *Antiquities from the City of*

Benin and from other parts of West Africa in the British Museum, London, 1899.

98 ROTH, H. LING. *Great Benin, Its Customs, Art and Horrors*, Halifax, 1903.

99 RYDER, A. F. C. A reconsideration of the Ife–Benin relationship, *JAH*, VI, 1965, pp. 25–37.

100 SELIGMAN, C. G. and B. Z. *Pagan Tribes of the Nilotic Sudan*, London, 1932.

101 a SHAW, C. T. Nigeria's past unearthed, *West African Review*, December 1960, pp. 30–7.

b —— Excavations at Igbo-Ukwu, Eastern Nigeria; an interim report, *Man*, LX, 1960, 210.

c —— Royal tomb at Igbo, Eastern Nigeria; the regalia and ritual instruments of a Nigerian priest king: the treasure house of Igbo, Archaeological Sections 2101 and 2102, *ILN*, CCXLI, 1962, pp. 358–9 and 404–7.

d —— Field research in Nigerian archaeology, *JHSN*, II, 1964, pp. 449–64.

e —— Spectrographic analyses of the Igbo and other Nigerian bronzes, *Archaeometry*, VIII, 1965, pp. 86–95.

f —— Further excavations at Igbo-Ukwu, Eastern Nigeria: an interim report. *Man*, LXV, 1965, 217.

102 a SIEBER, ROY. The arts and their changing social function, *Annals of the New York Academy of Sciences*, XCVI, 1962, pp. 653–8.

b —— The insignia of the Igala Chief of Eteh, Eastern Nigeria, *Man*, LXV, 1965, 65.

103 SMITH, M. W., (editor). *The Artist in Tribal Society*, London, 1961.

104 STANTON, W. R. and WILLETT, F. Archaeological evidence for changes in maize-type in West Africa, *Man*, LXIII, 1963, 150.

105 STRUCK, B. Chronologie der Benin-Altertümer, *Zeitschrift für Ethnologie*, 55, 1923, pp. 113–66.

106 TALBOT, P. A. *The Peoples of Southern Nigeria*, 4 vols, London, 1926.

107 TEMPLE, O. *Notes on the Tribes, Provinces, Emirates and States of the Northern Provinces of Nigeria compiled from Official Reports*, Lagos, 2nd ed., 1922.

108 THORBECKE, F. Beiträge zur Völkerkunde des Ost-Mbamlandes (3 Teil: Im Hochland von Mittelkamerun) *Abhandlungen d. Hamburg. Kol. Inst.*, 41, 1919.

109 TROWELL, M. *Classical African Sculpture*, 2nd ed., London, 1964.

110 UNDERWOOD, LEON. *The Bronzes of West Africa*, London, 1949.

111 VAN DER SLEEN, W. G. N. Trade-wind beads, *Man*, LVI, 1956, 27.

112 VANSINA, J. R., MAUNY, R. and THOMAS, L. V. (editors). *The Historian in Tropical Africa*, London, Ibadan and Accra, 1964.

113 VON LUSCHAN, F. *Die Altertümer von Benin*, 3 vols, Berlin and Leipzig, 1919.

114 VON SYDOW, ECKART. *Afrikanische Plastik* (ed. G. Kutscher), Berlin, 1954.

115 WALKER, S. W. Gabi figures and Edigi, first king of the Nupe, *Man*, XXXIV, 1934, 193.

116 WALSH, M. J. The Edi festival at Ife, *African Affairs*, XLVII, 1948, pp. 231–8.

117 a WARD PRICE, H. L. *Land Tenure in the Yoruba Provinces*, Lagos, 1933.

b —— *Dark Subjects*, London, 1939.

118 WESCOTT, R. W. Did the Yoruba come from Egypt? *Odu*, IV, n.d., pp. 10–15.

119 a WILLETT, F. The discovery of new brass figures at Ife, *Odu*, VI, 1958, 29–34.

b —— A terracotta head from Old Oyo, Nigeria, *Man*, LIX, 1959, 286.

c —— Bronze figures from Ita Yemoo, Ife, Nigeria, *Man*, LIX, 1959, 308.

d —— Bronze and terracotta sculptures from Ita Yemoo, Ife, *The South African Archaeological Bulletin*, XIV, 1959, pp. 135–7.

e —— A hunter's shrine in Yorubaland, Western Nigeria, *Man*, LIX, 1959, 334.

f —— Ife and its archaeology, *JAH*, I, 1960, pp. 231–48.

g —— Recent archaeological discoveries in Ilesha, *Odu*, VIII, 1961, pp. 4–20.

h —— Investigations at Old Oyo, 1956–57, an interim report, *JHSN*, II, 1961, pp. 59–77.

i —— The ritual stools of ancient Ife, *Man*, LXI, 1961, 187.

j —— The introduction of maize into West Africa: an assessment of recent evidence, *Africa*, XXXII, 1962, pp. 1–13.

k —— L'art d'Ife, sa nature et son origine, *VIe Congrès International des Sciences Anthropologiques et Ethnologiques*, Paris, 1963, Vol. 2, pp. 487–9.

l —— A further shrine for a Yoruba hunter, *Man*, LXV, 1965, 66.

m —— Spectrographic analysis of Nigerian bronzes, *Archaeometry*, 7, 1965, pp. 81–3.

n —— On the funeral effigies of Owo and Benin, and the interpretation of the life-size bronze heads from Ife, *Man*, *JRAI*, N.S.I, 1966, pp. 34–45.

o —— Ife, the art of an ancient Nigerian aristocracy, in *The Aristocratic Traditions in African Art*, ed. Douglas Fraser and Herbert Cole (in the press).

p WILLETT, F. and DEMPSTER, A. N. Stone-carvings in an Ife style from Eshure, Ekiti, Western Nigeria, *Man*, LXII, 1962, 1.

q WILLETT, F., and PICTON, J. On the identification of individual sculptors, a study of ancestor shrine carvings from Owo, Western Nigeria. *Man, JRAI*, N.S.II, no.1 1967.

r [WILLETT, F. and SPEED, F.] *The Sculpture of Western Nigeria*, Ibadan, 1960.

120 a WILLIAMS, D. The iconology of the Yoruba *edan Ogboni*, *Africa*, XXXIV, 1964, pp. 139–66.

b —— Lost wax brass-casting in Ibadan, *Nigeria*, LXXXV, 1965, pp. 96–100.

121 a WYNDHAM, JOHN. Yoruba folklore: the creation, *Man*, XIX, 1919, 58.

b —— *Myths of Ife*, London, 1921.

List of Illustrations

Unless otherwise indicated, all pieces are in the Ife Museum. All photographs are by the author, except Plates 1, 23, 24, 26–28 and 39 which are by Francis Speed, and Plate 99 which is by William Fagg.

Colour Plates

Monochrome Plates

Ife

38 Terracotta left arm from Ife. Ht 8 ins. Reg. no. 57.

39 Terracotta male torso from the Iwinrin Grove, Ife. Ht 11 ins. Reg. no. 51.

40 Incomplete terracotta figure from the Osongongon Obamakin Grove, Ife. Ht 11 ins. Reg. no. 53.

41 Terracotta ram's head from Oshogbo. L. $5\frac{3}{4}$ ins. Reg. no. 138/61.

42 Terracotta dog's head from the Osongongon Obamakin Grove, Ife. L. 3 ins. Reg. no. 36.

43 Terracotta ram's head from the Obalufon shrine, Ife. L. $4\frac{5}{8}$ ins. Reg. no. 35.

44 Terracotta ram's head from St Philip's churchyard, Aiyetoro, Ife. L. $6\frac{1}{4}$ ins.

45 Terracotta ram's head from Abiri, L. 8 ins.

46 Terracotta sculpture of a tethered animal from the Osongongon Obamakin Grove, Ife. L. 7 ins. Reg. no. 37.

47, 48 Terracotta owl from Olumobi Compound, Ife. Ht 5 ins. Reg. no. 68/61.

49 Terracotta elephant head from Lafogido, Ife. Ht 6 ins. Reg. no. 63/24a.

50 Terracotta ape from the Osongongon Obamakin Grove, Ife. Ht 5 ins.

51 Terracotta chameleon from Ibadan Road, Ife. Ht $4\frac{1}{4}$ ins. Reg. no. 13/62.

52 Terracotta left foot from Wunmonije Compound, Ife. L. $4\frac{1}{4}$ ins. Reg. no. 48/61.

53 Terracotta foot from Nok. Jos Museum.

54 Terracotta left foot from Ita Yemoo. L. $7\frac{5}{8}$ ins. Excav. no. I.Y. 30/9,10.

AFTER PAGE 132

55 Terracotta head from the Ondo Road site. Ht $6\frac{3}{8}$ ins. Reg. no. 171/61 A & F.

56 Terracotta torso from the Ondo Road site. Ht $9\frac{1}{4}$ ins. Reg. no. 171/61J.

57 Terracotta right foot from Lagere, Ife. Ht $6\frac{1}{2}$ ins. Reg. no. 88/6IQ.

58 Terracotta arms from Lagere, Ife. L. $6\frac{1}{2}$ and $3\frac{1}{2}$ ins. Reg. no. 88/61 F & N.

59 Terracotta head from Mokuro stream. Ht $7\frac{3}{4}$ ins. Reg. no. 8/61.

60 Terracotta head from Ife. Ht 5 ins. Museum für Völkerkunde, Berlin, reg. no. III C 27533.

61 Four stylized terracotta heads. Left to right from Oronmiyon Memorial College, ht 5 ins, reg. no. 65/61; Osongongon Obamakin Grove, ht $7\frac{1}{2}$ ins, reg. no. 29; Ife, ht $6\frac{1}{2}$ ins, reg. no. 63/46; Abiri, ht. $6\frac{3}{8}$ ins.

62 Three stylized terracotta heads. Left to right from Ita Yemoo, ht $5\frac{11}{16}$ ins, excav. no. I.Y. 28; Osongongon Obamakin Grove, ht $5\frac{5}{16}$ ins; uncertain provenance, ht $3\frac{1}{2}$ ins, reg. no. 33.

63 Leg of a quartz vessel from Ife. Ht $3\frac{1}{8}$ ins. Museum für Völkerkunde, Berlin, reg. no. III C 27548.

64 Ritual potsherd from Ita Yemoo. W. $4\frac{3}{4}$ ins. Excav. no. I.Y. 28.

65 Excavation of terracotta fragments, Ita Yemoo, 1963.

66 Detail of pavement excavated at the Catholic Mission, Ife, 1958.

67 Terracotta head from Igbo Obameri, Ife. Ht 7 ins. Excav. no. I 3 A, I 3 C.

68 Terracotta head from the Ifewara Road. Ht 10 ins. Reg. no. 37/61.

69 Priests of Orishanla at the Itapa festival.

70 Terracotta head in the shrine of Orishanla.

71 The Oni of Ife, Sir Adesoji Aderemi, at the Olojo festival.

72 Granite mudfish in the Ogun Ladin shrine, Ife Palace. L. 29 ins.

73 The Opa Oronmiyon, or stone staff of Oronyon. Ht 17 ft.

74 Stone male figure from the Ore Grove, Ife. Ht $40\frac{1}{2}$ ins.

75 Stone carving from Eshure in Ekiti. Ht shown 3 ft 6 ins.

76 Terracotta sculpture from the Iwinrin Grove, Ife. Ht 30 ins. Reg. no. 257–266.

77 Quartz stool from the shrine of Oluorogbo. W. 27 ins, ht 21 ins. British Museum, reg. no. 96.11. 22.1.

78 Granite-gneiss stool from the Apere Oro Grove. L. $13\frac{1}{2}$ ins.

79 Broken white quartz stool from the Epinbodo shrine. L. 11 ins. ht 4 ins. Reg. no. 139/61A.

80 Terracotta head from the Gold Coffer Mine, Jemaa. Ht $8\frac{1}{8}$ ins. Jos Museum, reg. no. 58/19.

81 Terracotta head from Jemaa. L. $3\frac{3}{4}$ ins. Jos Museum.

82 Terracotta head from Nok. Ht 14 ins. Lagos Museum.

83 Terracotta head from Tsauni camp, Jemaa. Ht 9 ins. Jos Museum.

84 Terracotta human loins from Nok. Ht $4\frac{7}{8}$ ins. Jos Museum, reg. no. H.3.

85 Terracotta kneeling man from Bwari. Ht $4\frac{1}{8}$ ins. Jos Museum.

AFTER PAGE 184

86 Terracotta animal from Zuru. Ht 22 ins. Lagos Museum, reg. no. 45.2.40.

87 Terracotta head from Wukari. Ht 6 ins. Pitt Rivers Museum, Oxford, Wukari N.A. 1932.

88 Tiv terracotta head. Ht $6\frac{1}{4}$ ins. Pitt Rivers Museum, Oxford, Capt. R. M. Downes, 1933.

89 Ife figurine from Benin. Ht $4\frac{7}{8}$ ins. Benin Museum.

90 Benin pendant from Ife. Ht $6\frac{9}{16}$ ins.

91 Bronze mask from Benin. Ht $5\frac{3}{8}$ ins. Lagos Museum, reg. no. 51.5. 1.

92 Terracotta head from the Ogbon Oya quarter, Ife. Ht 4 ins. Reg. no. 63/20.

93 Bronze figure from Benin. Ht 25 ins. Lagos Museum, reg. no. 54. 15.8.

94 Bronze head from Benin. Ht $8\frac{1}{4}$ ins. Lagos Museum, reg. no. 54. 15.7.

95 Bronze head from Benin. Ht $11\frac{1}{2}$ ins. Ife Museum on loan from Lagos Museum.

Figures

All drawings are by Tom Cross, except for the map, Fig. 1, which is by Anthony Waters.

Index

Numbers in italics refer to plates

Oluorogbo, 16 (map), 123, 125; *77*
Ondo Road, 66, 81; *55, 56*